"This book develops the conceptual foundations required for the analysis of markets with asymmetric information, and uses them to provide a clear survey and synthesis of the theoretical literature on bubbles, market microstructure, crashes, and herding in financial markets. The book is not only useful to the beginner who requires a guide through the rapidly developing literature, but provides insight and perspective that the expert will also appreciate."

Michael Brennan
Irwin and Goldyne Hearsh Professor of Banking and Finance at the University of California, Los Angeles, and Professor of Finance at the London Business School
President of the American Finance Association, 1989

"This book provides an excellent account of how bubbles and crashes and various other phenomena can occur. Traditional asset pricing theories have assumed symmetric information. Including asymmetric information radically alters the results that are obtained. The author takes a complex subject and presents it in a clear and concise manner. I strongly recommend it for anybody seriously interested in the theory of asset pricing."

Franklin Allen
Nippon Life Professor of Finance and Economics at the Wharton School, University of Pennsylvania
President of the American Finance Association, 2000

"This timely book provides an invaluable map for students and researchers navigating the literature on market microstructure, and more generally, on equilibrium with asymmetric information. It will become highly recommended reading for graduate courses in the economics of uncertainty and in financial economics."

Hyun Song Shin
Professor of Finance at the London School of Economics

Asset Pricing under Asymmetric Information

Bubbles, Crashes, Technical Analysis, and Herding

MARKUS K. BRUNNERMEIER

OXFORD

UNIVERSITY PRESS

OXFORD
UNIVERSITY PRESS

Great Clarendon Street, Oxford OX2 6DP

Oxford University Press is a department of the University of Oxford.
It furthers the University's objective of excellence in research, scholarship,
and education by publishing worldwide in

Oxford New York

Athens Auckland Bangkok Bogotá Buenos Aires Calcutta
Cape Town Chennai Dar es Salaam Delhi Florence Hong Kong Istanbul
Karachi Kuala Lumpur Madrid Melbourne Mexico City Mumbai
Nairobi Paris São Paulo Shanghai Singapore Taipei Tokyo Toronto Warsaw

with associated companies in Berlin Ibadan

Oxford is a registered trade mark of Oxford University Press
in the UK and in certain other countries

Published in the United States
by Oxford University Press Inc., New York

British Library Cataloguing in Publication Data
Data available

Library of Congress Cataloging in Publication Data
Brunnermeier, Markus Konrad.
Asset pricing under asymmetric information: bubbles, crashes, technical
analysis, and herding / Markus K. Brunnermeier.
p.cm.
Includes bibliographical references and index.
1. Stocks—Prices   2. Capital assets pricing model.   3. Information theory in economics.
I. Title
HG4636 .B78 2000   332.63'222–dc21   00-064994
ISBN 0-19-829698-3
1 3 5 7 9 10 8 6 4 2
Typeset by Newgen Imaging Systems (P) Ltd., Chennai, India
Printed in Great Britain on acid-free paper by
T.J. International Ltd., Padstow, Cornwall

To Smita

CONTENTS

LIST OF FIGURES

PREFACE

Motivation

A vast number of assets changes hands every day. Whether these assets are stocks, bonds, currencies, derivatives, real estate, or just somebody's house around the corner, there are common features driving the market price of these assets. For example, asset prices fluctuate more wildly than the prices of ordinary consumption goods. We observe emerging and bursting bubbles, bullish markets, and stock market crashes.

Another distinguishing feature of assets is that they entail uncertain payments, most of which occur far in the future. The price of assets is driven by expectations about these future payoffs. New information causes market participants to re-evaluate their expectations. For example, news about a company's future earning prospects changes the investors' expected value of stocks or bonds, while news of a country's economic prospects affects currency exchange rates. Depending on their information, market participants buy or sell the asset. In short, their information affects their trading activity and, thus, the asset price. Information flow is, however, not just a one-way street. Traders who do not receive a piece of new information are still conscious of the fact that the actions of other traders are driven by their information set. Therefore, uninformed traders can infer part of the other traders' information from the current movement of an asset's price. They might be able to learn even more by taking the whole price history into account. This leads us to the question of the extent to which technical or chart analysis is helpful in predicting the future price path.

There are many additional questions that fascinate both professionals and laymen. Why do bubbles develop and crashes occur? Why is the trading volume in terms of assets so much higher than real economic activity? Can people's herding behavior be simply attributed to irrational panic? Going beyond positive theory, some normative policy issues also arise. What are the early warning signals indicating that a different policy should be adopted? Can a different design of exchanges and other financial institutions reduce the risk of crashes and bubbles?

If financial crises and large swings in asset prices only affect the nominal side of the economy, there would not be much to worry about. However, as illustrated by the recent experiences of the Southeast Asian tiger economies, stock market and currency turmoil can easily turn into full-fledged economic crises. The unravelling of financial markets can spill over and affect the real side of economies. Therefore, a good understanding of price processes is needed to help us foresee possible crashes.

In recent years, the academic literature has taken giant strides towards improving our understanding of the price process of assets. This book offers a detailed and up-to-date review of the recent theoretical literature in this area. It provides a framework for understanding price processes and emphasizes the informational aspects of asset price dynamics. The survey focuses exclusively on models that assume that all agents are rational and act in their own self-interest. It does not cover models which attribute empirical findings purely to the irrational behavior of agents. It is expected that future research will place greater emphasis on behavioral aspects by including carefully selected behavioral elements into formal models. However, models with rational traders, as covered in this survey, will always remain the starting point of any research project.

Structure of the Survey

The main aim of this survey is to provide a structural overview of the current literature and to stimulate future research in this area.

Chapter 1 illustrates how asymmetric information and knowledge in general is modeled in theoretical economics. Section 1.1 also introduces the concept of higher-order knowledge which is important for the analysis of bubbles. Prices are determined in equilibrium. There are two different equilibrium concepts which are common in market settings with asymmetric information. The competitive Rational Expectations Equilibrium (REE) concept has its roots in general equilibrium theory, whereas the strategic Bayesian Nash Equilibrium concept stems from game theory. The book compares and contrasts both equilibrium concepts and also highlights their conceptual problems. This chapter also introduces the informational efficiency and allocative efficiency concepts to the reader.

The first section of Chapter 2 provides a more tractable notion of common knowledge and the intuition behind proofs of the different no-trade theorems. The no-trade theorems state the specific conditions under which differences in information alone do not lead to trade. A brief introduction of the basics of asset pricing under symmetric information is sketched out in Section 2.2 in order to highlight the complications that can arise under asymmetric information. In an asymmetric information setting, it makes a difference whether markets are only "dynamically complete" or complete in the sense of Debreu (1959), that is, completely equitizable. Market completeness or the security structure, in general, has a large impact on the information revelation of prices. Section 2.3 provides definitions of bubbles and investigates the existence of bubbles under common knowledge. It then illustrates the impact of higher-order uncertainty on the possible existence of bubbles in settings where traders possess different information.

The third chapter illustrates different market microstructure models. In the first group of models, all market participants submit whole demand schedules simultaneously. The traders either act strategically or are price takers as in the competitive REE. The strategic models are closely related to share auctions or divisible goods auctions. In the second group of models, some traders simultaneously submit demand/supply schedules in the first stage and build up a whole supply schedule in the form of a limit order book. In the second stage, a possibly informed trader chooses his optimal demand from the offered supply schedule. A comparison between uniform pricing and discriminatory pricing is also drawn. Sequential trade models à la Glosten and Milgrom (1985) form the third group of models. In these models, the order size is restricted to one unit and thus the competitive market maker quotes only a single bid and a single ask price instead of a whole supply schedule. In the fourth group of models, the informed traders move first. The classical reference for these models is Kyle (1985).

Chapter 4 focuses on dynamic models. Its emphasis is on explaining technical analysis. These models show that past prices still carry valuable information. Some of these models also explain why it is rational for some investors to "chase the trend." Other models are devoted to the informational role of trading volume. The insiders' optimal dynamic trading strategy over different trading periods is derived in a strategic model setting.

Chapter 5 classifies different herding models. Rational herding in sequential decision making is either due to payoff externalities or information externalities. Herding may arise in settings where the predecessor's action is a strong enough signal such that the agent disregards his own signal. Informational cascades might emerge if the predecessor's action is only a noisy signal of his information. Herding can also arise in principal–agent models. The sequence in which agents make decisions can be either exogenous or endogenous.

Stock market crashes are explained in Section 6.1. In a setting with widely dispersed information, even relatively unimportant news can lead to large price swings and crashes. Stock market crashes can also occur because of liquidity problems, bursting bubbles, and sunspots. Traders might also herd in information acquisition if they care about the short-term price path as well as about the long-run fundamental value. Under these circumstances, all traders will try to gather the same piece of information. Section 6.2 discusses investigative herding models that provide a deeper understanding of Keynes' comparison of the stock market with a beauty contest. Section 6.3 deals with short-termism induced by the stock market. The survey concludes with a brief summary of bank runs and its connection to financial crises.

Target Audience

There are three main audiences for whom this book is written:

1. *Doctoral students* in finance and economics will find this book helpful in gaining access to this vast literature. It can be used as a supplementary reader in an advanced theoretical finance course which follows a standard asset pricing course. The book provides a useful framework and introduces the reader to the major models and results in the literature. Although the survey is closely linked to the original articles, it is not intended to be a substitute for them. While it does not provide detailed proofs, it does attempt to outline the important steps and highlight the key intuition. A consistent notation is used throughout the book to facilitate comparison between the different papers. The corresponding variable notations used in the original papers are listed in footnotes throughout the text to facilitate cross-reference.

2. *Researchers* who are already familiar with the literature can use this book as a source of reference. By providing a structure for this body of literature, the survey can help the reader identify gaps and trigger future research.

3. *Advanced undergraduate students* with solid microeconomic training can also use this survey as an introduction to the key models in the market microstructure literature. Readers who just want a feel for this literature should skim through Chapters 1 and 2 and focus on the intuitive aspects of Chapter 3. The dynamic models in Chapter 4 are more demanding, but are not essential for understanding the remainder

of the survey. The discussion of herding models in Chapter 5 and stock market crashes and the Keynes' beauty contest analogy in Chapter 6 are accessible to a broad audience.

Acknowledgments

I received constructive comments and encouragement from several people and institutions while working on this project. The book started taking shape in the congenial atmosphere of the London School of Economics. Sudipto Bhattacharya planted the seeds of this project in my mind. Margaret Bray, Bob Nobay, and David Webb provided encouragement throughout the project. I also benefited from discussions with Elena Carletti, Antoine Faure-Grimaud, Thomas de Garidel, Clemens Grafe, Philip Kalmus, Volker Nocke, Sönje Reiche, Geoffrey Shuetrim, and Paolo Vitale.

The completion of the book was greatly facilitated by the intellectually stimulating environment at Princeton University. Ben Bernanke, Ailsa Röell, and Marciano Siniscalchi provided helpful comments. The students of my graduate Financial Economics class worked through draft chapters and provided useful feedback. Haluk Ergin, Ümit Kaya, Jiro Kondo, Rahel Jhirad, and David Skeie deserve special mention for thoroughly reviewing the manuscript.

Economists at various other institutions also reviewed portions of the manuscript. In particular, I thank Peter DeMarzo, Douglas Gale, Bruce Grundy, Dirk Hackbarth, Thorsten Hens, David Hirshleifer, John Hughes, Paul Klemperer, Jonathan Levin, Bart Lipman, Melissas Nicolas, Marco Ottaviani, Sven Rady, Jean Charles Rochet, Costis Skiados, S. Viswanathan, Xavier Vives, and Ivo Welch while still retaining responsibility for remaining errors. I appreciate being notified of errata; you can e-mail me your comments at markus@princeton.edu. I will try to maintain a list of corrections at my homepage http://www.princeton.edu/~markus.

Phyllis Durepos assisted in the typing of this manuscript; her diligence and promptness are much appreciated. Finally, enormous gratitude and love to my wife, Smita, for her careful critique and editing of every draft of every chapter. Her unfailing support made this project possible.

Princeton, February 2000

1

Information, Equilibrium, and Efficiency Concepts

Financial markets are driven by news and information. The standard asset pricing theory assumes that all market participants possess the same information. However, in reality different traders hold different information. Some traders might know more than others about the same event or they might hold information related to different events. Even if all traders hear the same news in the form of a public announcement, they still might interpret it differently. Public announcements only rarely provide a direct statement of the value of the asset. Typically one has to make use of other information to figure out the impact of this news on the asset's value. Thus, traders with different background information might draw different conclusions from the same public announcement. Therefore, financial markets cannot be well understood unless one also examines the asymmetries in the information dispersion and assimilation process.

In economies where information is dispersed among many market participants, prices have a dual role. They are both:

- an index of scarcity or bargaining power, and
- a conveyor of information.

Hayek (1945) was one of the first to look at the price system as a mechanism for communicating information. This information affects traders' expectations about the uncertain value of an asset. There are different ways of modeling the formation of agents' expectations. Muth (1960, 1961) proposed a rational expectations framework which requires people's subjective beliefs about probability distributions to actually correspond to objective probability distributions. This rules out systematic forecast errors. The advantage of the rational expectations hypothesis over ad hoc formulations of expectations is that it provides a simple and plausible way of handling expectations. Agents draw inferences from all available information derived from exogenous and endogenous data. In particular, they infer information from publicly observable prices.

In short, investors base their actions on the information conveyed by the price as well as on their private information.

Specific models which illustrate the relationship between information and price processes will be presented in Chapters 3 and 4. In Sections 1.1 and 1.2 of this chapter we provide the basic conceptual background for modeling information and understanding the underlying equilibrium concepts. Section 1.3 highlights the difference between allocative efficiency and informational efficiency.

1.1. Modeling Information

If individuals are not fully informed, they cannot distinguish between different states of the world.

State Space

A state of the world ω fully describes every aspect of reality. A state space, denoted by Ω, is the collection of all possible states of the world ω. Let us assume that Ω has only finitely many elements.[1] A simplistic example illustrates the more abstract concepts below. Consider a situation where the only thing that matters is the dividend payment and the price of a certain stock. The dividend and the price can be either high or low and there is also the possibility that the firm goes bankrupt. In the latter case, the price and the dividend will be zero. A state of the world ω provides a full description of the world (in this case about the dividend payment d as well as the price of the stock p). There are five states $\omega_1 = \{d_{high}, p_{high}\}$, $\omega_2 = \{d_{high}, p_{low}\}$, $\omega_3 = \{d_{low}, p_{high}\}$, $\omega_4 = \{d_{low}, p_{low}\}$, and $\omega_5 = \{d = 0, p = 0\}$. An *event* E is a set of states. For example, the statement "the dividend payment is high" refers to an event $E = \{\omega_1, \omega_2\}$. One can think that a state is chosen, for example, by nature but the individual might not know which state is the true state of the world or even whether event E is true.

From Possibility Sets to Partitions

Information allows an individual to rule out certain states of the world. Depending on the true state of the world $\omega \in \Omega = \{\omega_1, \omega_2, \omega_3, \omega_4, \omega_5\}$ she might receive different information. For example, if an individual learns

---

[1] Occasionally we will indicate how the concepts generalize to an infinite state space Ω.

in ω_1 that the dividend payment is high, she can eliminate the states ω_3, ω_4, and ω_5. In state ω_1 she thinks that only ω_1 and ω_2 are possible. One way to represent this information is by means of possibility sets. Suppose her possibility set is given by $\mathcal{P}^{i'''}(\omega_1) = \{\omega_1, \omega_2\}$ if the true state is ω_1 and $\mathcal{P}^{i'''}(\omega_2) = \{\omega_2, \omega_3\}$, $\mathcal{P}^{i'''}(\omega_3) = \{\omega_2, \omega_3\}$, $\mathcal{P}^{i'''}(\omega_4) = \{\omega_4, \omega_5\}$, $\mathcal{P}^{i'''}(\omega_5) = \{\omega_5\}$ for the other states. Individual i knows this information structure. By imposing the axiom of truth (knowledge) we make sure that she does not rule out the true state. In other words, the true state is indeed in $\mathcal{P}^i(\omega)$, that is

$$\omega \in \mathcal{P}^i(\omega) \quad \text{(axiom of truth)}.$$

However, individual i has not fully exploited the informational content of her information. She can improve her knowledge by introspection. We distinguish between positive and negative introspection. Consider state ω_1 in our example. In this state of the world, agent i considers that states ω_1 and ω_2 are both possible. However, by positive introspection she knows that in state ω_2 she would know that the true state of the world is either ω_2 or ω_3. Since ω_3 is not in her possibility set, she can exclude ω_2 and, hence, she knows the true state in ω_1. More formally, after conducting positive introspection the possibility sets satisfy

$$\omega' \in \mathcal{P}^i(\omega) \quad \Rightarrow \quad \mathcal{P}^i(\omega') \subseteq \mathcal{P}^i(\omega) \quad \text{(positive introspection)}.$$

Thus the individual's updated possibility sets are given by $\mathcal{P}^{i'}(\omega_1) = \{\omega_1\}$, $\mathcal{P}^{i'}(\omega_2) = \{\omega_2, \omega_3\}$, $\mathcal{P}^{i'}(\omega_3) = \{\omega_2, \omega_3\}$, $\mathcal{P}^{i'}(\omega_4) = \{\omega_4, \omega_5\}$, $\mathcal{P}^{i'}(\omega_5) = \{\omega_5\}$. Even more information can be inferred from this information structure by using negative introspection. Consider state ω_4 in our example. In state ω_4, individual i would think that ω_4 and ω_5 are possible. However, in state ω_5 she knows that the true state of the world is *not* in $\{\omega_1, \omega_2, \omega_3, \omega_4\} = \Omega \backslash \{\omega_5\}$. From this she can infer that she must be in state ω_4 because she does not know whether the true state is in $\Omega \backslash \{\omega_5\}$ or not. The formal definition for negative introspection is given by

$$\omega' \in \mathcal{P}^i(\omega) \quad \Rightarrow \quad \mathcal{P}^i(\omega') \supseteq \mathcal{P}^i(\omega) \quad \text{(negative introspection)}.$$

After making use of positive and negative introspection, individual i has the following information structure: $\mathcal{P}^i(\omega_1) = \{\omega_1\}$, $\mathcal{P}^i(\omega_2) = \{\omega_2, \omega_3\}$, $\mathcal{P}^i(\omega_3) = \{\omega_2, \omega_3\}$, $\mathcal{P}^i(\omega_4) = \{\omega_4\}$, $\mathcal{P}^i(\omega_5) = \{\omega_5\}$. This information structure is a partition of the state space Ω.

Indeed, any information structure that satisfies the axiom of truth and positive and negative introspection can be represented by a partition. A *partition* of Ω is a collection of subsets that are mutually disjoint and have a union Ω. The larger the number of partition cells, the more information agent i has.

Knowledge Operator

The knowledge operator

$$\mathcal{K}^i(E) = \{\omega \in \Omega : \mathcal{P}^i(\omega) \subseteq E\}$$

is an alternative concept for representing agent i's information.[2] While the possibility set $\mathcal{P}^i(\cdot)$ reports all states of the world an individual considers as possible for a given true state of the world, the knowledge operator does the converse. It reports all the states of the world, that is an event, in which agent i considers a certain event E possible. That is, it reports the set of all states in which agent i knows that the true state of the world is in the event $E \subseteq \Omega$. In our example, individual i knows event $E' = \{\text{dividend is high}\} = \{\omega_1, \omega_2\}$ only in state ω_1, that is $\mathcal{K}^i(E') = \omega_1$. Without imposing any axioms on the possibility sets, one can derive the following three properties for the knowledge operator:

1. Individual i always knows that one of the states $\omega \in \Omega$ is true, that is

$$\mathcal{K}^i(\Omega) = \Omega.$$

2. If individual i knows that the true state of the world is in event E_1 then she also knows that the true state is in any E_2 containing E_1, that is

$$\mathcal{K}^i(E_1) \subseteq \mathcal{K}^i(E_2) \quad \text{for } E_1 \subseteq E_2.$$

3. Furthermore, if individual i knows that the true state of the world is in event E_1 and she knows that it is also in event E_2, then she also knows that the true state is in event $E_1 \cap E_2$. In short, if she knows E_1 and E_2 then she also knows $E_1 \cap E_2$. One can easily see that the converse is also true. More formally,

$$\mathcal{K}^i(E_1) \cap \mathcal{K}^i(E_2) = \mathcal{K}^i(E_1 \cap E_2).$$

---

[2] Knowledge operators prove very useful for the analysis of bubbles. For example, a bubble can arise in situations where everybody knows that the price is too high, but they do not know that the others know this too.

We restate the axiom of truth and the two axioms of introspection in terms of knowledge operators in order to be able to represent information in terms of partitions. The axiom of truth (knowledge) becomes

$$\mathcal{K}^i(E) \subseteq E \quad \text{(axiom of truth)}.$$

That is, if i knows E (for example, dividend is high) then E is true, that is the true state $\omega \in E$. This axiom is relaxed when one introduces belief operators. Positive introspection translates into the *knowing that you know* (KTYK) axiom

$$\mathcal{K}^i(E) \subseteq \mathcal{K}^i(\mathcal{K}^i(E)) \quad \text{(KTYK)}.$$

This says that in all states in which individual i knows E, she also knows that she knows E. This refers to higher knowledge, since it is a knowledge statement about her knowledge. The negative introspection axiom translates into *knowing that you do not know* (KTYNK).

$$\Omega \backslash \mathcal{K}^i(E) \subseteq \mathcal{K}^i(\Omega \backslash \mathcal{K}^i(E)) \quad \text{(KTYNK)}.$$

For any state in which individual i does not know whether the true state is in E or not, she knows that she does not know whether the true state is in E or not. Negative introspection (KTYNK) requires a high degree of rationality. It is the most demanding of the three axioms. Adding the last three axioms allows one to represent information in partitions.

Group Knowledge and Common Knowledge

The knowledge operator for individual i_1, $\mathcal{K}^{i_1}(E)$, reports all states in which agent i_1 knows event E, that is, he knows that the true state is in E. If the knowledge operator of another individual i_2 also reports the same state ω, then both individuals know the event E in state ω. More generally, the intersection of all events reported by the individual knowledge operators gives us the states of the world in which all members of the group G know an event E. Let us introduce the following group knowledge operator

$$\mathcal{K}^G(E) := \bigcap_{i \in G} \mathcal{K}^i(E).$$

The mutual knowledge operator reports all states of the world in which each agent in group G knows the event E. However, although everybody knows event E in these states, an individual might not know that the others know E too. Mutual knowledge does not guarantee that all members of the group know that all the others know it too. Knowledge about knowledge, that is second-order knowledge can be easily analyzed by applying the knowledge operator again, for example $\mathcal{K}^{i_1}(\mathcal{K}^{i_2}(E))$. An event is second-order mutual knowledge if everybody knows that everybody knows event E. More formally,

$$\mathcal{K}^{G(2)}(E) := \bigcap_{i \in G} \left(\bigcap_{-i \in G \setminus \{i\}} \mathcal{K}^i(\mathcal{K}^{-i}(E)) \right) \cap \mathcal{K}^G(E).$$

If the three above axioms hold, the second-order mutual knowledge operator simplifies to

$$\mathcal{K}^{G(2)}(E) = \mathcal{K}^G(\mathcal{K}^G(E)).$$

If an event E is second-order mutual knowledge, then everybody knows E and everybody knows that everybody knows E, but some individuals might not know that everybody knows that everybody knows that everybody knows E. The above definition can easily be generalized to any nth order mutual knowledge, $\mathcal{K}^{G(n)}(E)$. Given the above three axioms,

$$\mathcal{K}^{G(n)}(E) = \underbrace{\mathcal{K}^G(\mathcal{K}^G(\ldots(\mathcal{K}^G(E))))}_{n\text{-times}}.$$

An event E is common knowledge if everybody knows that everybody knows that everybody knows and so on ad infinitum that event E is true. In formal terms, E is common knowledge if

$$\mathcal{C}\mathcal{K}(E) := \bigcap_{n=1}^{\infty} \mathcal{K}^{G(n)}(E).$$

Note that as long as the three axioms hold $\mathcal{C}\mathcal{K}(E) = \mathcal{K}^{G(\infty)}(E)$.

Physical and Epistemic Parts of the State Space –
Depth of Knowledge
A model is called complete only if its state space and each individual's partitions over the state space are "common knowledge." The quotation marks indicate that this "meta" notion of "common knowledge" lies outside of the model and thus cannot be represented in terms of the knowledge operators presented above.

Since the partitions of all individuals are "common knowledge" we need to enlarge the state space in order to analyze higher-order uncertainty (knowledge). Another simple example will help illustrate this point. Individual 1 knows whether interest rate r will be high or low. Individual 2 does not know it. The standard way to model this situation is to define the following state space Ω', $\omega'_1 = \{r_{high}\}$, $\omega'_2 = \{r_{low}\}$. Individual 1's partition is $\{\{\omega'_1\}, \{\omega'_2\}\}$, while agent 2's partition is $\{\omega'_1, \omega'_2\}$. Given the assumption that partitions are common knowledge, it follows immediately that agent 1 knows that agent 2 does not know whether the interest rate is high or low and agent 2 knows that agent 1 knows it. The second-order knowledge is common knowledge. In other words, any event which is mutual knowledge is also common knowledge. One cannot analyze higher-order uncertainty without extending the state space. To analyze situations where agent 1 does not know whether agent 2 knows whether the interest rate is high or low, consider the following extended state space Ω with $\omega_1 = (r_{high}, 2 \text{ knows } r_{high})$, $\omega_2 = (r_{high}, 2 \text{ does not know } r_{high})$, $\omega_3 = (r_{low}, 2 \text{ knows } r_{low})$, $\omega_4 = (r_{low}, 2 \text{ does not know } r_{low})$. If agent 1 does not know whether agent 2 knows the interest rate, his partition is $\{\{\omega_1, \omega_2\}, \{\omega_3, \omega_4\}\}$. Agent 2's partition is $\{\{\omega_1\}, \{\omega_3\}, \{\omega_2, \omega_4\}\}$ since he knows whether he knows the interest rate or not. Note that the description of a state also needs to contain knowledge statements in order to model higher-order uncertainty. These statements can also be in indirect form, for example, agent i received a message m.

A state of the world therefore describes not only (1) the physical world (fundamentals) but also (2) the epistemic world, that is what each agent knows about the fundamentals or others' knowledge. In our simple example the fundamentals partition the state space $\Omega = \{E_{r_{high}}, E_{r_{low}}\}$ into two events, $E_{r_{high}} = \{\omega_1, \omega_2\}$ and $E_{r_{low}} = \{\omega_3, \omega_4\}$. The first-order knowledge components partition the state space $\Omega = \{E_{2 \text{ knows } r}, E_{2 \text{ does not know } r}\}$ into $E_{2 \text{ knows } r} = \{\omega_1, \omega_3\}$ and $E_{2 \text{ does not know } r} = \{\omega_2, \omega_4\}$. The state description in our example does not capture all first-order knowledge statements. In particular, we do not introduce states specifying whether agent 1 knows the interest rate r or not. A state space Ω whose states specify first-order knowledge is said to have a depth equal to one in terms of Morris, Postlewaite, and Shin's (1995) terminology. Note that a state space with *depth of knowledge* of one is insufficient for analyzing third or higher-order knowledge statements. Since partitions are common knowledge, any third or higher-order knowledge statements such as "agent 2 knows that 1 does not know whether agent 2 knows the interest rate" are common knowledge. To relax this constraint one has to enlarge the state space even further and increase the depth of the knowledge of the state space, that is one has to incorporate second- or higher-order knowledge statements into the state description.

Sigma Algebras

A σ-algebra or σ-field $\mathcal{F}$ is a collection of subsets of Ω such that (1) $\Omega \in \mathcal{F}$, (2) $\Omega \setminus F \in \mathcal{F}$ for all $F \in \mathcal{F}$, and (3) $\bigcup_{n=1}^{\infty} F_n \in \mathcal{F}$ for any sequence of sets $(F_n)_{n \geq 1} \in \mathcal{F}$. This implies immediately that $\emptyset \in \mathcal{F}$ and for any $F_1, F_2 \in \mathcal{F}$, $F_1 \cap F_2 \in \mathcal{F}$. If Ω' is the (possibly multidimensional) real space $\mathbb{R}^k$, then the set of all open intervals generates a Borel σ-algebra.

All possible unions and intersections of a finite Ω, that is Ω's power set, provide the largest σ-algebra, $\mathcal{F}$. The unions of all partition cells of a partition $\mathcal{P}$ and the empty set form the σ-algebra $\mathcal{F}(\mathcal{P})$ generated by partition $\mathcal{P}$. Thus σ-algebras can be used instead of partitions to represent information. The more the partition cells, the larger is the corresponding σ-algebra.

A partition $\mathcal{P}_{t+1}$ is finer than $\mathcal{P}_t$, if $\mathcal{P}_{t+1}$ has more partition cells than $\mathcal{P}_t$ and the partition cells of $\mathcal{P}_t$ can be formed by the union of some partition cells of $\mathcal{P}_{t+1}$. A field $\mathcal{F}_t$ is a subfield of $\mathcal{F}_{t+1}$ if $\mathcal{F}_{t+1}$ contains all elements of $\mathcal{F}_t$. A sequence of increasing subfields $\{\mathcal{F}_0 \subseteq \mathcal{F}_1 \subseteq \cdots \subseteq \mathcal{F}_{T-1} \subseteq \mathcal{F}_T\}$ forms a filtration. If individuals hold different information, then their σ-algebras $\mathcal{F}^i$ differ. The σ-algebra which represents the pooled information of all agent i's information is often denoted by $\mathcal{F}^{\text{pool}} = \bigvee_{i \in \mathbb{I}} \mathcal{F}^i$. It is the smallest σ-algebra containing the union of all σ-algebras $\mathcal{F}^i$. Information that is common knowledge is represented by the σ-algebra $\mathcal{F}^{CK} = \bigcap_{i \in \mathbb{I}} \mathcal{F}^i$.

A random variable is a mapping, $X(\cdot) : \Omega \mapsto \Omega'$. We focus on $\Omega' = \mathbb{R}^k$. If the inverse image of Borel sets of $X(\cdot)$ are elements of $\mathcal{F}$, then the random variable $X(\cdot)$ is called $\mathcal{F}$-measurable. In other words, a random variable is $\mathcal{F}$-measurable if one knows the outcome $X(\cdot)$ whenever one knows which events in $\mathcal{F}$ are true. $\mathcal{F}(X)$ denotes the smallest σ-algebra with respect to which $X(\cdot)$ is measurable. $\mathcal{F}(X)$ is also called the σ-algebra generated by X.

Probabilities

$(\Omega, \mathcal{F}, P)$ forms a probability space, where P is a probability measure. Agents may also differ in the probabilities they assign to different elements of the σ-algebra. Let us denote the prior belief/probability distribution of agent i by P_0^i. Agents update their prior distribution and form a conditional posterior distribution after receiving information. Two probability distributions are called equivalent if their zero-probability events coincide. The state space Ω is generally assumed to be common knowledge. Often one also assumes that all individuals share the same prior probability distribution over the state space and that this distribution is common knowledge. This common prior assumption is also known as the Harsanyi doctrine and acts as a scientific discipline on possible equilibrium outcomes (Aumann 1987).

Agents' signals are also part of the state space. After a signal realization has occurred, individuals can update their probability distribution conditional on the observed realizations. The conditional distribution is derived by applying Bayes' rule

$$P^i(E_n|D) = \frac{P^i(D|E_n)\,P^i(E_n)}{P^i(D)}$$

whenever possible. For $P^i(D) = 0$ we assume that the posterior $P^i(E_n|D)$ is exogeneously specified. If the events $E_1, E_2, \ldots, E_N$ constitute a partition of Ω then Bayes' rule can be restated as

$$P^i(E_n|D) = \frac{P^i(D|E_n)\,P^i(E_n)}{\sum_{n=1}^{N} P^i(D|E_n)\,P^i(E_n)}.$$

Bayes' rule has direct implications for calculating the conditional distribution of random variables X and Y. Let $f_{XY}(x, y)$ denote the joint density function of the random variables X and Y. The marginal density is given by $f_X(x) = \sum_y f_{XY}(x, y)$. Although we have mostly ignored the complications involved when Ω is infinite, let us simply extend the above definitions to density functions of continuous random variables X and Y. In the continuous case, the marginal density of x is $f_X(x) = \int f_{XY}(x, y)\,dy$. The conditional density of X given $Y = y$ is $f_{X|Y}(x|y) = f_{XY}(x, y)/f_y(y)$ for $f_y(y) \neq 0$ in the discrete and the continuous case.

Belief Operators

Due to the axiom of truth, individuals were able to rule out certain states of nature. Without imposing the axiom of truth, individuals are only able to rule out certain states of the world with a certain probability. The p-belief operator reports all states of the world in which agent i considers event E to be at least likely with probability p:

$$B^{i,p}(E) = \{\omega \in \Omega | P^i[E \cap \mathcal{P}^i(\omega)|\mathcal{P}^i(\omega)] \geq p\}.$$

The probability distribution $P^i[\cdot|\mathcal{P}^i(\omega)]$ is conditional on the element $\mathcal{P}^i(\omega)$ of possibility set $\mathcal{P}^i$. This indicates that the belief operator can also be applied solely to the remaining states of the world which are not ruled out by the possibility sets. Let us define group belief operators that are analogous to the group knowledge operators. An event E is p-mutual belief if all individuals believe that the event is true with at least probability p. An event is p-common belief if everybody believes at least with probability p that E is true and that everybody believes with at least probability p that everybody believes with at least probability p and so on ad infinitum that event E is true with at least probability p. The p-mutual belief operator and p-common belief operator are defined analogous to the mutual knowledge operator and common knowledge operator respectively. The terms "certainty," "mutual certainty," and "common certainty" are used when $p = 1$. Note that the difference between knowledge operators and certainty operators is only due to the axiom of truth. Without the axiom of truth, an event might still occur even though individual i assigned zero probability to it. Dekel and Gul (1997) discuss the distinction between $(p = 1)$-beliefs and knowledge in greater detail.

Belief operators are also useful for judging whether models with a simplified information structure provide accurate predictions despite the fact that the information structure is much more complicated in reality. For example, although in reality individuals often do not know whether the other market participants received a signal or not, many economic models ignore higher-order uncertainty and thus implicitly assume that the depth of knowledge is zero. Belief operators provide an indication of when it is reasonable to restrict the analysis to an event $\Omega^{\text{restricted}} \subset \Omega$ with a lower depth of knowledge rather than to focus on the whole state space Ω. Morris, Postlewaite, and Shin (1995) illustrate this point and highlight its usefulness in the context of bubbles.

Signal Extraction – Conditional Distributions

In many models, agents have to update their prior probability distribution after receiving a signal. The resulting posterior distribution is conditional on the signal realization. Before restricting our attention to certain commonly used distributions, let us illustrate the *monotone likelihood ratio property* (MLRP) which allows us to rank different signal realizations.

Let us consider a two-dimensional state space $\Omega = \{v, S\}$ where $v \in \mathbb{R}$ is the only payoff-relevant variable and $S \in \mathbb{R}$ is a signal about v. A signal realization S^H is more favorable than signal realization S^L

if the posterior conditional on S^H dominates the posterior conditional on S^L. First-order stochastic dominance is one possible form of ranking posterior distributions. A conditional cumulative distribution $G(v|S^H)$ first-order stochastically strictly dominates $G(v|S^L)$ if $G(v|S^H) \leq G(v|S^L)$ for any realization of v and strictly smaller for at least one value of v. Stated differently, any individual with an increasing utility function $U^i(v)$ would prefer a gamble $G(\cdot|S^H)$ to a gamble $G(\cdot|S^L)$, since $\int U^i(v)\,dG(v|S^H) > \int U^i(v)\,dG(v|S^L)$. Surely the first-order stochastic dominance ranking is in general not complete, that is, not all distributions can be ranked according to this criterion. In other words, there are many possible distributions where for some v, $G(\cdot|S) \leq G(\cdot|S')$ and for other v, $G(\cdot|S) > G(\cdot|S')$. However if $f_S(S|v)$, the density of the signal distribution conditional on the payoff-relevant state v, satisfies the strict monotone likelihood ratio property (MLRP), then for any nondegenerated unconditional prior distribution $G(v)$ the conditional posterior distributions $G(v|S)$ can be ranked according to the first-order stochastic dominance criterion. The MLRP takes its name from the fact that the ratio of densities $f_S(S|v)/f_S(S|\bar{v})$ is monotonically increasing (decreasing) in S if $v > (<)\,\bar{v}$. Stated differently for all $v' > v$ and $S' > S$

$$\frac{f_S(S|v)}{f_S(S|v')} > \frac{f_S(S'|v)}{f_S(S'|v')}.$$

A formal proof and clear exposition of this result is given by Milgrom (1981). If the two random variables S and v satisfy the MLRP, they are also called affiliated (Milgrom and Weber 1982). Many of the commonly used probability functions and densities satisfy the MLRP. Examples are the normal distribution (with mean v), the exponential distribution (with mean v), the Poisson distribution (with mean v), the uniform distribution on $[0, v]$, and the chi-square distribution (with noncentrality parameter v).

Whereas the posterior of a probability distribution can take on any possible form, certain joint probability distributions of the state space lead to a nice closed-form solution of the conditional posterior distribution. Some distributions remain in the same class after updating. For example, if the prior is *uniformly distributed* and the signal provides an upper or lower bound for the posterior support, then the new distribution is also uniformly distributed. The same is true for the (double) *exponential distribution* $f(x) = \frac{1}{2}a \exp\{-a|x|\}$ with $x \in \mathbb{R}$. This property proves useful for calculating conditional means like $E_x[x|x \geq s]$. If the signal does not provide a lower or upper bound on the support of the conditional distribution, the conditional distribution might still fall into the same class of distributions. For example, this is the case for *normally distributed* random variables. Normal distributions are fully characterized by their mean and variance. The projection theorem is very useful for deriving the conditional mean and variance. Consider an n multidimensional random variable $(\vec{X}, \vec{S}) \sim \mathcal{N}(\mu, \Sigma)$ with means $\mu \in \mathbb{R}^n$ and variance–covariance matrix $\Sigma \in \mathbb{R}^{n \times n}$. $\vec{X}$ is a vector of n_X random variables and $\vec{S}$ is a vector of $n_S := n - n_X$ random variables. The mean vector and variance–covariance matrix can be written as

$$\mu = \begin{bmatrix} \mu_X \\ \mu_S \end{bmatrix}_{n \times 1} ; \qquad \Sigma = \begin{bmatrix} \Sigma_{X,X} & \Sigma_{X,S} \\ \Sigma_{S,X} & \Sigma_{S,S} \end{bmatrix}_{n \times n} .$$

The marginal distribution of S is then $N(\mu_S, \Sigma_{S,S})$ and the conditional density of X given $S = s$ can be derived by determining the conditional mean and variance using the projection theorem

$$(X|S = s) \sim \mathcal{N}(\mu_X + \Sigma_{X,S}\Sigma_{S,S}^{-1}(s - \mu_S), \Sigma_{X,X} - \Sigma_{X,S}\Sigma_{S,S}^{-1}\Sigma_{S,X}).$$

The proof of the projection theorem can be found in almost any statistics book.[3]

Note that the conditional variance–covariance matrix for normally distributed random variables is deterministic and does not depend on the signal realization, s. This is a special feature of the normal distribution.

The reciprocal of the variance of a normally distributed variable $X \in \mathbb{R}$, $1/\text{Var}[X]$, is often referred to as the *precision* τ_X of the random variable X.

The projection theorem is simplified for certain specific signal structures. For example, the conditional mean and variance of a one-dimensional random variable X given N signals $S_n = X + \varepsilon_n$, where

---

[3] The proof for the easiest version of the projection theorem

$$E[X|S = s] = E[X] + \frac{\text{Cov}[X, S]}{\text{Var}[S]}(s - E[S])$$

can be seen by multiplying both sides of the linear regression $X = \alpha + \beta S + \varepsilon$ by $(S - E[S])$. Taking expectations $E[XS] - E[X]\,E[S] = 0 + \beta(E[(S)^2] - E[S]^2)$, since ε is orthogonal to S. Thus, $\beta = \text{Cov}[X, S]/\text{Var}[S]$.

the noise terms ε_n have mean zero and are independent of $X \in \mathbb{R}$ and each other, are

$$E[X|s_1,\ldots,s_N] = \mu_X + \frac{1}{\tau_X + \sum_{n=1}^{N} \tau_{\varepsilon_n}} \sum_{n=1}^{N} \tau_{\varepsilon_n}(s_n - \mu_X)$$

$$\text{Var}[X|s_1,\ldots,s_N] = \frac{1}{\tau_X + \sum_{n=1}^{N} \tau_{\varepsilon_n}},$$

that is, the conditional precision is

$$\tau_{X|s_1,\ldots,s_N} = \tau_X + \sum_{n=1}^{N} \tau_{\varepsilon_n}.$$

If, in addition, all ε_n are identically distributed, that is, the variances of all ε_n are the same for all n, then

$$E[X|s_1,\ldots,s_N] = \mu_X + \underbrace{\frac{1}{\tau_X + N\tau_{\varepsilon_n}}}_{\text{Var}[X|s_1,\ldots,s_N]} N\tau_{\varepsilon_n}\left(\sum_{n=1}^{N} \frac{1}{N}s_n - \mu_X\right).$$

$\bar{s} := \sum_{n=1}^{N}(1/N)s_n$ is a *sufficient statistic* for observing the realization of all N signals $s_1,\ldots,s_N$. In general, a statistic is a function of observable random variables that does not contain any unknown parameters. A statistic is sufficient for observable random variables if the statistic leads to the same conditional distribution as the observable random variables.

The Kalman filter is also derived from the projection theorem. The Kalman filter technique is especially useful for steady state analysis of dynamic models, as shown in Chapter 4. The problem has to be brought in state space form:

$$z_{t+1} = Az_t + Bx_t + \epsilon_{t,1}$$
$$S_t = Cz_t + \epsilon_{t,2},$$

where the error terms $\epsilon_{t,1}$, $\epsilon_{t,2}$ are i.i.d. normally distributed. The first equation is the transition equation, which determines how the state vector z_t moves depending on the control vector x_t. The second equation is the measurement equation, which describes the relationship between the signal S_t and the current state z_t.

Normal distributions have the additional advantage that they fall into the class of stable distributions.[4] That is, any (weighted) sum of normally distributed random variables is also normally distributed. This property

---

[4] The Cauchy, Gamma and Bernoulli distributions are also stable distributions.

proves especially useful for portfolio analysis. If the assets' values are normally distributed, so is the value of the whole portfolio.

In many situations it is sufficient to model the relevant effects with a simple binary signal structure. A binary signal gives the right indication with probability q. However, one draws the wrong conclusion with probability $(1 - q)$. The (possibly state dependent) probability q is also called the binary signal's *precision*. Note that the term "precision" in the context of binary signals differs from the definition of precision in the context of normally distributed variables.

In summary, there are two components to modeling information. First, partitions or the associated σ-algebras capture the fact that information may allow us to distinguish between states of the world and to rule out certain states. Second, information also enables us to update the distribution over the remaining states of the world. This leads to an updated posterior probability distribution.

1.2. Rational Expectations Equilibrium and Bayesian Nash Equilibrium

There are two competing equilibrium concepts: the *Rational Expectations Equilibrium* (REE) concept and the game-theoretic *Bayesian Nash Equilibrium* (BNE) concept. In a REE, all traders behave competitively, that is, they are price takers. They take the price correspondence, a mapping from the information sets of all traders into the price space as given. In a BNE, agents take the strategies of all other players, and not the equilibrium price correspondence, as given. The game theoretic BNE concept allows us to analyze strategic interactions in which traders take their price impact into account.

Both equilibrium concepts are probably best explained by illustrating the steps needed to derive the corresponding equilibrium. Only a descriptive explanation is provided below. For a more detailed exposition one should consult a standard game theory book such as Fudenberg and Tirole (1991) or Osborne and Rubinstein (1994).

1.2.1. Rational Expectations Equilibrium

A possible closed-form solution of a *REE* can be derived in the following five steps.[5]

---

[5] Bray (1985) provides a nice illustration of the REE concept using the futures market as an example. Section 3.1.1 illustrates each step using Grossman (1976) as an example.

Step 1: Specify each traders' prior beliefs and propose a price function (conjecture) $P : \{\mathcal{S}^1, \ldots, \mathcal{S}^I, u\} \rightarrow \mathbb{R}_+^J$. This is a mapping from all I traders' information sets $\{\mathcal{S}^1, \ldots, \mathcal{S}^I, u\}$ consisting of individual σ-algebras and individual probability distributions to the prices of J assets. u allows one to incorporate some noise in the pricing function. All traders take this mapping as given. One actually proposes a whole set of possible price conjectures $\mathbf{P} = \{P|P: \{\mathcal{S}^1, \ldots, \mathcal{S}^I, u\} \rightarrow \mathbb{R}_+^J\}$ (for example parametrized by undetermined coefficients) since the true equilibrium price function is not known at this stage of the calculations.

Step 2: Derive each trader's posterior beliefs about the unknown variables, given the parametrized price conjectures and the fact that all traders draw inferences from the prices. These beliefs are represented by a joint probability distribution and depend on the proposed price conjecture, for example on the undetermined coefficients of the price conjecture.

Step 3: Derive each individual investor's optimal demand based on his (parametrized) beliefs and his preferences.

Step 4: Impose the market clearing conditions for all markets and compute the endogenous market clearing price variables. Since individuals' demands depend on traders' beliefs, so do the price variables. This gives the actual price function $P : \{\mathcal{S}^1, \ldots, \mathcal{S}^I, u\} \rightarrow \mathbb{R}_+^J$, the actual relationship between the traders' information sets $\{\mathcal{S}^1, \ldots, \mathcal{S}^I\}$, the noise component u, and the prices for a given price conjecture.

Step 5: Impose rational expectations, that is, the conjectured price function has to coincide with the actual price function. Viewed more abstractly, the REE is a fixed point of the mapping $\mathcal{M}_P : \mathbf{P} \rightarrow \mathbf{P}$. $\mathcal{M}_P(\cdot)$ maps the conjectured price relationship $\{\mathcal{S}^1, \ldots, \mathcal{S}^I, u\} \rightarrow \mathbb{R}_+^J$ onto the actual price functions. At the fixed point $\mathcal{M}_P(P(\cdot)) = P(\cdot)$, the conjectured price function coincides with the actual one. If one uses the method of undetermined coefficients, equating the coefficients of the price conjecture with those of the actual price function yields the fixed point.

The REE concept can be generalized to a dynamic setting with multiple trading rounds. Investors have many trading opportunities in these settings. The information of the investors changes over time as they observe more signals and the price process evolves. The unfolding of information for an individual investor $i \in \mathbb{I}$ can be modeled as a sequence of information sets consisting of a filtration, that is (increasing) σ-algebras, and associated probability distributions. A state ω in the dynamic state space Ω^{dynamic} describes a whole history (path) from $t = 0$ to $t = T$.

As before, the state consists of a fundamental and an epistemic part. In each period t individuals take the price function from the information sets of all investors at time t as given. In other words, all investors conjecture a price *process* function, which maps the sequence of information sets for each i into the price process space. Investors update their information at each time t since they can trade conditional on the price process up to time t. After deriving each individual's demand, the market clearing condition has to be satisfied in each trading round. Rationality dictates that the actual price process coincides with the conjectured one. Dynamic REE models – as covered in Chapter 4 – are often solved by using backward induction or by using the dynamic programming approach.

1.2.2. *Bayesian Nash Equilibrium*

In a competitive equilibrium, each agent thinks that his action does not affect the price and thus has no impact on the decisions of others. Game theory on the other hand allows one to model the strategic interaction between the agents. Games can be represented in two forms. The normal form representation of a game Γ specifies at least a set of players $i \in \mathbb{I}$, an action set A^i, and a payoff function U^i for each player. The extensive form of a game also specifies the order of moves and the information sets at each decision node and is best illustrated by means of a decision tree. A pure strategy determines player i's action at each decision node. It consists of a sequence of action rules. An action rule is a mapping from player i's information set into his action space at a certain point in time. A randomization over different pure strategies is a mixed strategy. If a player chooses random actions at each of his decision nodes independently, then he applies a behavioral strategy. A Nash equilibrium is formed by a profile of strategies of all players from which no single player wants to deviate. In a Nash equilibrium all players take the strategies of all the other players as given. A player chooses his own optimal strategy by assuming the strategies of all the other players as given. The Nash equilibrium of an extensive form game is given by the Nash equilibrium of its normal-form representation. If players face uncertainty and hold asymmetric information, the equilibrium concept generalizes to the BNE provided agents update their prior beliefs using Bayes' rule. Uncertainty is modeled by a random move of nature. Players learn from exogenous signals and from the moves of other players.

Simultaneous Move Games

Before extending the analysis to multiperiod, sequential move games, let us first illustrate the steps involved in the derivation of a BNE. This highlights the differences between a BNE and a REE.[6]

Step 1: Specify the players' prior beliefs and conjecture a strategy profile, that is a strategy for each player. More specifically, propose a whole set of profiles described either by a profile of general functions or by undetermined coefficients. These profiles also determine the joint probability distributions between players' prior beliefs, their information, and other endogenous variables like other traders' actions, demand, and prices. A single player's deviation from a proposed strategy profile alters this joint probability distribution and possibly the other players' beliefs. In a simultaneous move game, the other players cannot detect this deviation in time and there is no need to specify out-of-equilibrium beliefs.

Step 2: Update all players' beliefs using Bayes' rule and the joint probability distribution, which depends on the proposed set of strategy profiles, for example the undetermined coefficients.

Step 3: Derive each individual player's optimal response given the conjectured strategies of all other players and the market clearing conditions.

Step 4: If the best responses of all players coincide with the conjectured strategy profile, nobody will want to deviate. Hence, the conjectured strategy profile is a BNE. In other words, the BNE is a fixed point in strategy profiles. If one focuses only on equilibria in linear strategies, the proposed set of strategy profiles can be best characterized by undetermined coefficients. Each player's best response depends on the coefficients in the conjectured strategy profile. The BNE is then derived by equating the conjectured coefficients with the ones from the best response. The variational calculus method enables us also to derive the equilibria in which strategies can take any functional form.

Sequential Move Games

In sequential move (multiperiod) extensive form games, players take actions at different points in time. Let us focus first on perfect information games before analyzing games in which different traders hold different information. A strategy specifies the action at each node at

---

[6] An example which illustrates these steps for a sequential move game is given by Kyle's (1985) model in Section 3.2.3.

which a player makes a decision, independent of whether this decision node is reached in equilibrium or not. As before, a strategy profile forms a Nash equilibrium if nobody has an incentive to deviate from his strategy. Whether a deviation is profitable depends on how his opponents react after the player's deviation. The opponents' reactions after a deviation are also specified by their strategies. A Nash equilibrium does not require that the opponents' out-of-equilibrium (re-)actions are optimal. That is, many Nash equilibria rely on strategies which specify nonsequentially rational out-of-equilibrium actions. Subgame perfection rules out Nash equilibria which are based on empty threats and promises by requiring that the out-of-equilibrium action rules are also optimal after an observed deviation. In other words, the strategy is sequentially rational. An opponent cannot make a player believe that she will react to a deviation in a nonoptimal manner in the subsequent play. More formally, a Nash equilibrium is subgame perfect if the strategy profile is also a Nash equilibrium for any subgame starting at any possible (nonterminal) history, that is decision node. Subgame equilibria can be derived by backwards induction or by applying the dynamic programming approach.

Introducing Asymmetric Information in Sequential Move Games

In the case of imperfect information, a strategy specifies the actions of a player at any information set at which the agent is supposed to move. Players cannot distinguish between different histories contained in the same information set. Depending on the proposed candidate equilibrium strategy profile, agents have a joint probability distribution over the possible states of nature at each point in time. They use Bayes' rule to update their beliefs after each observed move or received signal. A deviation of one player from the proposed strategy profile might alter the subsequent players' beliefs about the true state of the world. Hence, whether a player considers a deviation profitable, depends on his beliefs about how his deviation affects the other players' beliefs and hence their subsequent actions. In other words, profitability of a deviation depends on the assumed out-of-equilibrium beliefs. Thus, the belief system consisting of equilibrium beliefs as well as out-of-equilibrium beliefs determine whether the proposed candidate equilibrium is a BNE. Note that as long as other players cannot detect any deviation, they assign zero probability to a deviation and there is no need to specify out-of-equilibrium beliefs. If, on the other hand, subsequent players observe the deviation, out-of-equilibrium beliefs need to be exogeneously specified. Out-of-equilibrium beliefs cannot be derived using Bayes' rule since these information sets are reached with probability zero in the (proposed) equilibrium.

Like the Nash equilibrium in the case of perfect information, the BNE refers to the normal form representation of the game and thus does not require sequential rationality. Hence, there are many BNE which rely on empty threats and promises. Subgame perfection has relatively little bite in imperfect information games since a subgame only starts at a decision node at which the player knows the true (single) history. Therefore, alternative refinements are applied for imperfect information extensive form games. A *sequential equilibrium* (i) requires that players are sequentially rational given their beliefs at each point in time, that is, at each of their information sets they optimize given the beliefs on the set of possible histories and (ii) it also restricts the possible set of out-of-equilibrium beliefs. To be able to derive these beliefs by means of Bayes' rule, we need to consider completely mixed behavioral strategies β. A mixed strategy is completely mixed if each pure strategy is played with strictly positive probability. Given this behavioral strategy profile, each terminal history is reached with strictly positive probability. That is, for a given prior distribution and β, one can derive the associated posterior belief system μ at each information set using Bayes' rule. This belief system μ together with the associated completely mixed behavioral strategy profile β is called an assessment (β, μ). If there exists a sequence of assessments $((\beta, \mu))_{n=1}^{\infty}$ that converges to a sequentially rational assessment, then the limit forms a sequential equilibrium. Note that only the limiting assessment has to satisfy sequential rationality, but it need not be completely mixed. The drawback of this refined solution concept is that existence is only formally proven for finite extensive games and it is not very easy to verify.

The simpler *Perfect Bayesian Equilibrium* (PBE) solution concept can be applied for a certain class of extensive form games. In these games all actions are observable and the asymmetry of information is modeled by an unobservable move of nature prior to the start of the game. Depending on the information/signal a player has received, the player is assigned a certain type. A PBE also requires sequential rationality and Bayesian updating after each observed action whenever possible. Any sequential equilibrium in this class of games is also a PBE.

In summary, the REE concept refers to a competitive environment where traders take the price function as given, whereas the BNE concept allows us to analyze environments where traders take their price impact into account. As the number of traders increases, the price impact of a single trader decreases. Therefore, one might be tempted to think that as the number of traders goes to infinity, the BNE of a trading game where all traders submit demand schedules might converge to the competitive REE. Kyle (1989), however, shows that this need not be the case.

Bayesian Implementation of REE

The REE provides a specific outcome for each possible realization of the signals. The question arises whether this mapping from information sets onto outcomes can be *implemented*. In other words, can an uninformed social planner design a mechanism or game form that would make it individually rational for all market participants to act as in the REE although they know that they might (partially) reveal their information? The mechanism design literature distinguishes between different forms of implementation. If there exists a mechanism whose equilibria *all* coincide with the REE allocation function, then the REE can be *fully implemented*. In this case, the "revelation principle" states that a direct mechanism with an equilibrium outcome identical to the REE outcome will also exist. In this direct mechanism each agent truthfully states his private information (type). A REE allocation function is *truthfully implementable* if a *possible* equilibrium of the direct mechanism coincides with the REE outcome. Truthful implementation does not require uniqueness of the equilibrium outcome. Due to the revelation principle any implementable function is also truthfully implementable. The converse need not be true. Laffont (1985) shows that the REE outcome is truthfully implementable for economies with a continuum of traders. For the case of finitely many traders, the REE outcome is only (truthfully) implementable if private information satisfies a kind of "smallness," Blume and Easley (1990). More precisely, the private information of a single individual alone must not have any impact on the equilibrium. Dubey, Geanakoplos, and Shubik (1987) show that no continuous mechanism (including the submission of demand functions to a market maker) can (uniquely) implement the REE correspondence even in the case of a continuum of traders. This occurs because the demand function game does not specify a unique outcome in the case of several market clearing prices. The actual trading outcome depends on the trading mechanism, which makes it clear that the market structure matters.

Epistemic Differences between BNE and REE

Both equilibrium concepts also differ in their epistemic assumptions. Assumptions about the cognitive capacity of agents are an important part of game theory. The study of epistemic foundations of game theoretic solution concepts is a recent and active research area. Common knowledge of the game and rationality of players alone do not imply the Nash equilibrium solution concept but only the weaker rationalizability solution concept. Aumann and Brandenburger (1995) provide sufficient conditions for a Nash equilibrium outcome. In a two-player game, mutual knowledge of the game, of the players' rationality, and of their conjectures implies that the conjectures constitute a Nash equilibrium. For games with more than two players, this condition is only sufficient if in addition all players share common priors and the conjectures are common knowledge.

In contrast, general equilibrium analysis makes no cognitive assumptions. In a REE each agent is assumed to know the mapping from traders' information onto prices, but nothing is assumed about what each agent knows about the other agents' cognitive capabilities and reasoning. In equilibrium all agents agree on the same price mapping (consensus) and point expectations (degeneracy), that is the mapping is deterministic. Dutta and Morris (1997) isolate the role of consensus and of degeneracy in achieving rational expectations.

Learning of REE

Both equilibrium concepts require that traders conduct complicated calculations. Thus, the question arises whether it is feasible to describe a plausible learning process which ultimately yields rational expectations if traders face the same situation repeatedly. It is shown by Bray and Kreps (1987) that rational learning of REE using a correctly specified Bayesian model is actually a more elaborate and informationally demanding form of REE. In such an extended REE, traders learn the "conventional" REE. Alternatively, if agents are boundedly rational in the sense that they are only using ordinary least square regressions to learn about the relationship between the price and the underlying information, the outcome converges under certain conditions to the REE (Bray 1982).

1.3. Allocative Efficiency and Informational Efficiency

Economists distinguish between two forms of efficiency. Allocative efficiency is concerned with the optimal distribution of scarce resources among individuals in the economy. Informational efficiency refers to how much information is revealed by the price process. This is important in economies where information is dispersed among many individuals.

Allocation

Before distinguishing between different forms of allocative efficiency, one has to define the term allocation. An *allocation* in a dynamic model determines not only the current distribution of commodities and production among all agents but it also specifies their redistribution at any point in time conditional on the state of the world. A current allocation, therefore, pre-specifies many future "transactions" which depend on the realization of the state. Agents pre-specify future transactions through standardized security contracts and their derivatives, such as futures, or through individual contractual arrangements. Pre-specified events trigger transactions determined by the allocation. It is important to distinguish these "intra-allocation transactions" from trades. In a general equilibrium setting, trades refer only to changes from one allocation to another. The applied finance literature does not always draw the distinction between transactions and trades.

In dynamic models, the state of the world describes the payoff-relevant history from $t = 0$ to $t = T$. The price process is part of the fundamental component as well as of the epistemological component of the state space Ω^{dynamic}. Price affects traders' payoff but is also a conveyor of information. An example of a possible state space is given by

$$\{\{\text{endowments}\}_{i \in \mathbb{I}}, \{\text{dividend of asset } j\}_{j \in \mathbb{J}}, \{\text{price of asset } j\}_{j \in \mathbb{J}},$$
$$\{\{\text{signals}\}_{j \in \mathbb{J}}\}_{i \in \mathbb{I}}\}_{t=0,\ldots,T}.$$

An allocation determines the distribution of resources for each date t along each possible terminal history ω from $t = 0$ to $t = T$. The so-called date-state (nonterminal history) in t for trader i is an event grouping all states (terminal histories) which cannot be ruled out by the information provided up to time t. The set of all possible terminal and nonterminal histories, that is the date-states (t, ω), is given by $\mathbb{T} \times \Omega^{\text{dynamic}}$, where $\mathbb{T} = \{0, 1, \ldots, T\}$. In general, the description of one date-state can be quite cumbersome. Symmetry and a recursive structure may allow one to simplify the state to a "sufficient date-state description."

Allocative Efficiency

An allocation[7] $\{\{x^i(\omega)\}_{\omega \in \Omega}\}_{i \in \mathbb{I}}$, or more generally a decision rule, is (*allocative*) *Pareto efficient* if there is no other allocation which makes

---

[7] In a dynamic model an allocation is given by $\{\{x^i(t_1\omega)\}_{(t_1\omega) \in \mathbb{I} \times \Omega}\}_{i \in \mathbb{I}}$.

at least one agent strictly better off without making somebody else worse off. However, in a setting with incomplete information, individuals' expected utilities – which determine the notion of "better off" and "worse off" – depend on their information. In such a setting, one distinguishes between forms of allocative efficiency: ex-ante, interim, and ex-post allocation efficiency. Ex-ante efficiency refers to the unconditional expected utility, interim efficiency refers to the expected utility conditional of private information sets S^i, for example, private signals S^i, and ex-post efficiency refers to expected utility conditional on all information, that is, the true state ω. Consequently, an allocation is ex-ante Pareto efficient if there is no other allocation which strictly increases one individual's (unconditional) expected utility $E[U^i(\cdot)]$ without reducing the other's (unconditional) expected utility level. Analogously, if we replace the unconditional expected utility with the expected utility $E[U^i(\cdot)|S^i(\omega)]$ conditional on each individual's signal S^i, we get the definition for interim Pareto efficiency. For the case of ex-post Pareto efficiency, one takes the expected utility $E[U^i(\cdot)|\omega]$ conditional on the true information state of the world ω. In financial market models, ex-ante efficiency mostly refers to the time before agents receive their signal, interim efficiency to the time after signal realization, and ex-post efficiency to the time after (perfect) information revelation through the price.[8] As illustrated by Holmström and Myerson (1983), these three notions of efficiency can also be represented via measurability restrictions on individual weights $\lambda^i(\omega) \in \mathbb{R}$ of a social welfare function $W(\{\{x^i(\omega)\}_{\omega \in \Omega}\}_{i \in \mathbb{I}})$.

$$W(\{\{x^i(\omega)\}_{\omega \in \Omega}\}_{i \in \mathbb{I}}) = \sum_{i \in \mathbb{I}} \sum_{\omega \in \Omega} \lambda^i(\omega) \Pr(\omega) U^i(x^i(\omega), \omega).$$

If one can find arbitrary constants λ^i for the welfare function, such that this allocation maximizes $W(\cdot)$, then this allocation is ex-ante efficient. For a given allocation, if one can find $\lambda^i(\omega)$ which are measurable only on the partitions associated with S^i, then this allocation is interim efficient. If one can find $\lambda^i(\omega)$ which depend on ω then the allocation is ex-post efficient. From this it follows immediately that ex-ante efficiency implies interim efficiency, which in turn implies ex-post efficiency. An alternative reasoning using negations is the following. If an allocation is interim inefficient, that is, an interim Pareto improvement is possible, then an ex-ante Pareto improvement is also possible.

---

[8] In some papers interim efficiency refers to the expected utility conditional on the private signal and the price signal.

Similarly, if an allocation is ex-post inefficient it is also interim inefficient. Intuitively, ex-ante Pareto efficiency does not only require that the allocation is Pareto efficient for each state ω but also that the allocation optimally insures all risk averse agents over the different states of the world.

So far we have not restricted the set of feasible allocations. Often there are not enough traded securities to ensure that an efficient allocation can be achieved. Constrained efficient outcomes and market completeness is the focus of Section 2.4. A further complication arises in a world with asymmetric information. An allocation might not be implementable if its implementation depends on information that individuals hold privately and are not willing to reveal. An allocation is only incentive compatible or individually rational if the individuals are willing to report their information, that is, their types. One can define ex-ante, interim, and ex-post incentive compatible efficiency as done above by restricting attention to the set of incentive compatible allocations.

In summary, in a world with asymmetric information, there are six notions of allocative efficiency: ex-ante, interim and ex-post efficiency within the set of all allocations and ex-ante, interim and ex-post efficiency within the set of incentive compatible allocations.

Informational Efficiency

Prices are informationally efficient if they fully and correctly *reflect* the relevant information. One can distinguish between strong, semi-strong, and weak forms of (market) informational efficiency, depending on the information reflected in the price. If the price reflects all publicly available as well as all private information then the price is *strong-form (informationally) efficient*. If it correctly reflects only public information then it is only *semi-strong form (informationally) efficient*, and if it reflects only the history of past prices and past returns, then the price is called *weak form (informationally) efficient*. This terminology of informational efficiency was originally coined in the empirical finance literature; see, for example, Fama (1970, 1976). If prices do not correctly and fully reflect public information, then there would be a profitable trading opportunity for individuals. In general, this is ruled out in models with rational, utility maximizing agents. If even the pooled private information is fully reflected in the price, then a public announcement of this private information would not alter the price.

Note that even if the price fully reflects information, it does not imply that everybody can *infer* this information from the price. *Information revelation* through prices is the focus of much of the theoretical literature on financial markets. Prices can be distinguished according to two criteria: (1) they can be fully revealing or partially revealing; and (2) they can be (strong-form) informationally efficient in a theoretical sense or not.

A price is *fully revealing* if agents can infer all private and public information from the price. This is the case if the pricing function, the mapping from the information sets into the price space for J assets, is invertible. Note that $P(\cdot) : \{\mathcal{S}^1, \ldots, \mathcal{S}^I\} \to \mathbb{R}^J$ might arise from a competitive REE or a strategic BNE. Prices are deemed to be *partially revealing* if traders can only partially infer the information which is dispersed in the economy.

Prices are (strong-form) informationally efficient in theoretical models if they reveal a sufficient statistic for all the information in the economy. In other words, observing the price will lead to the same equilibrium outcome as in a full communication equilibrium.[9] Fully revealing equilibria are obviously also informationally efficient.[10] Informationally efficient equilibria can be illustrated as follows. Let $\bar{S}$ be a sufficient statistic for all individual information sets $\{\mathcal{S}^1, \ldots, \mathcal{S}^I\}$. The function $\bar{S}$ is a sufficient statistic if the knowledge of $\bar{S}$ leads to the same posterior distribution as the knowledge of all individual information sets. If we can rewrite the price function as $P(\cdot) : \{\mathcal{S}^1, \ldots, \mathcal{S}^I\} \overset{g(\cdot)}{\to} \bar{S} \overset{f(\cdot)}{\to} P$ and if $f(\bar{S})$ is invertible, then the price is "fully informative" or (strong-form) informationally efficient in the theoretical sense of Grossman (1978). In contrast to the definition of informational efficiency in the empirical literature, the theoretical definition requires that traders can infer a sufficient statistic of all the information in the economy. In this book we will focus on informational efficiency in the theoretical sense.

If the price only (partially) reveals a sufficient statistic rather than all individual signals then the price also aggregates the information dispersed in the economy. *Information aggregation* allows market participants to capture a lot of information in the economy by simply observing a few prices.

[9] Radner (1979) defines a full communication equilibrium as one in which all information is shared among all market participants.

[10] Informationally efficient REE can be derived by considering the corresponding artificial economy in which all private information is treated as being public. The equilibrium of this artificial economy is a full communication equilibrium. Having solved for this equilibrium, one has to verify that it is a REE of the underlying diverse information economy.

Note that, in a dynamic setting, a price might be fully informative about the current information, yet the inferred sufficient statistic might not allow one to evaluate new future information as well as the current disaggregated information does. Section 4.1.1 sheds more light on this issue.

Interplay between Informational Efficiency and Allocative Efficiency: the Hirshleifer Effect

For informationally efficient REE, ex-post allocation efficiency is a direct implication of the first welfare theorem. REE which are only partially revealing are in general not ex-post efficient. Moreover, even an informationally efficient REE does not guarantee that the equilibrium allocation is interim efficient. Laffont (1985) provides an example of an informationally efficient REE which is interim inefficient and a partially revealing REE which is ex-post inefficient. The interim inefficiency can be due to a lack of optimal risk sharing.

Hirshleifer (1971) first noted that the expected revelation of information can prevent risk sharing. A simple example helps to illustrate his point. Consider a situation where two traders could perfectly insure each other. More specifically, after observing their private signal they still cannot distinguish between state ω_1, in which trader 1 gains and trader 2 loses, and state ω_2, in which trader 2 gains and trader 1 loses. Before they learn the true state ω, both traders are better off by insuring each other. After the true state is known, the winner is no longer interested in this deal. Demand functions allow traders to trade conditional on the equilibrium price, that is, conditional on the information revealed by the price. If the price reveals the true state ω, trade will not occur. The incentives to share risk ex-ante disappears if one knows the fully revealing price. In other words, price revelation can make ex-ante desirable insurance impossible.

Because of the Hirshleifer effect, it may be desirable to have a REE which only partially reveals the information of traders. Trade might be possible when prices reveal less information. On the other hand, partially revealing REE leads to a more severe adverse selection problem as uninformed investors can infer less information from prices. The trade-off between the Hirshleifer effect and the adverse selection effect is formally analyzed by Marin and Rahi (1996).

Grossman–Stiglitz Paradox

Informationally efficient prices lead to some of the more famous paradoxes. If prices are informationally efficient, that is, they are a sufficient statistic for all private signals, no trader will condition her demand on her private signal. But if traders' demand is independent of their signals, how can prices be informationally efficient? How do traders know whether the observed price is the rational expectations equilibrium price or an off-equilibrium price? Thus, the *Grossman paradox* arises.

In a model with endogenous information acquisition, informational efficiency precludes any costly information gathering. There is no incentive to gather costly signals if the sufficient statistic of all signals can be inferred from the prices for free. Acquiring information does not yield any advantage because other traders can immediately infer a sufficient statistic of it from the price. In other words, information acquisition results in a positive information externality to all the other traders. Consequently, an overall equilibrium with costly, endogenous information acquisition does not exist if markets are informationally efficient. This is known as the *Grossman–Stiglitz paradox*.

Jackson (1991) shows that the Grossman–Stiglitz paradox depends crucially on the price taking behavior of the traders. He develops a strategic BNE model in which a finite number of risk neutral traders submit demand functions. Thereby, he explicitly models the price formation process to illustrate how the signal is incorporated into the price. For specific parameters, costly information acquisition occurs in the BNE even though the price is informationally efficient. In other words, although some agents bear information acquisition costs, they do not have any informational advantage. In this setting, they acquire information because they are driven by the beliefs of the other agents about their information acquisition. Allowing for mixed strategies in a BNE also resolves the Grossman–Stiglitz paradox. Dubey, Geanakoplos, and Shubik (1987) show the resolution of this paradox in a market structure wherein traders can only submit market orders.

Partially Revealing Equilibria

There are many reasons for price changes, including information about the dividend/liquidation value of securities/assets, endowments shocks, preference shocks (for example, cross-sectional changes in risk aversion), and/or private investment opportunities. In *partially revealing equilibria*, incompletely informed traders face a signal extraction problem which does not allow them to infer the true reasons for the price change. This inference problem is illustrated in Figure 1.1.

As long as the price change is due to symmetric information, each trader knows the true reason for it. If some traders do not know the reasons for the price change they try to infer the asymmetric/differential

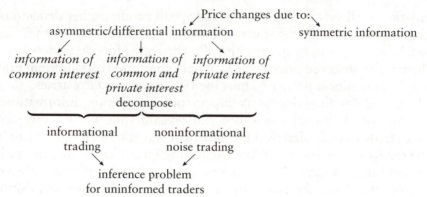

Figure 1.1. *Inference problem from price changes*

information leading to it. Typically agents can only infer the price impact of this asymmetric/differential information, but not of the actual information itself. The question uninformed agents face is whether this information is also relevant to their portfolio choice. In other words, is asymmetric/differential information of *common interest* or only of *private interest* for the other traders. More generally: to what extent is information of common interest?

To keep the analysis tractable, information which is partially of common interest and partially of private interest is assumed to be decomposable into these two parts. The literature refers to trade due to information of common interest as informational trading, whereas trade due to information of private interest is called uninformed trading or noise/liquidity trading. For example, information about the liquidation value of an asset is of common interest. On the other hand, information about trader i's inventory costs might concern only trader i's evaluation of a certain security as long as trader i's behavior has no impact on the aggregates. An endowment shock for a whole group of investors might affect the portfolio choice of all investors via a change in the equilibrium prices, yet it primarily concerns only those investors who experience the endowment shock. A further example of information of private interest is provided by Wang (1994). In his model, informed investors receive information about a private investment opportunity in which only they can invest. An equilibrium is partially revealing if less informed traders cannot determine whether the unexpected price changes are due to others' information of common interest or information of their private interest. Figure 1.1 provides an illustration of the different reasons for price changes.

Following Grossman and Stiglitz (1980) most models exogeneously introduce noise in order to make the equilibrium price only partially revealing. Chapters 3 and 4 will cover these models extensively. Allen (1981) provides a class of exchange economies where the price is "privately revealing." The traders' private signals combined with the price is a sufficient statistic for the pooled information of all traders. The full communication equilibrium of the artificial economy can still be used in such a setting for proving the existence of a REE. In a more general environment where the asymmetry of information persists in equilibrium, a different proof is needed. In order to apply the fixed point theorem, expected utility functions and, thus, the excess demand functions, must be continuous in prices. Ausubel (1990) presents a set of economies where every trader gets two signals. The first signal is a real number and the second signal is binary. The imposition of some differentiability conditions on marginal utility allows Ausubel (1990) to construct a partially revealing REE. There are also models where investors only observe a noisy signal of the price. In Allen (1985) the market clears only approximately since individuals' demands are based on this noisy price. According to the dominated convergence theorem, the noisy component smoothes out discontinuities in the excess demand function. This allows the author to apply the fixed point theorem on excess demand functions (instead of on the price mappings) and show the existence of a partially revealing REE. Even though traders observe only a noisy signal of the equilibrium price in Allen (1985), they know the equilibrium relationships between prices and parameters that describe the uncertain environment precisely. In other words, agents' models (beliefs) coincide with the true model. This rationality assumption is relaxed in Anderson and Sonnenschein (1982) and McAllister (1990). Their approach incorporates elements of bounded rationality and goes beyond the scope of this book.

The efficiency and equilibrium concepts introduced in this chapter provide the necessary background for a thorough analysis of asset prices and trading volume which is provided for a general setting in the next chapter and for more specific settings in the following chapters.

2

No-Trade Theorems, Competitive
Asset Pricing, and Bubbles

The concepts introduced in the previous chapter allow us to derive some results in a fairly general setting. In this chapter we demonstrate the general properties of equilibrium trades and asset prices. Before analyzing asset prices, we will first focus on equilibrium trades and trading volume in an asymmetric information setting. Section 2.1 illustrates different no-trade theorems and no-speculation theorems.

Sections 2.2 and 2.3 are concerned with the pricing of assets. Section 2.2 introduces the basics of standard competitive asset pricing under symmetric information and highlights the complications that arise if traders are asymmetrically informed. Information revelation by prices is closely linked to the security structure and market completeness. We will distinguish between dynamically complete markets and completely equitizable markets in multiperiod models with asymmetric information.

Dynamic asset pricing leads us to the analysis of bubbles. Bubbles that are common knowledge, like in a symmetric information setting, arise only under special circumstances. In contrast, in settings where market participants are asymmetrically informed, bubbles are typically not common knowledge. Necessary conditions for the existence of bubbles are derived in settings with higher-order uncertainty. Higher-order uncertainty and higher knowledge concepts were introduced in Section 1.1.

2.1. No-Trade Theorems

An immense number of transactions occur in financial markets. The large trading volume in the foreign exchange market is one illustrative example. Currency trading in foreign exchange markets amounts to more than ten times the value of imported and exported goods. One might think that this high trading volume cannot be explained without attributing it to speculation. Traders might speculate if they hold different opinions about the value of the assets. These varying opinions might be due to different information among traders. Therefore, one could be tempted to attribute high trading volume to differences in information among traders. This section illustrates that – counter to early intuition – asymmetric information alone cannot explain the high trading volume in financial markets. If the model is common knowledge and agents share common priors, different no-trade theorems show that asymmetry in information does not stimulate additional trade. On the contrary, asymmetric information might reduce the trading volume and might lead to market breakdowns. On the other hand, difference in information might lead to a higher trading volume in models where noise traders guarantee a certain random order flow and the other market participants hold different pieces of information.

An Equivalent, Tractable Definition of Common Knowledge

We need to extend our formal knowledge of partitions and knowledge operators in order to understand the major arguments and no-trade theorems presented in this section. In Section 1.1 we noted that an event E is common knowledge in a certain state ω if all agents know that the true state lies in this event and all know that all know this and so on, ad infinitum. Checking whether an event is common knowledge is very cumbersome since one has to verify an infinite number of conditions.

Aumann (1976) provided an equivalent, more tractable notion of common knowledge in terms of public events. Let us first introduce the following definitions.

1. An event E is *self-evident* for agent i if E is a union of i's partition cells $\mathcal{P}^i(\omega)$, that is, $\mathcal{P}^i(E) = E$. In other words, E is self-evident if for all $\omega \in E$, $\mathcal{P}^i(\omega) \subseteq E$.
2. Event E is a *public event* if it is simultaneously self-evident for all agents $i \in \mathbb{I}$.
3. A partition consisting of public events is called *common coarsening*. The *meet* $\mathcal{M} := \bigwedge_i^I \mathcal{P}^i$ is the finest common coarsening, that is a partition whose cells are the smallest public events $\mathcal{M}(\omega)$. The meet reflects the information which is common knowledge among all agents.
4. By pooling all individual's information, one can derive finer partitions. The *join* $\mathcal{J} := \bigvee_i^I \mathcal{P}^i$ is the partition which reflects the pooled information of all individuals in the economy.

Aumann (1976) shows that a public event $\mathcal{M}(\omega) \ni \omega$ is common knowledge at ω. Obviously, at this $\omega \in \mathcal{M}(\omega)$, any event $E' \supseteq \mathcal{M}(\omega)$ is also

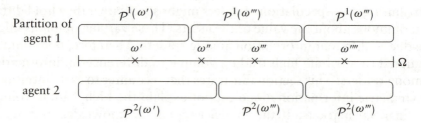

Figure 2.1. *Illustration of common knowledge events*

common knowledge. A public event $\mathcal{M}(\omega)$ can also be viewed as a set of states which are reachable from the true state ω. Let us use the example depicted in Figure 2.1 to illustrate this concept.

The state space Ω in this example is given by finitely many dots on the line. Agent 1's partition is illustrated above the line and agent 2's partition lies below the line. To illustrate the linkage between "reachability" and common knowledge, let us assume that ω' is the true state of the world. Consequently, agent 1 thinks that any $\omega \in \mathcal{P}^1(\omega')$ is possible. He knows that ω'' is not the true state of the world, but he also knows that agent 2 thinks that ω'' is possible. Therefore, the event $\mathcal{P}^1(\omega')$ is surely not common knowledge since ω'' is reachable through the partition cell $\mathcal{P}^2(\omega')$ of agent 2. Is event $\mathcal{P}^2(\omega')$ common knowledge? Consider state ω'''. Agent 1 and agent 2 know that ω'''' is not the true state, that is, the event $\mathcal{P}^2(\omega')$ is mutual knowledge in ω'. However, a state ω''' is still reachable. Although agent 1 is sure that agent 2 rules out state ω''', agent 1 knows that agent 2 is not sure whether agent 1 rules out state ω'''. Therefore, $\mathcal{P}^2(\omega')$ is not common knowledge. The public event $\mathcal{M}(\omega') = \mathcal{P}^1(\omega') \cup \mathcal{P}^1(\omega''')$ is common knowledge since any ω outside this event is not reachable. Consequently, the meet $\mathcal{M}$ for this example is given by $\{\mathcal{P}^1(\omega') \cup \mathcal{P}^1(\omega''), \mathcal{P}^1(\omega'''')\}$.

Agreeing to Disagree

This alternative notion of common knowledge allowed Aumann (1976) to show that rational players cannot "agree to disagree" about the probability of a given event. In other words, if the posterior probability of a rational player about a certain event is common knowledge, then the other player must have the same posterior probability. This result requires that all players use the Bayesian updating rule (that is, they are rational) from a common prior distribution and that the rationality of all players is common knowledge. The common prior doctrine states

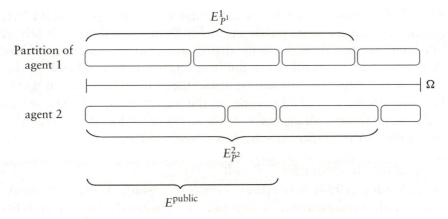

Figure 2.2. *Illustration of Aumann's agreement theorem*

that differences in probability assessments must be due to differences in information. Aumann's (1976) agreement result says intuitively that if a rational agent 1 has a different probability assessment than agent 2, then agent 2 must conclude that this can only be due to the fact that agent 1 has information agent 2 has not considered yet or vice versa. It is important to note that equal posterior probabilities do not mean that all traders followed the same reasoning to reach this common posterior. They need not have the same information.

Since it is a central result, let us also illustrate the formal proof. Figure 2.2 helps illustrate the outline of the proof.

Depending on the state ω, agent i receives a certain piece of information which allows him to update his prior distribution about the likelihood of a certain event D. Let us group all states ω in which the additional information leads to the same posterior P^i for agent i about event D and let us call this group of states $E^i_{P^i}$. In other words, for any $\omega \in E^i_{P^i}$, the posterior $P^i = \Pr(D|\mathcal{P}^i(\omega')) \ \forall \omega' \in E^i_{P^i}$ is the same. The event $E^i_{P^i}$ can be found for any agent i. Since the posteriors of all agents $\{P^i\}_{i \in \mathbb{I}}$ are common knowledge, the true state ω must lie in a public event $E^{\text{public}} \subseteq \bigcap_i E^i_{P^i}$. For all partition cells $\mathcal{P}^i(\omega) \subseteq E^{\text{public}}$, agent i's conditional probability concerning event D is the same. The proof relies on the fact that the conditional probability of D conditional on any union of $\mathcal{P}^i(\omega) \subseteq E^{\text{public}}$ including the public event E^{public} is also the same. Conditional probabilities satisfy this property which is known as the sure-thing principle. In short, conditioning on agent i's information partition cell leads to the same posterior as conditioning on the public event E^{public} does. This is true for any agent i. If all agents could have conditioned on the *same* public event E^{public} instead of on their private information, then their posterior distribution has to coincide provided they share a common prior distribution. The proof also makes clear that the posterior might be different from a setting where one pools all agents' information, that is, conditioning on the join $\mathcal{J} := \bigvee_i^I \mathcal{P}^i$. The reason is that even though all agents have the same posterior, the information set on which their posteriors are based might differ.

Generalization of Aumann's Result

Geanakoplos (1994) generalizes Aumann's result. Agents act conditional on their information. Action rules have to satisfy the measurability condition which states that an agent can only choose different actions conditional on states that he can distinguish from each other. Thus an action rule[1] can be viewed as a mapping from a trader's information set onto the action space. The same reasoning that Aumann applied for conditional probabilities can be applied to any action rule as long as the action rule satisfies the sure-thing principle. An action rule satisfies the sure-thing principle if whenever the rule assigns the same action a to $\mathcal{P}^i(\omega')$ as well as to $\mathcal{P}^i(\omega'')$, then it also assigns the same action a to the union of the information sets, $\mathcal{P}^i(\omega') \cup \mathcal{P}^i(\omega'')$. Then, the generalized agreement theorem states that if the actions chosen by players based on their private information are common knowledge, then there exists an environment with symmetric information which would lead to the same actions. More precisely, the action profile of all agents based on their individual private information is the same as the profile based on the public event E^{public}. This implies that in the case where all players follow the same action rule, and the actions are common knowledge, then the chosen action has to be the same for all players. As stated above, this theorem requires common priors and that the action rules satisfy the sure-thing principle. Geanakoplos (1994) calls this theorem "common knowledge of actions negates asymmetric information about events" to highlight the point that if the actions of players are common knowledge then asymmetric information has no impact.

Equilibrium with Commonly Observable Actions

The theorem stated above indicates that it makes a significant difference whether the actions of all players are common knowledge or not. Actions

---

[1] An action rule is a mapping from the partition into the action space at a certain point in time. A strategy (action plan) is a sequence of action rules for every possible partition.

are always common knowledge in a setting with only two players who agree on some contingent transfer of money. From Aummann's agreement theorem it immediately follows that two rational agents never bet against each other. This is because both agents would assign the same probability to the outcome of the bet in equilibrium.

There are many privately informed traders in a market environment and, thus, all traders' actions are not necessarily common knowledge. However, if all *net trade vectors are common knowledge*, the equilibrium outcome under asymmetric information coincides with the equilibrium in a symmetric information setting in which only the information revealed by the net trade vectors is made public. This is just an application of Geanakoplos' theorem that common knowledge of actions negates asymmetric information about events and holds for the REE concept and the BNE concept. In particular, if there is no trade under the equivalent symmetric information setting, there is also no trade under the asymmetric information setting. Note that common knowledge of all agents' net trades implicitly assumes that each trader can trade conditional on all others' net trades. However, no-trade results can also be derived even when the net trade vectors are not common knowledge, that is, each trader only knows his trading activity and observes the price and maybe the aggregate trading volume.

No-Trade Theorem for REE

In the standard REE setting, only the price vector is commonly known in equilibrium but the actions of each individual trader are typically not common knowledge. One of the first no-trade theorems states that if it is common knowledge that all traders are rational and the current allocation is ex-ante Pareto efficient, then new asymmetric information will not lead to trade, provided traders are strictly risk averse and hold concordant beliefs. There are many different ways to derive this result. Milgrom and Stokey (1982) originally proved this theorem using Aumann's agreement argument. Holmström and Myerson (1983) noted that interim efficiency of the initial allocation is sufficient and the theorem follows directly from the fact that interim efficiency implies ex-post efficiency.[2]

Another way to prove the no-trade theorem is to utilize the fact that all gains from trade sum up to zero if it is common knowledge that the initial allocation is interim efficient and all agents share a common prior. Kreps (1977) and Tirole (1982) prove the no-trade theorem by

---

[2] The relationship between the different forms of Pareto efficiency are explained in Section 1.3.

employing this reasoning and the fact that more knowledge never hurts a Bayesian optimizer in a nonstrategic (single-player) environment.

No-Trade Theorem for BNE

The no-trade theorem holds for Bayesian games as well. If it is common knowledge that the current allocation is interim Pareto optimal, then the trading game is a zero-sum game. Common knowledge of rationality implies that everybody tries to maximize his trading gains. Intuitively, anyone who receives a trading offer can infer that her opponent wants to make money by using her superior information. Since the opponent can only gain if somebody else loses, nobody will be willing to trade except at prices that already incorporate her information. In other words, passive investment is a (weakly) dominant strategy. The proof of the theorem uses the zero-sum game argument and the fact that additional information cannot hurt in a single-player environment.

Asymmetric Information Reduces Trade – Market Breakdowns

So far we have shown that asymmetric information alone does not stimulate trade if the initial allocation is interim Pareto efficient and thus no trade will occur under a symmetric information setting. We now illustrate that asymmetric information might even inhibit trade which would otherwise occur. In other words, asymmetric information can deter trade even when the current allocation is not interim Pareto optimal.

One kind of no-trade theorem is due to the Hirshleifer effect (Hirshleifer 1971). In this case the anticipated information revelation through prices prevents agents from risk-sharing trade. Trading provides a means for ex-ante Pareto improving risk sharing in a world with uncertainty where one group of risk averse traders is better off in one state and the other group in the other state. After the uncertainty is resolved, the group of traders which is better off is no longer willing to trade, because every allocation is ex-post Pareto efficient. Consider an information structure wherein no trader can distinguish between both states, but the combined information, that is, the join, provides knowledge about the true state. Now, if the price reveals the true state and traders trade conditional on the price, knowledge of the price prevents trading. Trade will not take place in the first place in anticipation of the information revelation of the price.

Another group of no-trade theorems is related to Akerlof's market for lemons (Akerlof 1970). These theorems relate to situations where the current allocation is not ex-ante Pareto efficient and agents want to trade for both informational and noninformational reasons. This is, for example, the case in a setting where all informed traders know the true value of the stock. Thus, informed investors trade to exploit their informational advantage, while uninformed traders only trade for the purpose of risk sharing. Uninformed traders face an adverse selection problem because they cannot discern the extent to which the price change is due to informed or uninformed hedging demand. Therefore, informed traders can extract an information rent from the uninformed traders. If the number of informed traders or the informational advantage of the insiders is too large, then the loss that the uninformed traders incur through the information rent for the insiders can outweigh their hedging gains. In this case they are unwilling to trade and one observes a market breakdown. Bhattacharya and Spiegel (1991) analyze market breakdowns for the case of a single information monopolist who trades with infinitely many competitive, uninformed investors. In their model the information monopolist trades strategically, that is, he takes into account the fact that his order will have an impact on information revelation through prices.

No-trade theorems can even arise in a setting with heterogeneous prior beliefs. Morris (1994) shows that incentive compatibility considerations can preclude trading.

Increased Trading Volume due to Asymmetric Information

He and Wang (1995) show that new asymmetric information need not lead to a no-trade outcome if the information is dispersed among many traders. Dispersed information can even lead to a higher trading volume than the volume that would result under symmetric information. In their model there are noise traders who trade for reasons exogenous to the model. Consequently, the initial allocation is not interim Pareto efficient, or at least it is not common knowledge and, thus, the classic no-trade theorems do not apply. In this setting, asymmetrically informed traders engage in trading in order to profit from the expected losses that noise traders incur. He and Wang's (1995) dynamic REE model is discussed in more detail in Section 4.3.

2.2. Competitive Asset Prices and Market Completeness

The trading opportunities available to investors and the possible sets of equilibrium allocations depend on the number and nature of tradeable assets. The security structure also affects how much information prices reveal. The basic ideas are best illustrated in a static setting before analyzing the dynamic case. In both settings, we summarize the key results for the symmetric information case[3] and then illustrate the complications that arise when asymmetric information is introduced. Like the literature, this section focuses primarily on a competitive market setting.

2.2.1. Static Two-Period Models

There is only one trading round in static models. Investors trade assets and form their portfolios in period $t = 0$. In $t = 1$ each asset j pays a dividend $X^j(\omega)$, which depends on the state of nature ω. In a model with symmetric information, a market is complete if there are enough assets with linearly independent payoffs such that each possible state of the world is insurable. A state is insurable if the security structure is such that buying or selling a certain combination of assets only alters the payoffs in this single state. In formal terms, the market is complete if the payoff (dividend) matrix $X_{|\Omega| \times J} = [X^1, \dots, X^J]$ has rank $|\Omega|$, that is, the rank of X is equal to the number of states ω. For complete markets, there also exists an alternative security structure with Arrow–Debreu securities for each possible state which leads to the same equilibrium outcome. An Arrow–Debreu security for state ω pays one unit only in state ω and nothing otherwise. The price of these Arrow–Debreu securities q are called *state prices*. The absence of arbitrage guarantees the existence of a unique (competitive) state price $q(\omega)$ for each state, provided the agents' utility functions are increasing. Assuming smooth utility functions, individual optimality guarantees that the state prices $q(\omega)$ coincide with each investor's marginal rate of substitution between the current consumption good and the consumption in state ω, that is

$$q(\omega) = \frac{\partial U^i / \partial c(\omega)}{\partial U^i / \partial c_0} =: MRS^i_{0,\omega} \quad \forall \omega.$$

From this it follows directly that the equilibrium outcome is Pareto efficient.

Three Asset Pricing Formulas
The (competitive) asset prices of the original securities are given by the weighted sum of state prices. The weights are such that the payoff of

---

[3] For a detailed exposition of the standard asset pricing theory, see for example Cochrane (2000), Duffie (1996), Huang and Litzenberger (1988), Ingersoll (1987), or Magill and Quinzii (1996).

the portfolio of Arrow–Debreu securities replicates the final payoff X^j of the original asset j:

$$p^j = \sum_{\omega \in \Omega} q(\omega) \, X^j(\omega).$$

The price of a riskless bond which pays one unit in each state of the world, that is, $X^{\text{bond}}(\omega) = 1 \; \forall \omega$ is $p^{\text{bond}} = \sum_{\omega \in \Omega} q(\omega)$. This also defines the risk-free rate r^f which is given by $p^{\text{bond}} = 1/(1 + r^f)$.

Let us define a *stochastic discount factor* $m(\omega) = q(\omega)/P^i(\omega)$ for a given probability distribution P^i. Hence, the pricing equation can be rewritten as the expectations of the product mX^j:

$$p^j = \sum_{\omega \in \Omega} P^i(\omega) \, m(\omega) \, X^j(\omega) = E^{P^i}[mX^j].$$

All prices are in terms of current consumption, that is, the price of current consumption is one. Changing the numeraire of the prices allows us to interpret state prices in terms of probabilities. Let us normalize the state prices $q(\omega)$ such that their sum is equal to one. The numeraire of these new state prices $\hat{q} = q(\omega)/\sum_{\omega \in \Omega} q(\omega)$ is a riskless bond which pays one unit in each state of the world, that is, $X^{\text{bond}}(\omega) = 1 \; \forall \omega$. Thus, the asset price in terms of a bond is the expectations with respect to the *equivalent martingale probability measure* $\hat{Q}$ formed by the state prices $\hat{q}$. The asset price in terms of current consumption can therefore also be written as

$$p^j = E^{\hat{Q}}\left[\frac{1}{1 + r^f} X^j \right],$$

where r^f is the risk-free rate reflecting the bond price.

The equivalent martingale measure (EMM) allows risk neutral pricing of assets (Harrison and Kreps 1979). Imagine a risk neutral investor whose subjective probability distribution over the states of the world happens to coincide with the normalized state prices $\hat{q}$. His discounted expected value of any asset j's payoff is then equal to the equilibrium asset price p^j.

Representative Consumer Economy – Aggregation

As long as markets are complete, the first welfare theorem implies that the equilibrium outcome is Pareto efficient in an environment with symmetric information. The derivation of (competitive) state prices q in a market with heterogeneous agents can be very computationally demanding. Pareto optimality implies that one can find a representative agent economy with the same asset prices. Calculating the asset prices of this economy is much easier. The prices have to be such that it is optimal for the representative agent to consume the aggregate endowment. The utility (welfare) function of the representative agent is a weighted sum of the individuals' utility functions, that is $U^{\text{repr}}(c) = \sum_i \lambda^i U^i(c)$. Unfortunately, the individual weights λ^i generally depend on the initial distribution of endowments.

An exceptional case is a setting in which all agents have a utility function $U^i(c)$ with *linear risk tolerance* (LRT), that is,

$$-\frac{\partial U^i/\partial c}{\partial^2 U^i/\partial c^2} = \alpha^i + \beta c$$

with a common coefficient of marginal risk tolerance β. These utility functions are also called *hyperbolic absolute risk aversion* coefficient (HARA) utility functions and encompass utility functions with constant absolute risk aversion and with constant relative risk aversion. This class of utility functions is further explained in the beginning of Chapter 3.

The aggregation property of LRT economies was derived in many steps. Gorman (1953) initiated the research on aggregation of heterogeneous agents. He showed that the equilibrium prices in an exchange economy do not depend on the initial distribution of endowments if and only if asset demands are affine functions of wealth with the same slope. Pollak (1971) characterized utility functions which allow Gorman aggregation. Utility functions which satisfy the von Neumann–Morgenstern axioms have to exhibit linear risk tolerance (LRT). This was first pointed out by Tobin (1958) and Cass and Stiglitz (1970) within the theory of fund separation. Rubinstein (1974) proved that LRT is sufficient for Gorman aggregation in an Arrow–Debreu setting. In other words, if all agents have LRT utility functions with a common constant β, then any λ_i weights for the representative consumer's utility function will lead to the same asset prices.

Incomplete Markets

If the asset structure does not allow one to insure each state ω individually, then the markets are said to be incomplete. In this case, the rank of the payoff matrix $\mathbf{X}_{|\Omega| \times J}$ is strictly smaller than the number of states $|\Omega|$. The absence of arbitrage still guarantees the existence of (competitive) state prices q. However, the state prices are not unique given certain asset prices p. There are many state prices $q > 0$ for which the pricing equation is $p^j = \sum_{\omega \in \Omega} q(\omega) X^j(\omega)$ and thus no-arbitrage holds. Consequently, there are also many possible stochastic discount factors and equivalent martingale measures.

For states ω which are individually insurable, state prices $q(\omega)$ still coincide with all agents $MRS^i_{0,\omega}$. That is, in equilibrium the $MRS^i_{0,\omega}$ for these ω's are the same for all agents i. However, for states which cannot be individually traded without changing the payoff in other states as well, the state price $q^i(\omega)$ might not be equal to all investors' $MRS^i_{0,\omega}$. Therefore, the equilibrium outcome is typically not Pareto optimal in an incomplete market setting because certain combinations of states cannot be traded. Nevertheless, it is still constrained Pareto efficient, that is, a Pareto improvement within the restricted trading set is not possible. If markets are incomplete, the trading space is restricted since certain states are not individually insurable. There are, however, some exceptional cases where a Pareto efficient outcome can be still achieved even though the markets are not complete. One well-known exception is an economy where all investors have LRT utility functions with a common constant β and each individual's endowments are tradable. In this case, the Pareto efficient outcome is characterized by a linear risk-sharing rule, that is, every investor holds a certain fraction of the aggregate risk. The Pareto optimal allocation can be achieved if each investor sells his endowment and buys a fraction of the aggregate endowment. Representative consumer analysis – as described earlier for the complete markets case – can also be used to derive the equilibrium asset prices for these incomplete market economies.

Introducing Asymmetric Information

The state space Ω also contains all individual signals in a setting with asymmetric information. The security structure not only determines which states are insurable, but also has an important impact on information revelation. Limiting the number of assets restricts the number of observable price signals and the trading possibilities of the informed investors. Thus, there might be many information constellations which lead to the same price vector, or even to the same trading behavior. Obviously not only the number of traded securities matters, but also which securities are traded is important. The actual security design has a significant impact on information revelation and has motivated the optimal security design literature. We restrict out attention to conditions which guarantee the existence of a fully revealing REE. We direct interested readers to Allen and Gale (1994) and Duffie and Rahi (1995) for a general treatment of the optimal security design literature.

Existence of Fully Revealing REE

The crucial condition for the existence of a fully revealing REE is that the mapping from signals onto prices is invertible. As the number of assets increases, so does the dimensionality of the price space. If there is only a finite number of possible signals (for example {high, middle, low}) and prices can be any vector in $\mathbb{R}^J_+$, the invertibility of the mapping from signals onto prices only fails in special circumstances. Radner (1979) concludes that a REE exists and is fully revealing for a generic set of economies. Kreps (1977) provides a well-known counterexample, where a fully revealing equilibrium does not exist. Kreps' example is, however, not robust since a small change in the parameters destroys the nonexistence result.

If the signal structure is more general, in the sense that signal realizations can take on any value on $\mathbb{R}$, or even $\mathbb{R}^m$, then the dimensionality of the signal space plays a crucial role. Allen (1982) shows that if the number of relative prices is larger than the dimensionality of the signal space, then a REE does exist and is fully revealing for a generic set of economies. For the case where the dimension of the signal space is equal to the number of relative prices, there exists an open set of economies with no REE (Jordan and Radner 1982). If the dimension of the signal space is higher than the dimension of the relative price space, then there exists a generic set of economies with non-fully revealing REE (Jordan 1983). Note that the signal space is part of the state space Ω. Consequently, if markets are complete, that is, a price can be derived for each state ω, then the set of prices is fully revealing. Similar results may apply for the existence of informationally efficient REE where prices only reveal a sufficient statistic of the signals. In this case the dimensionality of the space of the sufficient statistic rather than the signal space is crucial.

Quasi-complete Economies

If incomplete markets are *quasi-complete*, a (strong-form) informationally efficient REE exists independently of the dimensionality of the signal space and price space. DeMarzo and Skiadas (1998) essentially define incomplete markets as quasi-complete if (1) an equivalent martingale measure exists, and (2) all equilibrium outcomes are interim Pareto efficient given private information and the information revealed by prices. In general, an equivalent martingale measure $\hat{Q}$ need not exist if markets are incomplete and information is dispersed among many investors. Duffie and Kan (1991) provide a nonexistence example. As in the case for complete markets, an equivalent martingale measure also exists for quasi-complete markets. Although quasi-complete economies share many features of complete markets economies, they can also support equilibria that do not perfectly reveal agents' private information. DeMarzo and Skiadas (1998, 1999) show that (strong-form) informationally efficient equilibria are singletons and derive conditions for the additional existence of partially revealing equilibria. Furthermore, interim efficiency of the equilibrium allocation leads to a tractable characterization of the equilibrium trades.

Examples of quasi-complete economies are economies where the security structure allows everybody to sell his endowment, where investors have a common prior, and either (1) there is no aggregate risk, or (2) there is at least one risk neutral trader. An economy in which every investor has a linear risk tolerance (hyperbolic absolute risk aversion) (LRT, HARA) utility function with a common constant marginal risk tolerance β is also quasi-complete, provided individuals' endowments are tradable.

Equilibrium *trade vectors* can be computed in terms of the price vector. This is due to the assumed interim Pareto efficiency of the equilibrium allocation for quasi-complete economies. While interim efficiency has been commonly used to prove the no-trade theorem, DeMarzo and Skiadas (1998) extend the same logic to derive a trade result. Obviously, if the initial allocation is already interim efficient, all trades are zero and the no-trade outcome prevails. The authors illustrate the equilibrium trades for some examples of quasi-complete economies. In an economy with at least one risk neutral investor, all risk averse agents sell their endowment to this risk neutral investor in any REE. This occurs even if they hold different private information about the value of the stock. A tractable expression for the interim efficient trades can also be derived for economies where all agents have LRT (HARA) utility functions with a common constant β. Agents trade so that their fractional ownership of the aggregate endowment of each risky asset is equal to the ratio of their equilibrium risk tolerance to the aggregate risk tolerance. This is independent of whether the equilibrium is informationally efficient or not.

The existence of an equivalent martingale measure $\hat{Q}$ allows us to focus on risk neutral *pricing*. If $\hat{Q}$ is an EMM and p is a REE price vector, then $p = E^{\hat{Q}}[v|S^i, p]$ for each investor i. Applying the conditional expectations operator $E^{\hat{Q}}[\cdot|p]$ to both sides, the law of iterative expectations implies that $p = E^{\hat{Q}}[v|p]$. The same is true for expectations conditional on the price and on events which are common knowledge. This holds for partially revealing and informationally efficient REE. An informationally efficient price has to be equal to $p = E^{\hat{Q}}[v| \bigvee_{i \in \mathbb{I}} S^i, p]$. DeMarzo and Skiadas (1998, 1999) use this point to show that the fully (strong-form) informationally efficient price vector is a singleton. There might, however, also exist additional partially revealing equilibria with possibly different prices $p = E^{\hat{Q}}[v|S^i, p]$. As in Aumann's generalized agreement result presented in Section 2.1, all agents i have to share the same posterior estimate of v, $E^{\hat{Q}}[v|S^i, p] = p \; \forall \; i$. However, this posterior might be different from the posterior that is based on the pooled information. DeMarzo and Skiadas (1998, 1999) provide the necessary and sufficient conditions for the existence of additional partially revealing REE in quasi-complete economies.

DeMarzo and Skiadas (1998) also show that the Gorman *aggregation* can be extended to LRT economies with asymmetric information. In this case, the representative agent only needs to know the information revealed by the prices.

2.2.2. Dynamic Models – Complete Equitization versus Dynamic Completeness

There are many trading rounds $t = 0, 1, \ldots, T$ in a multiperiod model. Investors can restructure their portfolio in each period. In a dynamic setting, a state $\omega \in \Omega$ describes a whole history (path). Dynamic models can be classified into two groups depending on whether investors consume only in the final period $t = T$ or in each period. If consumption can only take place in the final period $t = T$, then markets are complete in the sense of Debreu (1959) if the consumption good can be traded in $t = 0$ conditional on every state ω. In models where investors consume in each period t, markets are only Debreu complete if all individuals can trade the consumption good conditional on any state ω and on any time t. In other words, markets are complete if any so-called date-state $(t, \omega) \in \mathbb{T} \times \Omega$ is insurable. Grossman (1995) calls these markets *completely equitizable* since there are enough securities with linearly independent payoffs such that conditional trading on any possible date-state is insurable through a once-and-for-all trade in $t = 0$. In other words, there will be no re-trade in later trading rounds and the dynamic setting is essentially the same as the static setting. Consequently, all the results of the static setting apply directly to the dynamic setting as long as markets are completely equitable. All the pricing formulas still apply, where the payoff of an asset in $t + 1$, $X_{t+1}(\omega) = d_{t+1}(\omega) + p_{t+1}(\omega)$, consists of the dividend payment in $t + 1$ plus the price in $t + 1$ in terms of consumption in $t = 0$.

Trading Strategies versus Traded Securities

In contrast to a static model, a dynamic setting has the advantage that it allows investors to adjust their portfolio as information unfolds over time. Trading in later trading rounds has the advantage that one can condition one's trading activities on the prior history. Many more payoff streams can be generated by using dynamic trading strategies. Dynamic trading strategies already specify in $t = 0$ issues such as at what time, in which states, which and how many assets are bought or sold. Arrow (1953) first observed that the possibility of trades in later trading rounds can make up for the absence of certain traded security markets. Markets are called *dynamically (or synthetically)* complete if all states are insurable through dynamic trading strategies.[4] The number of linearly independent assets only has to be larger than the maximum splitting index. In a model with symmetric information, the *splitting index* at time t reports the number of branches in which the path/history can possibly proceed starting from the current event in t to $t + 1$. As long as markets are dynamically complete, any additional asset is redundant and thus does not alter the economy. The price of this redundant asset can be derived from the prices of the other assets. In short, dynamically complete markets lead essentially to the same equilibrium allocation as completely equitable markets as long as all investors hold the same information.

Introducing Asymmetric Information

The previous result changes dramatically if traders are asymmetrically informed. In the asymmetric information setting, it makes a big difference whether markets are completely equitable or only dynamically complete. The main problem for the uninformed traders under asymmetric information is that they cannot distinguish between the case where

---

[4] For example, if the dividend payment of one asset is normally distributed, then the number of states is already infinite and, therefore, any market with finitely many assets is incompletely equitable. In a continuous time model in which trade occurs in any instant, the market can still be dynamically complete.

the opponent trades for informational reasons from the case where he just follows his pre-specified dynamic trading strategy. Grossman (1995) illustrates this point by means of an informal example.

He considers a dynamic pure exchange economy with no aggregate uncertainty. There are two types of investors in this economy whose income streams differ only in timing but share the same net present value. He compares two settings that differ only in their asset structures. In the first setting, markets are completely equitized because investors have the possibility of trading annuities. Annuity trading in $t = 0$ allows investors to perfectly smooth their income over time. Each investor consumes his per capita share of the aggregate income in equilibrium. At $t = 0$, each investor sells his income stream in exchange for a fixed annuity. Thus, no future trades are necessary for income smoothing.

In contrast, zero-coupon bonds are traded in the second setting. Investors have to trade bonds in each period to smooth their income over time. More formally, the markets are not completely equitizable because every date-state (t, ω) cannot be insured at $t = 0$. However, this asset structure is still dynamically complete. Thus, the equilibrium allocation is the same as in the case with annuities. This is the case as long as information is symmetric.

However, the equivalence of both settings evaporates if the model is enriched to incorporate uncertainty and asymmetric information. The noninformational bond trading in the setting without annuities provides informed traders noise to disguise their informed trading. That is, allocative trading can create noise, thereby, causing a signal extraction problem for uninformed traders. This is in sharp contrast to the setting with annuities where investors do not trade after $t = 0$ to smooth their income. Consequently, all trading activity after $t = 0$ has to be due to asymmetric information. This information is then revealed in the bond prices.

A second example provided by Grossman (1988) illustrates that adding another security increases the number of observable prices. This might reveal additional information. The author also points out the important informational difference between a synthesized and a real option. If the option is traded, the implied volatility of the underlying asset can be inferred through the option price. This is not possible if the option is synthesized by dynamic trading strategies. This model will be explained in more detail in Section 6.1.1 which focuses on stock market crashes. Grossman and Zhou (1996) extend the analysis. They show that in economies where the average risk aversion is decreasing in income, synthesized options lead to higher volatility and mean reversion in returns. In a dynamically complete market setting, any payoff stream can be synthesized using dynamic trading strategies. Therefore, in an incomplete equitization setting, noninformational trading, possibly over the whole trading horizon, can occur in order to obtain the desired income stream. Uninformed traders face an inference problem since insiders also trade to make use of their private information. They do not know the extent to which the price change is due to insider trading. Therefore, the price is only partially revealing.

The question arises whether a notion of dynamic completeness under asymmetric information can be specified as well. In the case of asymmetric information, the traders' information sets differ and, thus, their dynamic trading strategies have to satisfy different measurability conditions. This condition states that at any time a trader can only apply different trading rules for different states if he is able to distinguish between them. The splitting index can also differ from trader to trader. The splitting index at t reports the number of subpartitions the information partition can be split into when a trader receives new additional information at $t + 1$. Taking the maximum splitting index at each point in time might lead to further insights, but I am not aware of any research addressing this issue.

2.3. Bubbles

Famous historical examples of dramatic price increases followed by a collapse include the Dutch Tulip Mania (1634–7), the Mississippi Bubble (1719–20), and the South Sea Bubble (1720). The historical details and possible explanations for these episodes are elaborated by Kindleberger (1978) and Garber (1990). The more recent empirical findings of the excess volatility literature, starting with LeRoy and Porter (1981) and Shiller (1989), illustrate that the variability of asset prices cannot be explained by variations in dividend streams. The major quarrel in the literature relates to the question of whether large changes in prices are due to shifts in the fundamentals or departures of the asset price from the fundamental value. A bubble is said to occur if an asset price exceeds its fundamental value. The difficulty lies in determining the fundamental value of an asset. The fundamental value of an asset is generally not exogenously given; it is endogenously determined in equilibrium. This fundamental value determines whether a bubble occurred at all and which component of the price is due to a bubble. The following section highlights the difficulty in determining the fundamental value of an asset. This literature focuses on prices in a competitive market environment.

2.3.1. Growth Bubbles under Symmetric Information

Fundamental Value – Speculation and Re-trade

A trader is only willing to buy or hold an asset at a price which is higher than its fundamental value if he thinks that he can resell the asset at an even higher price in a later trading round. Harrison and Kreps (1978) call this trading behavior "speculation." They attribute this definition to Keynes (1936). A trader speculates if his foremost interest is in cashing in capital gains rather than enjoying a future dividend stream. Consequently, one might think the fundamental value might be the price which an investor is willing to pay if he is forced to hold the asset forever, that is, if he is not allowed to re-trade. In a setting without uncertainty the fundamental value of a future dividend stream in terms of current consumption is its discounted value, where the equilibrium discount factor also depends on the asset structure. One can easily extend the analysis to a setting with uncertainty by taking the expectations of the possible dividend payments as long as the agents are risk neutral. Risk averse agents, however, may value dividend payments in different date-states (t, ω) differently since their endowment might be different in different date-states. However, with completely equitizable markets, a Pareto efficient equilibrium allocation can be achieved in a once-and-for-all trade in $t = 0$. Thus, all individual marginal rates of substitution $(MRS^i_{0,(\omega,t)})$ coincide in equilibrium. In this case, one can take expectations with respect to the equivalent martingale measure (EMM) $\hat{Q}$. In summary, this definition of fundamental value seems reasonable as long as markets are completely equitizable or all agents are risk neutral, in which case the agents' $MRS^i_{0,(\omega,t)}$ do not depend on the allocation. This need not necessarily be the case with incomplete markets, for a setting with asymmetric information, or a setting without common priors.

If markets are only incompletely equitizable, re-trade in later trading rounds is not only due to speculation. The definition of fundamental value presented above does not take into account the fact that there might be re-trade not only for speculative reasons but also to replicate the payoffs of nontraded securities. With incomplete equitization and no re-trade, a Pareto optimal allocation is usually not achieved in equilibrium. Consequently, agents' $MRS^i_{0,(\omega,t)}$ differ at the equilibrium allocation. Re-trade usually leads to a different equilibrium allocation and, thus, it also effects the equilibrium $MRS^i_{0,(\omega,t)}$ and, hence, the EMM^i. Let EMM^i be one of the possible equilibrium EMM which corresponds to the MRS^i of agent i at the equilibrium allocation. Taking the expected value using the equivalent martingale measure (EMM^i) that is associated with agent i's MRS^i results in agent i's evaluation of the dividend stream under the condition that re-trade is not allowed. If agents' MRS^i differ, so do their fundamental valuation of the asset. The value of a stream of dividends depends crucially on the market security structure. The equilibrium allocation can change as the number of assets increases. Therefore, the equilibrium MRS^i's and thus the EMM^i's can also change. Dynamic trading strategies allow traders to replicate the payoffs of missing securities, that is, they allow traders to complete markets. Hence, they change the equilibrium EMM^i's. The definition of fundamental value based on a "buy and hold strategy" has the shortcoming that it ignores the fact that re-trade also occurs to replicate payoffs of nontraded securities, which alters the equilibrium allocation and, thus, the EMM. The following example should demonstrate this point.

Consider an economy with two types of agents where trading takes place in $t = 0$ and $t = 1$ and a single risky security pays a dividend $d_T(\omega)$ in $t = 2 = T$ depending on the state $\omega \in \Omega = \{\omega_1, \omega_2\}$. Both states are equally likely and the true state is revealed prior to trading in $t = 1$. The MRS of the agents is such that type 1 agents value the dividend $d_T(\omega_1)$ as one unit of current consumption in state ω_1 and zero in state ω_2, whereas the consumption value for type 2 agents is the other way around. If we ignore discounting, both types of agents assign the asset a value of $1/2$ in $t = 0$ if they have to hold it until $T = 2$. However, if they are allowed to re-trade in $t = 1$, then the value of the asset is 1, since re-trade ensures that the asset will be in the hands of the agents who value the dividend most highly. Consequently, the price of the asset in $t = 0$ will be 1 and, hence, an "expected bubble" of $1/2$ arises if one follows the definition of a fundamental value which is based on a buy and (forced) hold strategy. The problem associated with this definition can be seen if one slightly changes the security structure. Instead of a single asset which pays a dividend in both states, let us now assume that there are two assets. One asset pays a dividend $d(\omega_1)$ in state ω_1 and zero otherwise and the other asset pays a dividend $d(\omega_2)$ in state ω_2 and zero otherwise. In $t = 0$ the price of each asset is $1/2$, that is, the sum of both prices is 1. The price of the assets coincides with its fundamental value and, hence, no bubble exists. This illustrates the argument that the fundamental value – defined in a buy and forced hold context – depends crucially on the security structure. Despite this weakness, some papers define bubbles with respect to this definition of the fundamental value.

If we focus only on buying and holding strategies we ignore the fact that re-trade via dynamic trading strategies might increase the trading space and, thus, enhance the possible allocation which can be reached in equilibrium. Taking the possible $MRS^i_{0,(\omega,t)}$ at the equilibrium allocation in this enlarged trading space and evaluating the income stream accordingly results in a fundamental value definition which is immune to the criticism presented above. Santos and Woodford (1997) employ this definition of fundamental value. Since there are many possible MRS^i as long as markets are (dynamically) incomplete, there might still be multiple fundamental values of an asset. A bubble certainly occurs if the asset price exceeds the highest of these fundamental values. Obviously, it is much harder to demonstrate the existence of bubbles using this revised definition.

Changes in Fundamental Value due to Sunspots

Large price swings might also be due to large shifts in the fundamental value driven by sunspots. *Sunspots* are publicly observable extrinsic events that do not affect the technologically feasible set, agents' preferences, information, endowments, and so on. Nevertheless, they serve as a coordination device for the agents in the economy to select a particular static price equilibrium in the case of multiple equilibria. Azariadis (1981) and Cass and Shell (1983) develop models where this extrinsic uncertainty matters. Allen, Morris, and Postlewaite (1993) illustrate sunspot equilibria using a simple example wherein a dynamic equilibrium consists of a sequence of static equilibria. Suppose the dynamic discrete-time economy can be described as a repetition of a one-period exchange economy. Agents live only for one period and they are replaced by identical agents in the next period. That is, preferences and endowments are the same in each period. Furthermore, let us assume that there are at least two static Walrasian equilibria with different prices in each one-period economy. Any sequence of the static equilibria forms a dynamic equilibrium of the dynamic economy. The selection of the static equilibrium in each period might depend on sunspots. Prior to trading, agents observe the realization of the public signal "sunspot" which alters their beliefs about the other agents' trading behavior and thus their optimal trade. In short, prices will change from period to period, depending on the realization of the sunspot. A bit of care is needed to extend this example to a setting where assets pay dividends over time and agents consume in more than one period. It is easy to see that the consumption value of the dividend payments in each period and, thus, the fundamental value of an asset, depends on the realization of the sunspot. In short, even though agents' preferences, information, endowments, and so forth do not change, the fundamental value might change over time. In a setting with asymmetric information, even more complications arise in determining the fundamental value. We will discuss this issue after illustrating bubbles in a symmetric information environment.

Securities of Finite Maturity and Backwards Induction
Independently of whether sunspot equilibria arise, the pricing formulas due to the no-arbitrage condition in the static setting can be generalized to a dynamic setting. The individual's intertemporal optimization problem links the price of an asset in t to the asset's payoff in $t + 1$, that is, to the sum of the asset's price in $t + 1$ and the dividend payment, d_{t+1}:

$$p_t = E_t^{P^i}[m_{t,t+1}(p_{t+1} + d_{t+1})],$$

where the equilibrium $MRS^i_{(\omega,t),(\omega,t+1)}$ of any agent i forms a possible stochastic discount factor $m_{t,t+1}$. $E_t^{P^i}[\cdot]$ are the expectations with respect to the probability measure P^i conditional on all information up to time t. As explained for the static case in Section 2.2, taking expectations with respect to the EMM $\hat{Q}$ allows one to rewrite the above stochastic Euler equation as

$$p_t = E_t^{\hat{Q}}\left[\frac{1}{1 + r_{t,t+1}^{f,i}}(p_{t+1} + d_{t+1})\right].$$

The risk-free rate $r_{t,t+1}^{f,i}$ is the same for all agents i if a risk-free portfolio is part of the trading space.

Backward induction can be used to pin down the current equilibrium price p_t for securities with finite maturity T^{mat}. By iterating the above difference equation, the law of iterative expectations implies that the equilibrium price is given by the expected discounted value of the future dividend stream. The equilibrium price exactly coincides with the asset's fundamental value. Consequently, no bubble emerges for assets with finite maturity. If all traders are rational, backward induction rules out bubbles, provided that there are only a finite number of trading rounds. If there are infinitely many trading opportunities, a bubble might exist even in a finite horizon model (Bhattacharya and Lipman 1995).

Growth Bubbles for Securities of Infinite Maturity

The fundamental value of the securities with infinite maturity is still given by the expected discounted value of the future payoff stream of the asset. Free disposal of assets guarantees that the fundamental value p^f exists (Santos and Woodford 1997). The stochastic Euler equation also holds for securities with infinite maturity. However, the backward induction argument fails since there is no well-determined starting point. A bubble might occur due to a "lack of market clearing at infinity." The bubble at time t is given by the price of the asset minus its fundamental value, that is, $b_t = p_t - p_t^f$. The stochastic Euler equation for the price p_t for each t and the definition of the fundamental value as the expected discounted value of the dividend stream imply that the bubble component b_t has to satisfy the following expectational difference equation:

$$b_t = E_t^{\hat{Q}}\left[\frac{1}{1 + r_{t,t+1}^{f,i}} b_{t+1} \right].$$

In other words, any bubbles has to grow over time in expectations. The expected growth depends on the *EMM* $\hat{Q}$.

Deterministic bubbles have to grow at the risk-free rate. As long as investors are risk neutral, the *EMM* coincides with the objective probability of states. Consequently, in this case the expected growth rate of any bubble has to coincide with the risk-free rate (Blanchard and Watson 1982). For illustrative purposes, Blanchard and Watson (1982) also consider an example where the bubble bursts in each period with probability $1 - \pi$, and continues with probability π. If the bubble persists, it has to grow by a factor $(1 + r_{t,t+1}^f)/\pi$ in order to compensate for the probability of bursting. This faster growth is necessary to achieve an expected growth rate equal to the risk-free rate as prescribed by the expectational difference equation specified above. Even though the probability that the bubble bursts tends to one as time evolves, the expected value of the bubble increases to infinity as the time horizon goes to infinity.

The expectational difference equation specified above allows us to eliminate many potential bubbles. Note that this difference equation also has to hold for negative bubbles. However, a negative bubble would imply that the stock holders expect that the stock price becomes negative at a finite future date. Free disposal rules out negative security prices and thus negative bubbles (Blanchard and Watson 1982; Diba and Grossman 1988). A similar argument can also be employed for positive bubbles on assets with nonzero net supply as long as the aggregate endowment is bounded by a portfolio plan.

Loosely speaking, potential bubbles which outgrow the economy cannot occur. The intuition behind this argument is as follows. At any point in time τ, the aggregate wealth of the economy contains this growing bubble component, b_τ. Thus, the expected net present value at t of the aggregate wealth in τ does not converge to zero, even as time τ goes to infinity. On the other hand, if aggregate consumption is bounded, the net present value of aggregate consumption in τ goes to zero, as τ goes to infinity. Hence, in an economy with a bubble the present value of some household's wealth exceeds the present value of the aggregate consumption for all periods that are sufficiently far in the future. This is inconsistent with optimization by this household since an optimizing household would consume part of its wealth. This argument can be used to rule out bubbles in equilibrium; see for example, Brock (1979, 1982) and Scheinkman (1988).

Santos and Woodford (1997) provide the most comprehensive analysis by allowing for short-lived agents, incomplete markets settings, and borrowing limits. Their setting also encompasses overlapping generation models. To apply the above reasoning, the future aggregate endowment has to be bounded by a portfolio trading plan. Santos and Woodford (1997) derive the necessary additional restrictions on preferences which are needed for the result to hold in full scope. The authors show that bubbles on securities with nonzero net supply cannot exist under fairly general conditions even if the maturity of these securities is infinite. They conclude that the known bubbles in the literature are only exceptional cases.

One exception is economies where the pure existence of bubbles enlarges the trading space. In other words, a bubble might emerge if it provides further trading opportunities and thus allows a different equilibrium allocation. This typically results in different marginal rates of substitution, $MRS^i_{0,(\omega,t)}$, and thus in a different EMM. This generally changes the fundamental value of the asset. Nevertheless, a bubble might exist even with respect to the new fundamental value. The most famous example is fiat money in an overlapping generations (OLG) model. Samuelson (1958) shows that fiat money has a positive price although its (intrinsic) fundamental value is zero. In Samuelson's OLG model, each generation lives only for two periods. Diamond (1965) and Gale (1973) generalize this setting. In each period there is a young generation and an old one. One period later, the old people die, the young folks become old, and a new young generation is born. Consider a simplified example where only young people are endowed with a consumption good, while the older generation has no endowment. Ideally, the young people would like to smooth their consumption and save some of their endowment for their retirement. However, this is impossible without money. Whom should the young people lend money to in order to save for retirement? The old people will not be alive to repay their debt. The actual problem is that the market with the future generations is not open. Introducing fiat money with a value of zero does not help. But if the price of fiat money is positive, there exists a trading opportunity with future generations. Let us denote the equilibrium price by p^{fiat}. The young generation sells some of their endowment in return for money to the current old generation. In the next period the now old generation uses this money to buy consumption goods from the new young generation. In short, fiat money is a bubble that enlarges the trading space by serving as a store of value that enables all generations to smooth their consumption. These OLG economies can even support two or more types of fiat money. Indeed, every pair of nonnegative prices p^{fiat_1} and p^{fiat_2} such that $p^{\text{fiat}} = p^{\text{fiat}_1} + p^{\text{fiat}_2}$ would lead to the same equilibrium consumption allocation. This also highlights the indeterminacy of equilibrium exchange rates (Santos and Woodford 1997).

Tirole (1985) considers a deterministic OLG model where capital is an input factor of production. Capital as well as fiat money can be used for intertemporal transfer of wealth. The economy grows at a rate n. Since there is no uncertainty in his model, a potential bubble has to grow at a risk-free interest rate of $r^f_{t,t+1}$. Savings in the bubble crowd out capital accumulation in the economy and thus the equilibrium interest rate increases from the "no-bubble interest rate" $\bar{r}^f_{t,t+1}$ to $r^f_{t,t+1}$. No bubble equilibrium exists for $\bar{r}^f_{t,t+1} > n$ since a bubble would outgrow the economy. This is not the case if the economy grows faster than the bubble, that is, $0 < \bar{r}^f_{t,t+1} < n$. Even though they do not enlarge the trading space, bubbles are feasible in this case because they cannot outgrow the economy.

Bewley's (1980) monetary model is another example where a fiat money bubble occurs because it generates additional trading opportunities. In this deterministic model, fiat money is the only traded security between two infinitely lived households. Both households' endowment stream is perfectly negatively correlated and both would like to smooth their consumption. However, complete smoothing is not possible due to the household's borrowing constraints and missing traded securities. A positive bubble in the form of fiat money not only enlarges the trading space but also relaxes the agents' borrowing limits. The borrowing constraints are less restrictive since fiat money adds to agents' wealth. Santos and Woodford (1997) present three additional examples where equilibrium pricing bubbles are possible under special circumstances.

In summary, bubbles under a symmetric information setting can only arise in special circumstances. Bubbles on securities of finite maturity are ruled out by backwards induction. Infinite horizon bubbles are also generally excluded. They are only possible in special cases, such as when they enlarge the trading space or in the unlikely case where the aggregate endowment of the economy is not bounded by a portfolio plan. This means that the "no-bubble interest rate" in a deterministic environment is smaller than the growth rate of the economy.

2.3.2. Information Bubbles

The existence of a bubble is common knowledge in a symmetric information setting. This follows directly from the fact that the model itself is common knowledge. Our earlier discussion illustrated the point that commonly known bubbles generally do not arise in equilibrium. In this section, we will analyze whether bubbles can still be ruled out if they are not commonly known. One can envision a situation where everybody knows that the price is above the fundamental value, that is, the bubble is mutual knowledge, yet each individual does not know that the others know it too. They might still hold the asset since they believe that the others will value the asset even higher in the future. Settings with asymmetric information and higher-order uncertainty provide further insights about the existence of bubbles.

Dynamic Knowledge Operators

Traders have to forecast the other market participants' future information in order to predict the future price path of an asset. The state space Ω^{dynamic} has to be both dynamic and of higher depth of knowledge in order to capture higher-order uncertainty. Agents' information about the value of an asset as well as their information about others' knowledge changes over time. In other words, their information partitions $\mathcal{P}_t^i$ become finer and finer. Therefore, we denote the partitions at time t with an additional subscript t. The associated knowledge operator of agent i at t is therefore denoted by $\mathcal{K}_t^i(E) = \{\omega \in \Omega^{\text{dynamic}}: \mathcal{P}_t^i(\omega) \subseteq E\}$. Note that the partition at time t also reflects the information which market participants infer from the price process up to time t. For an extended discussion of a dynamic state space, we refer the interested reader to Geanakoplos (1994).

Expected Bubbles versus Strong Bubbles

If traders have asymmetric information they also have different beliefs about the other traders' dynamic trading strategies. This makes it even more difficult to disentangle re-trades which are due to dynamic trading strategies in order to complete missing markets from purely speculative re-trade. Therefore, the fundamental value in this section is defined as the value of a "buy and hold to maturity strategy" which rules out any form of resale. Consequently, the shortcomings of this definition discussed earlier might also arise in this setting. These shortcomings are less prominent in models in which the risky assets pay a single dividend only at maturity, all agents have state-independent risk neutral linear utility functions, and they all share common priors. Since agents' information about the future dividend stream differs, their marginal evaluations of the "buy and hold to maturity strategy" are not the same. If the price is greater than the maximum of these values, a bubble surely exists. Allen, Morris, and Postlewaite (1993) distinguish between "expected" and "strong bubbles." If at a date-state (t, w) the price is higher than every agents' marginal valuation of the asset, then an *expected bubble* occurs. In other words, each agent's expected value of the asset is lower than the asset price. A *strong bubble* occurs if there is a state of the world ω in which all agents know that the price is higher than the value of any possible dividend stream outcome. That is, no possible dividend realization can justify this price.

Necessary Conditions for Information Bubbles

Expected or strong bubbles can be ruled out if the necessary conditions for expected and strong bubbles are not satisfied. Tirole (1982) shows that in a dynamic REE, bubbles cannot occur if the initial allocation is ex-ante Pareto efficient. In other words, interim Pareto *in*efficiency is the first necessary condition for expected bubbles. The proof makes use of the fact that rational traders are not willing to buy a bubble asset since some traders have already realized their gains and have left a negative-sum game for the other traders. The reason is analogous to the zero-sum argument in the proof of the no-trade theorem. Obviously, if the initial allocation is interim Pareto efficient, bubbles will not occur, independently of whether there are short-sale constraints or not. In Tirole's dynamic setting, the asset pays a dividend in each period and all traders are risk neutral. Given risk neutrality, any initial allocation is ex-ante Pareto efficient.

Agents can be risk averse in Allen, Morris, and Postlewaite (1993). There is only a single risky asset of finite maturity in their model and money serves as the numeraire. The risky asset pays a dividend of $d_T(\omega)$: $\Omega \mapsto \mathbb{R}_+$ at T depending on the state of the world ω. The authors show that the existence of an expected bubble requires that short-sale constraints strictly bind in some future contingency. If an agent i assigns positive probability to being short-sale constrained at some future time in some contingency, he might be willing to hold on to an asset, even if the price is strictly higher than his marginal valuation of the asset. The second necessary condition for an expected bubble is that each trader i is short-sale constrained at some future contingency.

The two conditions listed above are necessary for expected bubbles as well as for strong bubbles since any strong bubble is also an expected bubble. Additional necessary conditions can be derived for strong bubbles. If a strong bubble occurs, each trader knows that the current stock market price is above any possible realization of the dividend d_T. To make this happen in equilibrium, traders must believe that the other traders do not know this fact. Consequently, strong bubbles can only occur if each trader has private information (Allen, Morris, and Postlewaite 1993). From this it also follows that strong bubbles can never arise in a market setting where net trades of all agents are common knowledge. As shown in Section 2.1, the common knowledge of actions, that is, net trades, negates asymmetric information about events (Geanakoplos 1994). In particular, bubbles cannot arise in economies with less than three traders since in a two-trader market, both would know each others' trades.

Morris, Postlewaite, and Shin (1995) illustrate the linkage between higher-order knowledge and the existence of information bubbles. The model setup is the same as in Allen, Morris, and Postlewaite (1993) except that all market participants are risk neutral. This simplifies the derivation of the price process. In any REE, the price at maturity T is equal to the dividend payment in T, that is, $p_T = d_T$. The prices in earlier periods can be derived using backward induction, that is, $p_t = \max_{i \in \mathbb{I}} E_t^i[p_{t+1}|\mathcal{P}_t^i]$ for all $\omega \in \Omega$ and $t = 1, \ldots, T$. In the states ω in which it is mutual knowledge among all traders that the final dividend payment is zero, that is $d_T = 0$, any strictly positive asset price is a strong bubble. Morris, Postlewaite, and Shin (1995) focus their analysis on this case, that is, on the event $E_T^{d_T=0} = \{\omega \in \Omega | d_T(\omega) = 0\}$ of the states of the world where the final dividend payoff, d_T, is zero. The authors show that such a strong bubble can be ruled out at time t if it is mutual knowledge in t that in period $t+1$ it will be mutual knowledge that ... in $(T-1)$ it will be mutual knowledge that the true asset value is zero. More formally, $\{\omega \in \Omega | p_t(\omega) = 0\} = \mathcal{K}_t^G \mathcal{K}_{t+1}^G \cdots \mathcal{K}_{T-1}^G (E_T^{d_T=0})$. This result is derived by induction. If it is mutual knowledge at $T-1$ that $d_T = 0$ then the price $p_{T-1} = 0$, if at $T-2$ everybody knows that $p_{T-1} = 0$ then $p_{T-2} = 0$, and so forth. The knowledge operators refer to different time periods and also reflect the information which traders can infer from the price itself. Therefore, the above statement is only a "reduced form" statement. A corollary that relies on knowledge at t alone follows directly from the above result. If it is $(T-t)$th order mutual knowledge that the final dividend payment is zero, then a strong bubble can be ruled out from period t onwards. In formal terms, $\mathcal{K}_t^{G(T-t)}(E_T^{d_T=0}) \subseteq \{\omega \in \Omega | p_t(\omega) = 0\}$. If everybody in t already knows that everybody knows, and so on, that $d_T = 0$, then at t everybody knows that everybody will know in $t+1$ that everybody will know in $t+2$, and so on, that $d_T = 0$. This follows directly from the fact that knowledge can only improve over time. In short, a bubble can only exist at or after time t if the true asset value is not $(T-t)$th order mutual knowledge at time t. Obviously, if the state space Ω only allows us to model higher order uncertainty up to a degree of nth order, then nth order mutual knowledge of $E_T^{d_T=0}$ implies that $d_T = 0$ is also common knowledge and thus no bubble can exist. In the case where the depth of knowledge of the state space and the number of remaining trading rounds is higher than the order of mutual knowledge of the true asset value, some bounds for the size of the bubble can still be provided. p-belief operators as defined in Section 1.1 are useful for this exercise. Morris, Postlewaite, and Shin (1995) show that the asset price is not more than $(1-p)(T-t)d_T^{\max}$ if every trader p-believes in t that everybody will p-believe in $t+1$ that … every trader will p-believe in $T-1$ that the final dividend $d_T = 0$. The result is derived by using the same reasoning for belief operators instead of knowledge operators.

Examples of Information Bubbles

The necessary conditions provide the minimal requirements to construct information bubbles. Allen, Morris, and Postlewaite (1993) provide a partial converse of the necessary conditions by illustrating four examples of strong bubbles. In these examples there are at least three traders, at least three remaining time periods, and prices are not fully revealing. The gains from trade are generated in the four examples either by (1) heterogeneous beliefs among the traders, (2) state-dependent utility functions, (3) random endowments and identical concave utility functions, or by (4) an interim Pareto inefficient initial allocation in a setting where traders have different concave utility functions. In Allen, Morris, and Postlewaite (1993) the fundamental value is defined by the valuation of a "buy and hold strategy" that rules out any form of resale.

It remains to be seen whether the setting is robust to the more general definition of fundamental value which allows for allocative re-trade in order to complete missing markets.

Bubbles might also emerge in principal–agent settings where traders invest other people's money. In these models there are positive gains from trade for the direct market participants. These gains are at the expense of the principals.

In Allen and Gorton (1993) there are positive gains from trade for portfolio managers who trade on behalf of the investors. Investors lose in this setting since the overall game is a zero-sum game. Investors face an agency problem. They cannot distinguish between good and bad fund managers. Good fund managers are able to pick the stock with positive net present value whereas bad managers are not. Bad managers pool in equilibrium by buying stocks with negative expected value. Bad fund managers "churn bubbles" since due to their limited liability their payoff function exhibits a call option feature.

In Allen and Gale (2000) traders borrow money to invest in the stock market. That is, their stock market investment is debt financed. This principal–agent setting results in the classic risk-shifting problem. If the borrower buys risky assets, he cashes in on all the upside potential but can shift downside risk on to the lender. The loser is the lending party. This makes very risky assets more attractive and increases their price. The authors argue convincingly that most bubbles emerge at times of financial liberalization. The resulting credit expansion leads to exuberant asset prices. The bubble is larger, the larger the credit expansion and the more risky the asset.

This section illustrates that assuming that all traders have the same information can easily lead to wrong conclusions. Whereas almost all bubbles can be ruled out in a symmetric information setting, this is not the case if different traders have different information and they do not know what the others know.

3

Classification of Market Microstructure Models

The results presented in the last chapter were derived in a very general setting without specifying particular utility functions or return distributions. One needs to describe the economy in more detail in order to go beyond these general results. The loss of generality is compensated for by the finding of closed-form solutions, comparative static results, and a more detailed analysis of the economic linkages. Models in the current chapter take a closer look at the market microstructure and its role in the revelation of information. This chapter is devoted to classifying static models where each trader trades only once and thus does not have to worry about the impact of his trading on the future price path. Dynamic models are discussed in Chapter 4.

Classification Dimensions

Market microstructure models can be classified along at least four dimensions: type of orders, sequence of moves, price setting rule, and competitive versus strategic structure. These alternative classification schemes are described below.

Traders submit different *types of orders* depending on the market structure. The three basic types of orders are market orders, limit orders, and stop (loss) orders. A trader who submits a market order can be sure that his order will be executed, but bears the risk that the execution price might fluctuate a lot. Limit orders allow one to reduce this risk since a buy (sell) order is only executed if the transaction price is below (above) a certain limit. Stop orders set the opposite limits. They trigger a sell (buy) transaction if the price drops below (rises above) a pre-specified level. However, the trader faces an execution risk with limit and stop orders since these orders will not be filled if the equilibrium price does not reach the specified limit. The trader can form a whole demand schedule by combining many limit and stop orders. Demand schedules specify the number of stocks that a trader wants to buy or sell for each possible equilibrium price. Therefore, the trader can avoid both the execution risk and the risk of fluctuating prices. Note that a demand schedule becomes a supply schedule when it specifies a negative demand.

The *sequence of moves* of different market participants is also different in various market microstructure models. In models where all traders simultaneously submit demand schedules, the auctioneer's only task is to set the market clearing price. In reality, the market makers play an important role in certain financial markets. They take on positions and trade on their own account. One can classify financial markets into quote driven and order driven markets. In quote driven markets, like the NASDAQ, the market maker sets a bid and ask price or a whole supply schedule before the possibly informed trader submits his order. Since the market maker guarantees the price, the trader faces no execution risk. In contrast, in order driven markets the informed trader submits his order before the market maker sets the price. Both settings differ in their sequence of moves. In both settings the less informed market maker faces an adverse selection problem when a possibly informed trader arrives. In order driven markets, the market maker offers bid and ask prices or a whole supply schedule to screen out different informed traders. Therefore, these models fall into the class of screening models. On the other hand, an informed trader who submits his order first reveals some of his private information. Thus, order driven models are closer to signaling models.

In addition to the timing, markets also differ in their *price setting rule*. With uniform pricing, the price of every unit is the same. This is not the case with discriminatory pricing. For example, when a trader faces a limit order book, he picks off the different limit orders at different limit prices. As he "walks along the book", his execution price for the additional units becomes worse and worse.

Finally, as outlined in Chapter 2, we can distinguish between *competitive and strategic models*. In competitive models, all traders take the price as given, whereas in strategic models, traders take their impact on the equilibrium price into account. To highlight this difference let us look at the demand of an individual trader. A risk neutral price taker demands infinitely many stocks if his estimate of the stock value exceeds the competitive price. Thus, the assumption of risk aversion is essential in competitive models to restrain individual demands. In strategic models, the trader also takes into account the fact that the price moves against him if he demands a large quantity. In other words, both risk aversion and strategic considerations restrain his demand.

Given the four classification dimensions described above, the market microstructure models surveyed in this chapter are classified as follows:

- simultaneous submission of demand schedules
  - competitive rational expectation models
  - strategic share auctions
- sequential move models
  - screening models where the market maker offers a supply schedule
    uniform price setting
    limit order book analysis
  - sequential trade models with multiple trading rounds
  - strategic market order models where the market maker sets prices ex-post.

In addition, search and matching models can also be found in the literature. For commodities like housing, individuals often have to search for suitable trading partners or they are randomly matched. Agents are matched in the first stage and bargain in the second stage. However, these search and matching models are less relevant for financial markets. This is because transactions in financial markets mostly occur in a centralized place. This centralization and the provision of immediacy by market makers guarantee that there is, in general, sufficient liquidity to find a counter-party for each trade. Thus, instead of covering this interesting but tangential strand of literature in this survey, we refer the reader to the overview provided by Spulber (1999).

Utility Functions with Linear Risk Tolerance

Certain utility functions and return distributions simplify the analysis in various market microstructure models. Therefore, it is worthwhile to illustrate these utility functions and distributions up front before we dive into the specifics of the different model setups.

Most tractable utility functions $U(W)$ are encompassed in the class of utility with linear risk tolerance (LRT). Risk tolerance, $1/\rho$, is defined as the reciprocal of the Arrow–Pratt measure of absolute risk aversion

$$\rho(W) := -\frac{\partial^2 U/\partial W^2}{\partial U/\partial W}.$$

The risk tolerance is linear in W if

$$\frac{1}{\rho} = \alpha + \beta W.$$

Table 3.1.

Class	Parameters	Utility function $U(W)$
Exponential utility (CARA)	$\beta = 0, \alpha = 1/\rho$	$-\exp\{-\rho W\}$
Generalized power utility	$\beta \neq 1$	$(1/(\beta - 1))(\alpha + \beta W)^{(\beta-1)/\beta}$
(a) quadratic utility	$\beta = -1, \alpha > W$	$-(\alpha - W)^2$
(b) log utility	$\beta = +1$	$\ln(\alpha + W)$
(c) power utility (CRRA)	$\alpha = 0, \beta \neq 1, -1$	$(1/(\beta - 1))(\beta W)^{(\beta-1)/\beta}$

LRT utility functions are sometimes also called hyperbolic absolute risk aversion (HARA) utility functions. As described in Section 2.2, economies are quasi-complete if all agents have LRT utility functions with common β and all endowments are tradable. Table 3.1 illustrates special utility functions within this class of utility functions.

CARA-Gaussian Setup

The CARA-Gaussian setting simplifies the trader's utility maximization problem for two reasons. First, the normal distribution allows us to make extensive use of the projection theorem described in Section 1.1. Second, the certainty equivalent of a normal random variable is linear in its mean and variance, if the utility function is exponential.

The exponential (CARA) utility function $U(W) = -\exp(-\rho W)$ with a constant absolute risk aversion coefficient

$$\rho = -\frac{\partial^2 U(W)/\partial(W)^2}{\partial U(W)/\partial W}$$

is the most commonly used utility function. The expected utility resembles a moment generating function and makes it easy to calculate the certainty equivalent of the random wealth W:

$$E[U(W)|\mathcal{S}^i] = \int_{-\infty}^{+\infty} -\exp(-\rho W) f(W|\mathcal{S}^i) \, dW$$

$$= -\exp\left[-\rho\left(\underbrace{E[W|\mathcal{S}^i] - \frac{\rho}{2}\text{Var}[W|\mathcal{S}^i]}_{\text{certainty equivalent}}\right)\right].$$

Maximizing the expected utility conditional on the appropriate information set $\mathcal{S}^i$ is equivalent to maximizing the certainty equivalent. The resulting quadratic objective function leads to simple linear demand functions.

The normality assumption is also very tractable for portfolio analysis given that the weighted sum of normally distributed variables is also normally distributed. In other words, if the liquidation value of each stock v^j is normally distributed, so is the value of the portfolio $\{x\}_{j \in \mathbb{J}}$, $\sum_j v^j x^j$.

Multinomial random variables and χ^2 distributed variables might arise in models with endogenous information acquisition and multi-period models. The certainty equivalent extends to multinomial random variables $\mathbf{w} \sim \mathcal{N}(0, \mathbf{\Sigma})$ with a positive definite (co)variance matrix $\mathbf{\Sigma}$. More specifically,

$$E[\exp(\mathbf{w}^T \mathbf{A} \mathbf{w} + \mathbf{b}^T \mathbf{w} + d)]$$

$$= |\mathbf{I} - 2\mathbf{\Sigma}\mathbf{A}|^{-1/2} \exp[\tfrac{1}{2}\mathbf{b}^T(\mathbf{I} - 2\mathbf{\Sigma}\mathbf{A})^{-1}\mathbf{\Sigma}\mathbf{b} + d],$$

where $\mathbf{A}$ is a symmetric $m \times m$ matrix, $\mathbf{b}$ is an m-vector, and d is a scalar. Note that the left-hand side is only well-defined if $(\mathbf{I} - 2\mathbf{\Sigma}\mathbf{A})$ is positive definite.[1]

The tractable CARA-Gaussian setup has two shortcomings. First, normally distributed stock values can become negative with strictly positive probability, and second, an investor with an exponential utility always invests a fixed amount of his wealth in the risky asset, independent of his wealth. Both features are not in line with reality.

CRRA-Lognormal Setup

These specific shortcomings do not arise if all traders' risk preferences exhibit constant relative risk aversion and the stock value is lognormally distributed. In contrast to normally distributed stock values, lognormally distributed stock values are never negative. The power (CRRA) utility function guarantees that an investor increases his investment in risky stocks as his wealth increases. Indeed, an investor with a CRRA utility function always invests a constant fraction of his wealth in the risky portfolio.

The certainty equivalent for a CRRA utility function

$$U(W) = \frac{1}{1 - \gamma}(W)^{1-\gamma}$$

---

[1] For an example of an application see the discussion on Brown and Jennings (1989) in Section 4.1 of this survey. Additional details about normally distributed variables can be found in Anderson (1984, Chapter 2).

with a constant relative risk aversion coefficient

$$\gamma = -\frac{\partial^2 U(W)/\partial(W)^2}{\partial U(W)/\partial W} W$$

is given by

$$E[U(W)] = U\big(\underbrace{E[W] \exp[-\tfrac{1}{2}\gamma\sigma^2]}_{\text{certainty equivalent}}\big),$$

where the wealth W is lognormally distributed, that is $\ln[W] \sim \mathcal{N}(\mu, \sigma^2)$.

Unfortunately, the sum of lognormally distributed random variables is not lognormally distributed. This makes portfolio analysis more complicated. In addition, individual demand functions are not necessarily linear.

Equipped with these technical details, we are now ready to take a closer look at the different market microstructure models.

3.1. Simultaneous Demand Schedule Models

Many market microstructure models allow traders to submit orders such as limit and stop orders that are conditioned on the equilibrium price. More generally, traders are able to submit whole demand schedules. These demand schedules allow traders to trade conditional on the equilibrium price. Therefore, the equilibrium price can be thought of as being part of the traders' information sets.

As outlined in Chapter 1, one can distinguish between competitive REE and strategic BNE. In a competitive REE, each trader takes the price function from the information sets into the price space as given. Furthermore, each trader believes that his trading does not impact the equilibrium price. In contrast, in a strategic setting, each trader takes his price impact into account. Competitive models are described in Section 3.1.1 and strategic models are examined in Section 3.1.2.

3.1.1. Competitive REE

The underlying market microstructure of a competitive REE can be thought of as a setting where each trader submits whole demand schedules. In competitive models traders take the price as given when forming their optimal demand schedules. Investors believe that their trading activity does not influence the price. To justify such behavior one could assume that each trader is only a point in a "continuum of clones" with identical private information. However, this price taking behavior rules out any analysis of price manipulation.

We begin our presentation of competitive models by describing informationally efficient REE and noisy REE and then turn to models with endogenous information acquisition.

Informationally Efficient REE

Grossman (1976) describes one of the first models with a closed-form REE solution. In his model, information about the liquidation value v of a single risky asset is dispersed among many traders. Each trader receives a noisy signal about the true payoff v,

$$S^i = v + \epsilon_S^i,$$

where $\{\epsilon_S^i\}_{i=1}^I$ are mutually independent and identically normally distributed. The riskless bond is traded at an exogenously fixed price with perfectly elastic supply. The bond pays a fixed interest rate r. All random variables are normally distributed and traders have exponential utility functions with the same absolute risk aversion coefficient (CARA-Gaussian setup).

As illustrated in Section 1.2.1, the standard way to solve for the REE is to follow the five steps summarized below:

Step 1: First propose a price conjecture. In this case,

$$P = \alpha_0 + \alpha_S \bar{S},$$

where $\bar{S} = I^{-1} \sum_i^I S^i$. Since $\bar{S}$ is a sufficient statistic for all individual signals $\{S^i\}_{i=1}^I$, the price is (strong-form) informationally efficient.

Step 2: Given this price signal and the individual private signal S^i, each trader updates his beliefs about the final payoff of the risky stock v using the projection theorem. Since P reveals $\bar{S}$ which is a sufficient statistic for all S^i, $E[v|S^i, P] = E[v|\bar{S}] = \lambda E[v] + (1 - \lambda)\bar{S}$ and $\text{Var}[v|S^i, P] = \text{Var}[v|\bar{S}] = \lambda \text{Var}[v]$, where

$$\lambda := \frac{\text{Var}[\epsilon]}{I \, \text{Var}[v] + \text{Var}[\epsilon]}.$$

Step 3: As a third step, the individual demand for the risky asset is derived. Trader i's terminal wealth after having invested in x shares and b bonds is $W^i = vx^i + b^i(1 + r)$. Given his initial endowments of e_0^i bonds, his bond holding is $b^i = e_0^i - Px^i$. In a CARA-Gaussian setup the demand function maximizes the certainty equivalence $E[vx^i + (e_0^i - Px^i)(1 + r)|S^i, P] - \frac{1}{2}\rho(x^i)^2 \text{Var}[v|S^i, P]$. The demand function is given by

$$x^{i,*}(P) = \frac{E[v|S^i, P] - P(1 + r)}{\rho \text{Var}[v|S^i, P]}.$$

Step 4: Imposing market clearing $\sum_i^I x^{i,*}(P) = X^{\text{supply}}$ leads to the actual relation between the information sets and price. That is

$$P = \frac{\lambda}{1 + r}\left(E[v] - \rho \text{Var}[v]\frac{1}{I}X^{\text{supply}}\right) + \frac{1 - \lambda}{1 + r}\bar{S}.$$

Step 5: Finally, rationality is imposed by equating the undetermined coefficients α_0 and α_S. This yields the REE.

Grossman (1976) uses a different method to derive the linear REE. He first solves for the equilibrium of an artificial economy in which all private information is treated as being public. Radner (1979) calls the equilibrium of this artificial economy a "full communication equilibrium." Having solved for this equilibrium, Grossman (1976) verifies that the full communication equilibrium is a (linear) REE of the underlying diverse information economy. It is possible to solve for the equilibrium in this manner as long as the REE price is (strong-form) informationally efficient. DeMarzo and Skiadas (1998) demonstrate that the markets in Grossman (1976) are quasi-complete even though only one risky asset and a bond are traded. They prove uniqueness of the informationally efficient REE in this CARA-Gaussian setting and show that a minor deviation from the normality assumption leads to the additional existence of partially revealing REE.

Admati (1989) provides an intuitive explanation for why the trader's individual demand in Grossman (1976) does not depend on (1) trader's income; (2) their private signals; and (3) the equilibrium price. The CARA utility function formulation implies that each trader's demand for stock is independent of his income. The private signal has no impact on a trader's demand since the price reflects all information and is a sufficient statistic for it. This raises the question of how the price can reflect all information if the aggregate demand does not depend on the individual signals. This is the Grossman paradox that was discussed earlier in Section 1.3. More surprisingly, the demand functions do not even depend on the price itself, even though it serves as a sufficient statistic for all information in the economy. In general, a change in price alters the demand through the income and substitution effect. In a setting with asymmetric information there is a third effect: the information effect. In an economy with a single risky asset, a price increase indicates a higher expected payoff for this asset. More formally, $E[v|S^i, P] = E[v|P] = \lambda E[v] + (1 - \lambda)\bar{S} = \lambda E[v] + (1 + r)(P - \alpha_0)$. If one inserts this expression into the demand function, one can show that the information effect exactly offsets the substitution effect. Moreover, the income effect plays no role in a setting with CARA utility function and a single risky asset.

An informationally efficient price reveals all relevant information for free. Consequently, in a setting with endogenous information acquisition, no trader has an incentive to collect any costly information. However, if nobody gathers information, the price cannot reveal it. In short, as discussed in Section 1.3, a competitive equilibrium with costly endogenous information acquisition does not exist (Grossman–Stiglitz paradox).

Noisy REE

Noisy REE models were developed to address the conceptual problems of strong-form informationally efficient equilibria illustrated in the last two paragraphs. Grossman (1976) makes very strong assumptions to reach a strong-form efficient equilibrium. Not only do all traders share a common prior distribution, they also commonly know each other's risk preferences, trading motives, aggregate supply, and so on. In addition, higher-order uncertainty is ignored in Grossman (1976). In short, the only uncertainty traders face pertains to the liquidation value v. In reality, however, there are many uncertain factors which affect the equilibrium price but not necessarily the liquidation value. The simplest way to capture this additional uncertainty is to introduce some noisy aggregate supply $u \sim \mathcal{N}(0, \sigma_u^2)$. This noise term makes prices only partially revealing because traders cannot disentangle the price change due to the noise component from the change which is due to informed trading. The REE price function now has an additional term $\alpha_u u$ and can be written as

$$P = \alpha_0 + \alpha_S \bar{S} + \alpha_u u.$$

It is impossible to perfectly infer the sufficient statistic $\bar{S}$ of all signals from the price because of the exogenous random supply u.

The REE can still be derived following the five steps outlined earlier.[2]

Introducing a noisy aggregate supply u can be thought of as a simplified reduced form of modeling. A random price inelastic demand by liquidity traders makes the residual supply noisy. Liquidity traders trade for reasons exogenous to the model. Explicit modeling of liquidity trades, which are not driven by information of common interest, often unnecessarily complicates the analysis. Nevertheless, there are many different ways to endogenize uninformative trading. For example, in Wang (1994) investors have high liquidity demand when they have highly profitable private investment opportunities. These private investment opportunities are investor specific and, hence, they are not equitizable, that is, trade conditional on their dividend streams is not possible.

The noisy REE setup was initiated by three main papers: Grossman and Stiglitz (1980), Hellwig (1980), and Diamond and Verrecchia (1981). Grossman and Stiglitz (1980) introduces a random aggregate supply u in a simplified setting. In their model there are only two groups of traders: the informed (those who have bought an identical signal $S = v + \epsilon$) and the uninformed. Given the price conjecture $P = \alpha_0 + \alpha_S S + \alpha_u u$, the price signal $S^P = S + (\alpha_u / \alpha_S) u$ provides additional information to the uninformed traders. Uninformed traders, however, can only partially infer the signal of the informed traders. The price provides no additional signal for informed traders since they already know S.

Grossman and Stiglitz's (1980) model captures the (partial) information transmission role of prices, but does not illustrate the information aggregation role of prices. This is because information is not dispersed among the traders in their model. This additional aspect is analyzed by Hellwig (1980) and Diamond and Verrecchia (1981). As in Grossman (1976), both papers assume that the signals are conditionally independent of each other given the true payoff. In other words, $S = v + \epsilon^i$, where the error term ϵ^i differs among the traders. Whereas in Hellwig (1980) the aggregate supply of the risky asset is assumed to be random, in Diamond and Verrecchia (1981) each investor's endowment is random

---

[2] For solving the algebra it proves useful to rewrite the price conjecture as the price signal

$$S^P = \bar{S} + \frac{\alpha_u}{\alpha_S} u = \frac{P - \alpha_0}{\alpha_S}.$$

Instead of simultaneously solving for α_S and α_u, one can focus on the fraction α_u / α_S.

and therefore the average supply is also random as long as the number of traders does not go to infinity. The price is only partially revealing in both models. Given the CARA-Gaussian setup, one can demonstrate the existence and uniqueness of the equilibrium and derive comparative static results.[3] Additional details of these models are presented in Section 4.1.2. Hellwig (1980) shows that the REE in the "high noise limit" (where the variance of aggregate endowments u goes to infinity) corresponds to the equilibrium in which market participants do not try to learn something from the equilibrium price. The REE at the "low noise limit" corresponds to the informationally efficient REE illustrated in Grossman (1976). The same is true when investors are almost risk neutral. In this case, investors are willing to take on large positions of the risky asset, that is, their demand schedules are very flat. This reduces the price impact of the random aggregate supply. In other words, there is a lot of informed trading relative to the random supply.

Admati (1985) extends Hellwig's (1980) setting to a model with multiple risky assets and infinitely many agents. In her model, the price of an asset does not necessarily increase with its payoff or decrease with its actual supply. This is the case because a price change in one asset can provide information about other risky assets. Admati's model illustrates that not only the correlation between financial assets' returns (which is the focus of CAPM), but also the correlation between the prediction errors in traders' information is important for determining equilibrium relations.

The main focus of Pfleiderer (1984) is the role of volume and variability of prices. He analyzes how a change in the signal's precision alters expected trading volume. His results are extended in He and Wang (1995) which is discussed in greater detail in Section 4.3.

Introducing a Risk Neutral Competitive Fringe
All traders were risk averse in the models discussed so far. Risk aversion restrains privately informed investors from taking on an infinitely large position. Some more recent models introduce a fraction of uninformed traders who are risk neutral. These scalpers, floor traders, or other market makers have no private information. They only observe the aggregate demand of the other traders, that is the limit order book. Introducing this risk neutral competitive fringe simplifies the derivation of REE since the equilibrium price is always determined by the conditional expectations

---

[3] In Hellwig (1980) the relevant fraction of the equilibrium coefficient, α_S/α_u, is given by the solution of a cubic equation.

given the information of the competitive fringe. Introducing this fraction of risk neutral traders disentangles the risk-sharing aspect from the information aspect. That is, a risk averse trader who has no informational advantage is unwilling to hold any risky asset in equilibrium. He only takes on a risky position if he holds some private information which is not revealed in the limit order book. In other words, his only motive of trade is to exploit his informational advantage. Models with a risk neutral competitive fringe are covered in more detail in Sections 4.1.2 and 5.4.2.

Endogenous Information Acquisition and Selling of
Information prior to Trading

Grossman and Stiglitz (1980) not only introduce a random aggregate supply but also endogenize the information acquisition decision to explicitly analyze the Grossman–Stiglitz paradox. Prior to trading, each trader decides whether to acquire a common information signal $S = v + \epsilon$ at a certain cost. The certainty equivalent for exponential utility functions given normally or χ^2-distributed random variables again proves to be very useful in deriving the private value of the signal. The signal's value depends on the trader's risk aversion as well as on information revelation of the price, that is, the amount of noise trading and the fraction of informed versus uninformed traders. In the equilibrium, traders are indifferent between acquiring the signal S or just relying on the price signal $S^P = S + (\alpha_u/\alpha_S)u$. That is, their willingness to pay for the signal coincides with the cost for the signal. Grossman and Stiglitz (1980) derive some interesting comparative statics concerning the equilibrium fraction of informed traders. Verrecchia (1982) generalizes the information acquisition decision. In his model, traders gather different signals and they can choose the quality of the private signal $S^i = v + \epsilon^i$ they purchase. He assumes that the signal's cost increases in the precision of its error term ϵ^i in a convex manner.

Admati and Pfleiderer (1986, 1990) analyze how an information monopolist should sell his information to competitive traders. The more this information is revealed by the price, the lower is the traders' incentive to pay for this information. The authors show that it is optimal for a seller to add noise to his information when his information is very precise. This increases the fraction of market participants that would be willing to pay to become better informed. When the number of traders is large, it is better to sell personalized signals, that is, signals with an idiosyncratic noise term. In this case, the information monopolist sells identically distributed signals to all traders and not only to a fraction of the market participants. The information monopolist can also sell his information indirectly by using it to create an investment fund. Admati and Pfleiderer (1990) show that the informed fund manager always makes full use of his information. The authors also illustrate that the degree to which information is revealed by the market price determines whether an indirect sale or direct sale of information leads to higher revenue for the information seller.

Competitive REE Market Order Models

In most REE models, traders submit whole demand schedules and thus they can trade conditional on the current price. Therefore, the statistical inference from the price and market clearing occur simultaneously. In contrast, in Hellwig's (1982) market order model traders can only trade conditional on the past prices and not on the current price. Hellwig (1982) uses this market order model in order to resolve the Grossman–Stiglitz paradox. In this model a null set of the continuum of traders receives information in advance. In discrete time, this information is only revealed by the price one period later. This gives the insiders the opportunity to make use of their information to achieve a positive return. Therefore, traders have an incentive to acquire information. Even as the time span between the trading rounds converges to zero, insiders can make strictly positive returns and an informationally efficient outcome can be arbitrarily closely reached. In Hellwig (1982), traders are myopic and the individual demands are exogenously given rather than derived via utility maximization. Blume, Easley, and O'Hara (1994) analyze the informational role of trading volume within such a framework. Their model is described in greater detail in Section 4.4.

3.1.2. Strategic Share Auctions

As Hellwig (1980) pointed out, traders behave "schizophrenically" in a competitive REE. On the one hand, each trader takes prices as given. That is, he thinks that his and other's demand, which is based on private information, does not affect the price. On the other hand, he tries to infer information from the price, which means that he thinks that private information is reflected in the price. This, however, can only be the case if their demand impacts the price. This behavior can only be justified in a setting with infinitely many traders, where each individual trader's demand has a negligible impact on the price, while the aggregate demand of all the other traders does not.

In contrast to the competitive REE models, in a strategic BNE model traders take into account the fact that their trading affects the price. Each trader knows that *prices will move against him* when he trades larger quantities. Therefore, he incorporates this effect while forming his optimal demand correspondence.

Kyle (1989) develops a symmetric BNE in demand schedules using a CARA-Gaussian setting. In this model there are informed, uninformed, and liquidity traders. Each trader's strategy is a demand schedule which is submitted to an auctioneer. Informed traders' demand schedules $x^{in}(p, S^i)$ also depend on their individual signal $S^i = v + \epsilon^i$. The liquidity traders' aggregate demand is exogenously given by the random number $-u$. One can also view u as an additional random supply. The auctioneer collects all individual demand schedules and derives the market clearing price.

Interpretation as Share Auction

Kyle's (1989) setup can also be viewed as a share auction. Informed and uninformed bidders bid for the random excess supply (negative demand) u of the stock provided by the liquidity traders. Share auctions were first analyzed by Wilson (1979). Each trader can acquire a fraction of the total supply. This distinguishes share auctions or divisible goods auctions from standard auction theory where each bidder demands a fixed quantity. Thus, share auctions or multi-unit auctions with divisible goods have features that are quite distinct from the standard unit demand auctions.

Before analyzing a setting with asymmetric information as in Kyle (1989), let us focus on the symmetric information case. In Wilson (1979) the amount of liquidity trading u, that is the aggregate supply, is not random and is normalized to one. In a Nash equilibrium each trader takes the demand schedules of the other traders as given. Given the demand schedules of the other traders and the fixed aggregate supply, each bidder faces a residual supply curve. Trader i acts like a monopsonist and picks his optimal point on the residual supply curve. If the residual supply curve is very steep, that is, the other bidders submitted steep demand schedules, the bidder prefers a lower quantity at a lower price. With uniform pricing a marginal quantity increase leads not only to a higher price for the next marginal unit but also increases prices for all other units as well. A bidder is indifferent between any demand schedule as long as it goes through his optimal point on the residual supply curve. However, his demand schedule is determined in equilibrium since his demand determines the residual supply curve for the other bidders and, hence, their optimal bidding function. Nevertheless, there are multiple equilibria. Wilson (1979) shows that many prices can be sustained in equilibrium. To illustrate this, let us focus on the special case where the value of the stock $\bar{v}$ is commonly known. It is easy to verify that the following demand schedules for the I bidders support any equilibrium price p^* in the range $[0, \bar{v})$:

$$x^i(p) = \frac{1}{I}(1 + \beta_p(p^* - p)), \quad \text{where } \beta_p = \frac{1}{(I-1)(\bar{v} - p^*)}.$$

If all bidders submit steep demand schedules (p^* is very low), then each bidder faces a steep residual supply curve. This steep residual supply curve makes each bidder reluctant to bid for a higher quantity since it would also increase the price for his other units given uniform pricing. In other words, the marginal cost of increasing the quantity is larger than $\bar{v}$. Therefore, the bidder in a share auction can sustain a price well below the asset's true value $\bar{v}$. Wilson (1979) concludes that the revenue for the seller will be much lower in share auctions than in standard unit demand auctions. In unit demand auctions, traders are in Bertrand competition with each other. This results in a unique equilibrium price of $\bar{v}$. The multiplicity of equilibria in share auctions carries over to the case of random values v. In this case, bidders look at the certainty equivalence of v and their bidding schedules depend on the assumed risk aversion.

Introducing a random aggregate supply, u, reduces the multiplicity problem. In the absence of this random supply component, each bidder's demand curve has to pass through his optimal point on the residual supply curve that he faces. Hence, with fixed aggregate supply there are many degrees of freedom to find a profile of demand functions such that the residual supply is very steep for each bidder. Thus, low equilibrium prices can be supported. In contrast, with a random aggregate supply, u, the residual demand curve faced by a bidder also depends on the realization of u. In such a setting, each bidder tries to submit a bid schedule which is optimal for each possible realization of u. This reduces the degrees of freedom of possible demand schedules that can form a best response. Hence, the set of possible equilibria is cut down. Klemperer and Meyer (1989) derive sufficient conditions for uniqueness in the case of a continuous unbounded distribution of u. Klemperer and Meyer (1989) employ a setting where oligopolistic firms compete against each other with supply schedules. In short, uncertainty in the aggregate supply, which is often generated by liquidity traders, significantly reduces the set of equilibria.

Necessary Conditions for Symmetric Nash Equilibrium

Some useful insights can be drawn from studying the necessary conditions for a symmetric Nash equilibrium with continuous downward sloping demand functions $x^*(p)$ for all I bidders. Let us restrict our attention to strategies which lead to market clearing. Market clearing $Ix^*(p) = u$ determines the equilibrium price. Since $x^*(p)$ is invertible, all bidders can infer the random supply u from the equilibrium price p. In other words, each equilibrium price p' corresponds to a certain realization of the random supply u'. Bidders trade conditional to the equilibrium price by submitting demand schedules. Thus, they implicitly condition their bid on the random supply u. Every bidder i prefers his equilibrium strategy $x^{i,*}(p)$ to any other demand schedule $x^i(p) = x^{i,*}(p) + h^i(p)$. To avoid the calculus of variation, let us focus on pointwise deviations at a single price p', that is, for a certain realization u' of u. For a given aggregate supply u', bidder i's utility, is $E_v[U((v - p(x^i))x^i)]$. Deviating from $x^{i,*}_{p'}$ alters the equilibrium price p'. The marginal change in price for a given u' is given by totally differentiating the market clearing condition $x^i_{p'} + \sum_{-i \in \mathbb{I} \setminus i} x^{-i,*}(p) = u'$. That is, it is given by

$$\frac{\mathrm{d}p}{\mathrm{d}x^i} = -\left[\sum_{-i \in \mathbb{I} \setminus i} \frac{\partial x^{-i,*}}{\partial p} \right]^{-1}.$$

The optimal quantity $x^{i,*}_{p'}$ for trader i satisfies the first-order condition

$$E_v\left[U'(\cdot)\left(v - p + x^{i,*}_{p'}\left[\sum_{-i \in \mathbb{I} \setminus i} \frac{\partial x^{-i,*}}{\partial p} \right]^{-1} \right) \right] = 0$$

for a given u'. This first-order condition has to hold for any realization of u, that is, for any possible equilibrium price p'. For distributions of u that are continuous without bound, this differential equation has to be satisfied for all $p \in \mathbb{R}$. Therefore, the necessary condition is

$$E_v\left[U'(\cdot)\left(v - p + \frac{x^{i,*}(p)}{\sum_{-i \in \mathbb{I} \setminus i} \partial x^{-i,*}/\partial p} \right) \right] = 0.$$

For a specific utility function $U(\cdot)$, explicit demand functions can be derived from this necessary condition.

$U'(\cdot)$ is a constant for *risk neutral* bidders. Thus, the necessary condition translates to

$$p = E[v] + \left[\sum_{-i\in\mathbb{I}\setminus i} \frac{\partial x^{-i,*}}{\partial p}\right]^{-1} x^{i,*}(p).$$

In words, the bidding function consists of two parts. The first term $E[v]$ reflects the bidder's value of an additional marginal unit. The second term is negative and is due to bid shading. After imposing symmetry among the bidders' demand schedules and solving the differential equation the necessary condition simplifies to $x(p) = (E[v] - p)^{1/(I-1)}k_0$. Hence, the demand function in inverse form is $p(x) = E[v] - (1/k_0)^{(I-1)}(x)^{(I-1)}$. Note that equilibrium demand schedules are only linear for the two-bidder case.

The exponential CARA utility function $U(W) = -e^{-\rho W}$ with *constant absolute risk aversion* coefficient ρ is another special case. The first-order condition simplifies to

$$\frac{\int e^{-\rho x^{i,*}v}vf(v)\,dv}{\int e^{-\rho x^{i,*}v}f(v)\,dv} - p + \left[\sum_{-i\in\mathbb{I}\setminus i} \frac{\partial x^{-i,*}}{\partial p}\right]^{-1} x^{i,*} = 0,$$

where $f(v)$ is the density function of v. The ratio of the integral is the derivative of the log of the moment generating function, $(\ln \Phi)'(-\rho x^{i,*}(p))$. In addition, if v is normally distributed then the first term simplifies to $E[v] - \rho x^{i,*}(p)\,\mathrm{Var}[v]$. Thus, the individual demand schedule is given by:

$$p = E[v] - \rho\,\mathrm{Var}[v]\,x^{i,*}(p) + \frac{1}{\sum_{-i\in\mathbb{I}\setminus i}\partial x^{-i,*}/\partial p}x^{i,*}(p).$$

As before, the demand schedule can be divided into two parts. The first two terms reflect the value of an additional marginal unit for bidder i. The third term is negative and is due to bid shading. After imposing symmetry, the solution of the differential equation in inverse form is given by

$$p(x) = E[v] - \rho\,\mathrm{Var}[v]\frac{I-1}{I-2}x - k_1(x)^{I-1}.$$

This also illustrates that demand functions are only linear for $I \geq 3$ and for the constant $k_1 = 0$.

Introducing Asymmetric Information

Kyle (1989) focuses exclusively on linear demand functions in a CARA-Gaussian setting. Traders are asymmetrically informed in his model. Informed traders receive an additional private signal $S^i = v + \epsilon^i$ and, hence, their demand schedule $x^{in}(p, S^i)$ depends not only on the price but also on their private signal. The uninformed traders' demand function, $x^{un}(p)$, depends only on the price p. Liquidity traders provide the aggregate supply u. u is independently normally distributed and can be positive or negative. The discussion about share auctions so far focused on the intuition for positive aggregate supply. The analysis is analogous for negative aggregate supply. Indeed, Kyle's (1989) model can also be viewed as a double share auction. Depending on the private information and the realization of u, traders buy or sell the stock. In a symmetric BNE with linear demand schedules each informed trader faces a linear residual supply curve $p = \alpha_I^i + \lambda_I x^i$, where α_I^i is random and λ_I is constant. The reciprocal of λ_I is interpreted as "market depth," the liquidity of the market. Whereas in competitive REE models the aggressiveness of informed traders is only restricted by their risk aversion, in strategic models agents trade less aggressively due to both their risk aversion and the price impact of their trades. Thus, in Kyle's setting traders try to avoid trading their informational advantage away.

Prices reveal less information in strategic models than in competitive REE models. Thus, strategic models facilitate costly information acquisition. Unlike Hellwig (1980), even in the limit, when noise trading vanishes or traders become almost risk neutral, prices do not become informationally efficient in Kyle (1989). Nevertheless, the profit derived from private information (the information rent) is driven down to zero. The reason is that the informed trader faces an extremely steep residual supply curve which makes the profit maximizing quantity zero. Kyle (1989) also shows that as the number of informed speculators increases to infinity, the model converges to a monopolistic competition outcome which need not be the same as that in a competitive environment. The limit coincides with the competitive REE only if the limit is taken by combining many replicas of smaller economies with identical structure.

Kyle (1989) analyzes the special case with a single information monopolist and many competitive outsiders in more detail. He derives a tractable closed-form solution for this case. Bhattacharya and Spiegel (1991) illustrate market breakdowns for this special case.

Uniform Pricing versus Discriminatory Pricing (Limit Order Book)

So far, we have focused on uniform pricing in share auctions. With uniform pricing, the first marginal unit costs the same as the last one. In other words, the total payment for bidder i is $px^i(p)$. In contrast, under discriminatory pricing, the bidder pays his actual bidding price for each marginal unit. For each additional marginal unit, the bidder has to pay the inverse of his demand schedule $x^{-1}(p)$. His total payment is the area below his demand schedule $\int_0^{x^i(p)} p(q)\,dq$, where $p(q)$ is the inverse of his demand function.

Price discrimination changes the nature of the strategic interaction between the bidders. Given the bid schedules of all other traders, each individual trader does not act as a monopsonist. Bidding for an additional marginal unit does not alter the price of the first units. Therefore, bidders have no incentive to restrain their bidding as is the case in a uniform price setting. This eliminates the equilibria which support prices which are below the commonly known value of the asset as described by Wilson (1979). Back and Zender (1993) explicitly make this argument and argue in favor of discriminatory pricing.

Discriminatory pricing also leads to different demand curves. As shown above, in a CARA–Gaussian setup, the bidding function under uniform pricing satisfies the following condition:

$$p = E[v] - \rho\,\mathrm{Var}[v]\,x^{i,*}(p) + \frac{1}{\sum_{-i\in\mathbb{I}\setminus i}\partial x^{-i,*}/\partial p}\,x^{i,*}(p).$$

This condition also holds in a setting where all agents maximize a mean–variance utility.[4] Viswanathan and Wang (1997) uses such a setup to highlight the difference in demand schedules between both auction structures.

The demand function under discriminatory pricing is

$$p = E[v] - \rho\,\mathrm{Var}[v]\,x^{i,*}(p) + \frac{1}{\sum_{-i\in\mathbb{I}\setminus i}\partial x^{-i,*}/\partial p}\,\frac{1}{H(u)}.$$

$H(u)$ coincides with the hazard rate of the random aggregate supply u, $g(u)/(1 - G(u))$, if the bidders maximize a mean–variance utility function over the stock value v. $G(u)$ is the cumulative distribution and $g(u)$

---

[4] Mean–variance utility functions are directly defined over the mean–variance space, that is, $U(E[W], \mathrm{Var}[W])$. An exponential von Neumann–Morgenstern utility function reduces to a mean–variance certainty equivalent if its argument W is normally distributed.

is the density function of u. This mean–variance utility formulation differs from an expected CARA utility specification to the extent that the bidders are risk neutral with respect to the price risk.

If one examines both demand schedules it is immediately clear that bidders differ in their bid shading term. In a uniform price share auction the shading is bid proportional to x^i, that is, it affects the slope of the demand functions. In contrast, in a discriminatory price setting, bid shading changes the intercept of the demand functions. The extent of bid shading in a discriminatory auction depends on the hazard rate of the random aggregate supply u.

Some papers illustrate share auctions where bidders are asymmetrically informed. The classical reference is Maskin and Riley (1989) who analyze share auctions from a mechanism design point of view. More recent articles are Ausubel and Cramton (1995) and Viswanathan and Wang (1999). The latter paper provides an explicit equilibrium characterization of a two-bidder share auction under price discrimination.

3.2. Sequential Move Models

In the last section, all traders submitted their demand schedules simultaneously. In other words, every trader submitted his order before observing the order of the other market participants. In the following sections, we allow for sequential order submission. Depending on the order of moves, one can distinguish between screening and signaling models. In the next two sections we focus on models in which the uninformed market participants act before the informed trader moves. The uninformed traders offer contracts or trading opportunities that allow them to screen the different types of informed agents. Consequently, these models fall into the class of screening models. In contrast, models in which the informed party moves first fall into the class of signaling models. While an equilibrium does not exist in many screening models, signaling models typically have multiple equilibria. This rules out clear-cut predictions since many equilibrium outcomes can be supported depending on the specified beliefs. Models where the informed party moves first are covered in Section 3.2.3. The next section looks at screening models.

3.2.1. Screening Models à la Glosten

A general feature of models in this section is that in the first stage, uninformed risk neutral traders submit whole supply schedules. The uninformed trader is either a single market maker or many market makers like floor traders, scalpers, day traders, and market timers. Given a single aggregate price schedule, the risk averse trader submits his utility-maximizing market order. He trades for informational reasons as well as for liquidity reasons and picks his optimal order size. This class of models focuses only on a one-time interaction.

Uniform Pricing

Glosten (1989) considers a uniform price setting, where the informed investor pays the same for the first marginal unit as for the last unit. This is in contrast to a limit order book where the investor can "walk along the book;" that is, where each additional unit becomes more and more expensive. In Glosten (1989) a risk averse informed trader with an exponential utility function experiences an endowment shock u and receives a private signal $S^i = v + \epsilon$ about the value v of a stock. As usual, u, v, and ϵ are independently normally distributed. The agent trades for liquidity reasons and informational reasons. Risk aversion causes him to adjust his portfolio after the endowment shock. He also wants to trade for information reasons to exploit his private information.

The market makers quote an aggregate price schedule prior to trading. A single risk averse trader observes the quoted price schedule and chooses his optimal order size. Glosten (1989) compares the "dealership market structure" consisting of many *perfectly* competitive market makers with the "specialist system" at the New York Stock Exchange where each investor has to trade through a monopolistic specialist. For the case of perfect competition among the market makers, the price schedule in Glosten (1989) is given by

$$P^{co}(x) = E[v|x].$$

Perfect competition among market makers requires that the expected profit for any order size x is zero. On average, market makers profit from trading with investors with large endowment shocks since these investors trade for rebalancing reasons, and lose to traders with small endowment shocks who trade for informational reasons. A competitive market setup might, however, not provide sufficient liquidity since the market will close down for large quantities. The reason is that competitive forces prevent the market makers from effectively screening the different types of traders. The market makers have to protect themselves against the adverse selection problem of large orders by making the price schedule steeper. However, market makers are unable to protect themselves against extremely large orders and, thus, the market closes down. A general problem in any screening setting with an unbounded continuous type space is that an equilibrium might not always exist as highlighted in Rothschild and Stiglitz (1976). However, Glosten (1989) defends his setting because of its tractability and qualitative similarity to a discretized version with finitely many types.

In contrast to the perfectly competitive dealer market, a monopolistic specialist commits himself to the following price schedule $P^{mo}(\cdot)$:

$$\arg \max_{P^{mo}(x^*(\cdot))} E[P^{mo}(x^*(\cdot))\, x^*(\cdot) - v x^*(\cdot)].$$

$x^*(\cdot)$ denotes the optimal order size of the trader which depends on his endowment shock and his information. The problem a single market maker faces can also be viewed as a principal–agent problem. The principal (specialist) sets a menu of contracts $(x, P^{mo}(x))$ from which the agent chooses the one which maximizes his expected utility. The crucial difference to the perfectly competitive market maker setting is that a monopolistic specialist has the ability to cross-subsidize different order sizes. He earns a larger profit from small trades, but makes losses on large trades in equilibrium. Small trades are more likely than large trades. Cross-subsidization enables him to induce a different trading behavior by the informed trader at the second stage. Large trades are unlikely to occur, but likely to result from information based trading. By keeping the ask price of large buy orders relatively low, the specialist guarantees that traders with extreme signals do not reduce their trade size in order to pool with trades with less extreme signals. This cross-subsidization is the reason why a market structure with a monopolistic specialist stays open for larger trade sizes than a market with multiple market makers.

Madhavan (1992) compares a two-stage game as in Glosten (1989) with the share auction setting similar to Kyle (1989). He uses this comparison to illustrate the difference between a quote-driven market such as NASDAQ or SEAQ and an order-driven market capturing some features of the NYSE.

Limit Order Book
Whereas in Glosten (1989) the risk averse informed trader faces a uniform price, in Glosten (1994) he picks off the limit orders from the limit order book at their limit prices. As in the case of price discrimination, the trader pays less for the first buy orders than for the later buy orders, provided that the supply schedule is increasing.

Glosten (1994) characterizes the equilibrium properties of the limit order book under perfect competition. He shows that under discriminatory pricing the average price will not be equal to the conditional expectation of v given the order size x even if market makers perfectly compete against each other. Instead, the competitive price for the next marginal (buy) order y is the "upper tail" conditional expectation

$$P^{co}(y) = E[v|x \geq y].$$

Traders who buy only a tiny marginal quantity have to pay a higher ask price than in a uniform price setting. The reason is that the competitive market makers do not know whether the trader only wants to buy the first marginal unit or whether he will go on to buy further units. The result is that even for tiny order sizes there is a substantial bid–ask spread. Similar to Glosten (1989), if there is a single monopolistic market maker, the limit order book cross-subsidizes across order sizes. The limit order book favors larger orders and, therefore, provides liquidity even for extremely large orders. Another feature of the limit order book is that it is immune to "cream skimming" of orders by competing exchanges. The competitive limit order book already offers the best price for an additional order. Suppose the trader can split his overall demand and can anonymously submit a number of smaller orders to different exchanges. If a competing exchange offers him a better price for part of his order, it has to make losses on average. Rather than outlining the exact details of Glosten (1994), let us focus on the model setup of Biais, Martimort, and Rochet (1997) which also captures the case of imperfect competition between a finite number of market makers.

Biais, Martimort, and Rochet (1997) provide a characterization of the unique BNE in an oligopolistic screening game. In the first stage I risk neutral market makers submit their supply schedules $p(x)$ to build up a limit order book.[5] In the second stage an informed trader buys $x = \sum_i^I x^i$ shares, where x^i is the number of shares bought from market maker i. His total transfer payment to the individual market maker i for x^i shares is $t^i(x^i) = \int_0^{x^i} p(q)\,dq$.

Let us focus on the optimal order size for the informed agent before deriving the optimal demand schedules for the market makers. Prior to trading, this agent experiences an endowment shock of u shares and receives a signal S about the value of the stock v. Contrary to most models, in Biais, Martimort, and Rochet (1997) nature independently

---

[5] The corresponding notation in the original article is $x^i = q_i$, $u = I$, $t^i(x^i) = T_i(q_i)$, $S = s$, $\rho = \gamma$.

chooses the signal S and the error term ϵ. The value of the stock is then determined by $v = S + \epsilon$. Only ϵ is normally distributed, whereas the probability distributions of u and S have bounded support.[6] This signal structure simplifies the trader's maximization problem since his wealth is $W = v(u+x) - \sum_i^I t^i(x^i)$ conditional on u and S is normally distributed and $E[v|S] = S$ and $\text{Var}[v|S] = \text{Var}[\epsilon]$. The certainty equivalent of the informed agent's exponential CARA utility function is

$$E[W|u, S] - \frac{\rho}{2}\text{Var}[W|u, S]$$

$$= (u + x)S - \frac{\rho\,\text{Var}[\epsilon]}{2}(u + x)^2 - \sum_i^I t^i(x^i).$$

This objective function can be split into two parts. The first part is independent of x and thus represents the agent's reservation utility; the second part

$$\left[(S - \rho\,\text{Var}[\epsilon]u)x - \frac{\rho\,\text{Var}[\epsilon]}{2}x^2 - \sum_i^I t^i(x^i)\right]$$

groups the terms which depend on x and, hence, affects the agent's optimal order size. The signal S and the endowment shock u affect only the linear term $(S - \rho\,\text{Var}[\epsilon]u)x$. Although agents might differ in u and S, the mean–variance utility specification and signal structure used by Biais, Martimort, and Rochet (1997) allow them to capture the different agent types via a one-dimensional variable $\theta = S - \rho\,\text{Var}[\epsilon]u$. This reduces a complicated two-dimensional screening problem to a much simpler one-dimensional problem.

Biais, Martimort, and Rochet (1997) derive as a benchmark the ex-ante efficient order size $x^*(\theta)$ for each type of agent θ. Since only the agent himself knows his type, the principal has to elicit this information from the agent. In other words, an information rent must be granted to the agent such that it is optimal for him to reveal his information θ.

---

[6] The signal structure $v = S + \epsilon$, where S and ϵ are independently distributed, is more tractable but less commonly used. In most models $S = v + \epsilon$, where v and ϵ are independently distributed. An exception is the common value unit demand auction with independent signals. Nature draws I independent signals S^i which determine the common value of the object, $v = \sum_i^I S^i$. Under this assumption the revenue equivalence theorem (RET) of private value auctions, as explained in Section 6.2, extends to the pure common value auction setting. Consequently, Milgrom and Weber's (1982) linkage principle does not apply to this case.

Instead of studying the allocations and tranfers, Biais, Martimort, and Rochet (1997) take the dual approach by working with the allocation and the agent's information rent directly to achieve this objective.

The authors first analyze the case of a single monopolistic market maker. The monopolistic market maker receives the total gains from trade except the agent's information rent since he has the commitment power to set the agent's supply schedule (limit order book). The market maker does not induce the agent to choose the efficient outcome since he maximizes his payoff, which is the total gains from trade minus the information rent. By distorting the allocation the market maker reduces the overall gains from trade but he is able to reduce the agent's information rent by even more. This increases his payoff. This is the classic rent-efficiency trade-off in screening models. This distortion lowers the trading volume $|x(\theta)|$. Biais, Martimort, and Rochet (1997) also show that the supply schedule is discontinuous around orders of size zero. In other words, there is a strictly positive bid–ask spread for infinitesimally small trades.

In the case of oligopolistic screening, I market makers submit supply schedules to build up a limit order book. Each market maker can only offer contracts contingent on his own trades x^i and not on the total trading volume x. Competition among the market makers reduces their possibility to distort the allocation in order to save information rent. As the number of market makers increases, the overall profit for the market makers declines and informational rent of the agent increases. Each individual market maker cannot control the rent-efficiency trade-off. This deepens the market and results in a larger trading volume $|x|$ than in the monopoly case. Nevertheless, the trading volume fails to reach the optimal risk-sharing level.

In the limiting case with infinitely many market makers, Biais, Martimort, and Rochet (1997) confirm the findings of Glosten (1994). Competition in supply schedules in this common value environment is limited. Although the market makers' aggregate profit converges to zero, a strictly positive small trade bid–ask spread remains.

Contrasting the Limit Order Book with Uniform Price Setting

Biais, Martimort, and Rochet (1997) limit their analysis to the case of discriminatory pricing. Röell (1998) and Viswanathan and Wang (1997) highlight the differences between discriminatory pricing and uniform pricing. Both papers focus exclusively on the first stage, the submission of supply (demand) schedules, since they assume that the agent's order size x is exogenous and thus is not affected by the equilibrium aggregate supply schedule. This simplifies the comparison between a uniform and discriminatory price setting because it reduces the problem to a share auction setting. *I* market makers de facto bid to execute a fraction of the agent's order of random size x. Share auctions are discussed in detail in Section 4.1.2.

Röell (1998) derives a nice linear closed-form solution for both price setting rules by assuming that x is double exponentially distributed. A large buy order x is a positive signal about the value of the stock. The conditional expectation $E[v|x] = v_0 + \gamma x$ is assumed to be linearly increasing in x. The double exponential distribution of x, $f(x) = \frac{1}{2}ae^{-a|x|}$, also leads to a simple linear expression for conditional expectations $E[\cdot|x \geq y]$. Linearity of conditional expectations $E[\cdot|x]$ leads to linear supply schedules in the uniform pricing setting, whereas the linearity of $E[\cdot|x \geq y]$ guarantees linear schedules for the limit order book. For the case of uniform prices, the linear aggregate supply function is given by

$$p^u(x) = v_0 + \frac{I-1}{I-2}\,\gamma x.$$

In contrast, the equilibrium limit order book is given by

$$p^d(x) = v_0 + \frac{I}{I-1}\frac{\gamma}{a} + \gamma x.$$

As noted earlier, the limit order book is deeper but less tight than under the uniform pricing rule. That is, the bid–ask spread is wider for small orders. Figure 3.1 plots the *average* market prices for different order

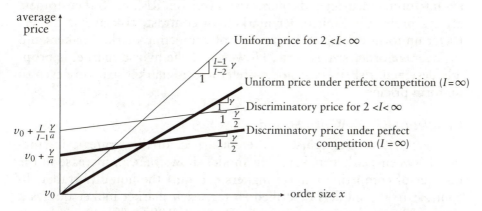

Figure 3.1. *Average market price schedules under uniform and discriminatory pricing*

sizes, x. It also illustrates the impact of competition between the market makers as their number I increases.

The simple closed-form solution allows us to directly see the implications of enhancing competition between the I market makers. As I increases, the supply schedules under uniform prices become flatter while the intercept stays the same. Under discriminatory pricing the slope of the supply schedules stays the same, but the intercept is reduced. In other words, increased competition makes the limit order book tighter. Röell (1998) also extends her analysis to a setting where the market makers face quadratic inventory costs instead of adverse selection costs.

Inventory considerations are also the focus of Viswanathan and Wang (1997). In their model market makers maximize a mean–variance utility function over the final payoff and thus they are not risk neutral. Since the agent's (sell) order x is purely random and without informational content, their setting resembles a share auction. Thus, the characterization of supply (demand) schedules of their model has already been described in Section 3.1.2. Viswanathan and Wang (1997) not only compare the discriminatory limit order book with the uniform price setting in a dealership market but also with a hybrid market setting. The authors assume a hybrid market structure in which all orders below a fixed size r are executed in a limit order book, whereas larger orders go to a dealership market with uniform pricing. The authors compare the three different market structures from the agent's ex-ante point of view. That is, the agent chooses, before he observes his random order size x, the market structure which maximizes his ex-ante mean–variance utility over proceeds from his sale. The analysis shows that the agent's ex-ante preference depends on his risk aversion. Risk neutral customers always prefer the limit order market. In contrast, risk averse traders prefer uniform pricing if the number of competing market makers and the average order size is large. However, if the hybrid market is properly designed, risk averse traders prefer hybrid market structure even to uniform pricing.

Competition May Widen Spread

Dennert (1993) highlights a different aspect of the strategic interaction between market makers. His model shows that an increase in the number of competing market makers can hurt the liquidity trader. In contrast to the models described so far, each market maker quotes a single bid and a single ask price in Dennert (1993). They pre-commit themselves to trade up to one unit of shares at this bid and ask price.

In the second stage, the trader chooses his optimal demand. An informed trader knows the true value of the asset $v \in \{-1, +1\}$. He trades with many market makers simultaneously as long as it is profitable for him. On the other hand, by assumption a liquidity trader only trades one unit with the market maker who offers him the best price. In short, only the market maker(s) with the best quote trade with a liquidity trader. Therefore, every market maker has an incentive to undercut his rival's quotes and consequently an equilibrium in pure strategies does not exist. Dennert (1993) derives the equilibrium price distribution for the symmetric mixed strategy equilibrium. In this equilibrium, all market makers make zero profit in expectations. The author shows that as the number of market makers increases, the transaction costs for the liquidity trader increase. Intuitively, as the number of registered market makers increases, the informed trader has more trading opportunities, while the liquidity trader still trades only with a single market maker who offers the best price. The adverse selection problem as a whole is more severe and thus the transaction costs for the liquidity traders increases. In the second part of this paper, Dennert (1993) shows that the results also generalize to a setting where market makers can set whole price schedules instead of a single bid and ask price.

3.2.2. Sequential Trade Models à la Glosten and Milgrom

In Section 3.2.1 we examined models in which the market makers submit whole supply functions. In this section, we restrict the order size to one unit. Therefore, the market maker quotes only two prices: a single bid price and a single ask price. This also restricts the screening possibilities of the market maker. The market maker's client is either an informed trader or a liquidity trader. Models in this section pioneered the analysis of bid–ask spreads due to asymmetric information. Most models in this class also assume that the market makers quote competitive bid and ask prices. The underlying Bertrand competition among the market makers is not explicitly modeled but is exogenously assumed. This simplifies the analysis and allows models with multiple trading rounds. In this setting, the market maker updates his quotes after each trade.

Monopolistic Market Maker
Copeland and Galai (1983) restrict their analysis to a one-time interaction, as in the models described in the last section.[7] In their setting

---

[7] These models are based on the intuitive reasoning presented by Bagehot (1971)—a pseudonym for Jack Treynor—who explains the bid–ask spread due to adverse selection.

there is also no competition among market makers. A single monopolistic market maker sets the bid and ask to maximize his own profit. The market maker is uninformed and faces an adverse selection problem. He either trades with an informed trader or with an uninformed liquidity trader. An informed trader arrives with probability μ. He knows the true value of the stock v. He buys only if the true value, v, is higher than the ask price and sells only if it is smaller than the bid price. In both cases, the market maker will lose out to the informed trader. The market maker profits if a liquidity trader arrives. This occurs with probability $1 - \mu$. A liquidity trader either buys or sells the stock or is inactive depending on his exogenous reasons for trading. As the spread widens, the probability increases that a liquidity trader might not trade at all. In Copeland and Galai (1983) the bid–ask spread is partly due to adverse selection and partly to the monopolistic power of the market maker. The authors compute the profit maximizing spread for the market maker and derive some comparative static results. As the probability of informed traders μ increases, the market maker widens his bid–ask spread.

Multiple Trading Rounds and Competitive Market Makers

In Copeland and Galai (1983) the true value of the stock v is made public after one trading round. In contrast, there are many trading rounds in the seminal paper of Glosten and Milgrom (1985). A single investor arrives exogenously in each period and the market maker adjusts his bid and ask prices after each trade. The investor trades for informational reasons with probability μ and for liquidity reasons with probability $1 - \mu$. Although Glosten and Milgrom (1985) analyze a multiperiod setting, each trader employs a static trading strategy since they trade at most once.

Another difference between Copeland and Galai (1983) and Glosten and Milgrom (1985) is that the latter assumes that the risk neutral market maker sets competitive bid and ask prices. In other words, the expected profit for the market maker is zero in each period. This simplifies the analysis since the market maker cannot cross-subsidize over time. Competitive price setting is justified as long as in each period a new risk neutral market maker could potentially enter the market in each period. The new entrant could Bertrand-compete all expected profits away. In contrast, in a setting with a monopolistic market maker, the market maker might be willing to accept some expected losses in the first trading round, if this would reveal more information in the early trading rounds. He could use this information to subsequently recuperate his losses. The assumed risk neutrality of the market maker also abstracts from inventory considerations.[8]

The trading strategy of an informed trader is to buy the stock if the ask price is below his expected value of the stock and sell it when the bid price is above the expected value. Since each informed trader trades only once and the prices are pre-set, he does not care how his trade affects the future price path. Liquidity traders in Glosten and Milgrom (1985) trade as long as liquidity needs exceed the ask (bid) price for the buy (sell) order. The literature has emphasized a simplified version of Glosten and Milgrom (1985) in which liquidity traders buy or sell a stock with equal probability independently of the set prices. Figure 3.2 illustrates the probability structure of the Glosten–Milgrom sequential trade model for the simplified case presented in Section 3 of Glosten and Milgrom (1985), where v is high, v_H, with probability π or low, v_L, with probability $1 - \pi$.

Potential Bertrand competition ensures that the ask price is the market maker's expected value of v conditional on an arriving buy order and the bid price is his expected value conditional on a sell order. In short,

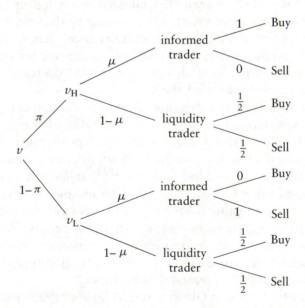

Figure 3.2. *Tree diagram of the trading probabilities*

[8] Inventory models provide an alternative explanation for spreads, Ho and Stoll (1981).

the ask price p^{ask} and bid price p^{bid} are

$$p^{\text{ask}} = E[v|\text{buy order, past order flow}]$$

and

$$p^{\text{bid}} = E[v|\text{sell order, past order flow}].$$

If the fraction of informed traders increases, the adverse selection problem becomes more severe and therefore the bid–ask spread ($p^{\text{ask}} - p^{\text{bid}}$) widens. On the other hand, a higher number of informed traders also increases the speed of information revelation. Increasing the number of informed traders also increases the serial correlation in the order flow.

As the market maker observes the incoming buy and sell orders, he updates his beliefs about the asset's value using Bayes' rule. As time goes by and the market maker observes more and more orders, his estimate about the true value of the stock becomes more precise. The market maker becomes more certain of the information held by the insiders and therefore the size of the spread falls. Glosten and Milgrom (1985) show that the bid and ask price eventually converge to the true value v.

In this simplified setting the market imbalance, that is the difference between sell and buy orders, is a sufficient statistic for the whole history of the past order flow. This also implies that a "no-trade event" does not alter the market maker's beliefs.

To further illustrate the dynamic aspects of this model, let us focus on an even simpler setting where the low value of the stock $v_{\text{L}} = 0$ and the high value $v_{\text{H}} = 1$ occur with equal probability. The market maker's expected value $E[v|\text{past order flow}]$ does not coincide with the midpoint between ask and bid $\frac{1}{2}(p^{\text{ask}} - p^{\text{bid}})$ unless the current conditional expected value is 0.5. To see this, let us consider the case where the current expected value is above 0.5. In this case, the market maker must have observed more buy orders than sell orders. An additional buy order will have a smaller impact on his posterior estimate than an additional sell order. More formally, $|p^{\text{ask}} - E[v|\cdot]| < |E[v|\cdot] - p^{\text{bid}}|$ and, therefore, the midpoint is biased downwards.

The transaction price in Glosten and Milgrom (1985) follows a martingale process, but the quoted ask and bid prices do not. The reason is that an additional trading round provides more information for the market maker and thereby tightens the spread over time. Since the spread size is not a martingale, it is impossible that both the bid and ask prices follow a martingale process. Nevertheless, the quoted ask and bid prices are still Markov processes.[9]

Introducing "Event Uncertainty"

Easley and O'Hara (1987) extend Glosten and Milgrom's (1985) sequential trading model in two ways. In Glosten and Milgrom (1985) traders' buy or sell orders are restricted to a fixed size of one unit. Consequently the market maker quotes only a single bid price and a single ask price. Easley and O'Hara (1987) allow order sizes of one and two units, that is, small and large orders. Furthermore, they introduce the concept of "event uncertainty." An information event occurs with probability α and the information structure is similar to that depicted in Figure 3.2. The information event does not occur with probability $(1 - \alpha)$ and no trader receives any information. In that case, all traders are uninformed and neither the market maker nor the uninformed traders know the true value of the stock. They also do not know whether an information event has occurred.

There are several trading rounds during the trading day. At the beginning of the trading day, nature selects whether an information event occurs or not. If information is released, the pool of infinitely many traders contains a fraction $(1 - \mu)$ of uninformed traders and a fraction μ of informed traders who receive a signal about the true value of the stock v. If no information event occurs only uninformed traders are in the pool. Uninformed investors trade for exogenous reasons and do not take informational aspects into account. They submit large and small orders in an ex-ante specified probabilistic way. Informed traders choose their optimal order size given the quoted bid and ask prices. If the quoted prices are the same for both quantities, they would always prefer to trade large quantities. Consequently, the market maker sets a larger spread for large trades in equilibrium. Informed traders do not take into account the fact that trading a large quantity can influence the future price process. This is reasonable given that the trader's chance to trade again is zero since there are infinitely many informed traders in the pool.

Two types of equilibria can arise depending on the parameter constellation. In the pooling equilibrium, informed traders submit small and large orders. Consequently, market makers demand a spread for both

---

[9] A price process follows a Markov process if a single state, for example, the current price, is a sufficient statistic for the whole history. It follows a martingale process if the expected future prices are equal to the current price, that is $E_t[p_{t+1}] = p_t$.

types of orders. The spread is larger for large trades since informed traders would otherwise always prefer large quantities. In contrast, in the (semi-) separating equilibrium all informed traders prefer to submit large orders despite the larger spread for large trades. Uninformed traders randomly submit small and large orders, as it is exogenously specified. Since only uninformed traders submit small trades in the (semi-) separating equilibrium, the competitive spread for small trades is zero.

"Event uncertainty" allows Easley and O'Hara to explain the partial price recovery that is observed after large (block) sales. A block sale reduces the market makers estimate of the value of the stock. Without event uncertainty, a subsequent small order would not alter his quoted prices because small orders are solely initiated by uninformed traders in a (semi-) separating equilibrium. In contrast, in the case of "event uncertainty" a small order increases the market maker's belief that no information event has occurred, which leads to a slight increase in quotes. In general, both the size and the sequence of trades matter when the market maker is uncertain whether there was an information release in the beginning of the trading day.

Easley and O'Hara (1992) focus solely on the impact of "event uncertainty." In this paper the trade size is restricted to one unit, as in Glosten and Milgrom (1985). Informed traders buy one share if their estimate of the value of the stock is above the ask price and sell one share if their estimate is below the bid price. Otherwise they might choose not to trade at all. This is in particular the case if they do not receive any information at the beginning of the trading day. Absence of trade, therefore, provides a signal that no information event has occurred. By observing the sequence of orders, the market maker can update his beliefs of both the true value of the asset as well as of whether some traders received insider information about this true value. Hence, in contrast to the simplified version of Glosten and Milgrom (1985), time per se is not exogenous to the price and the imbalance between buy and sell orders is not a sufficient statistic for the post order flow. Similarly the last transaction price is also not a sufficient statistic for the past order moves. Therefore, the transaction price process is no longer a Markov process. However, the transaction price is still a martingale. The numerical example presented above, where $v_L = 0$ or $v_H = 1$ with equal probability, is also very illustrative in the case of "event uncertainty." Absence of trade makes asymmetric information less likely and thus pulls the quotes towards 0. 5. If the current midpoint is at 0. 5, a competitive market maker reduces the spread. However, absence of trade need not always reduce the spread if the ask and bid do not straddle around 0.5.

Pagano and Röell (1992) contrast the standard Glosten–Milgrom (1985) setting with a batch auction market where market orders are collected before the market maker sets the competitive price. These batch models lead us to the next section.

3.2.3. Kyle Models and Signaling Models

In the previous two sections, we discussed sequential models where the uninformed market maker sets the prices before the informed trader submits his market order. In this section, we cover models where the informed party moves first and, thereby, signals some of his information to the uninformed individuals.

The Static Kyle (1985) Setup

Kyle's (1985) seminal paper is the classical reference for this class of models.[10] Its elegant solution made this setup very popular for analyzing many market microstructure issues such as insider trading, stock price manipulation, and front running.

This section focuses on the static version of Kyle (1985) where there is only one trading round. In this batch clearing model, there are three groups of risk neutral players: a single informed investor, many liquidity traders, and a market maker who sets the price after observing the aggregate order flow. In contrast to the previous model, multiple traders are active in the market place at the same time. Some trade for liquidity reasons, while the insider tries to exploit his private information. In other words, the informed insider and the liquidity traders submit their orders simultaneously. The market maker only observes the net order flow X. He does not observe each individual order and, thus, he does not know the informed trader's order size $x \in \mathbb{R}$. Kyle (1985) assumes that the market maker sets the execution price P_1 equal to his best estimate $E[v|X]$. The liquidity traders trade for reasons exogenous to the model. Their demand is given by the random variable $u \sim \mathcal{N}(0, \sigma_u^2)$. The total net order flow is $X = x + u$. The value of the stock v is normally distributed $\mathcal{N}(P_0, \sigma_{v,0}^2)$. The single, risk neutral, information monopolist is the only one who knows the true value of the risky asset, v. He trades to maximize his profit which equals his capital gain $(v - P_1)$ times the quantity of his stock holdings, x. Since he acts strategically, he takes into account the fact that his demand x will influence the price, P_1.

---

[10] The notation X and $\sigma_{v,0}^2$ used here corresponds to the notation y and Σ_0 used in the original article, respectively.

Kyle (1985) focuses on the BNE, where all strategies are linear in equilibrium. To derive the perfect BNE, let us follow the steps outlined earlier in Section 1.2. The first step is to propose equilibrium strategies for both the insider and the market. Let the proposed strategy for the insider be $x = \beta(v - P_0)$ and for the market maker be $P_1 = P_0 + \lambda X$. The coefficients β and λ will be determined in equilibrium. The insider maximizes his expected trading profit $E[\pi | v] = E[(v - P_1)x|v]$, where he takes into account the fact that according to his beliefs, $P_1 = P_0 + \lambda(x+u)$. His optimal stock holding is then given by $x^* = (1/2\lambda)(v-P_0)$.

The market maker observes the aggregate net order flow $X = x + u$. Given his beliefs about the insider's trading strategy, $x = \beta(v - P_0)$, he tries to infer the value of the stock v from X. Since v and u are normally distributed and the insider's demand x is linear in v, the projection theorem yields the conditional expectation

$$E[v|X] = P_0 + \frac{\text{Cov}[v, X]}{\text{Var}[X]}(X - E[X]) = P_1.$$

The perfect BNE is obtained by determining the coefficients λ and β. Given the best replies, the equilibrium coefficients are given by

$$\beta = \frac{1}{2\lambda} \quad \text{and} \quad \lambda = \frac{\beta\sigma_{v,0}^2}{\beta\sigma_{v,0}^2 + \sigma_u^2}.$$

In equilibrium $\lambda = \frac{1}{2}\sqrt{\sigma_{v,0}^2/\sigma_u^2}$ and $\beta = \sqrt{\sigma_u^2/\sigma_{v,0}^2}$. λ determines the price increase of an additional buy order. The reciprocal of λ can be viewed as the *market depth*. If λ is low, an additional order will not lead to a large price change and, thus, the market is very liquid. The small price impact of an additional order reflected by a low λ induces the insider to trade more aggressively.

The expected profit for the insider in equilibrium is given by $E[(v - P_1)x] = \frac{1}{2}(\sigma_u^2\sigma_{v,0}^2)^{1/2}$. His expected profit is increasing in $\sigma_{v,0}^2$ since $\sigma_{v,0}^2$ measures the informational advantage of the insider. A higher variance of u implies more liquidity trading which in turn provides more opportunity for the insider to disguise his information based trading. The market maker breaks even on average. He loses money to the insider but makes the same amount of money from the noise traders on average. Consequently, the insiders' expected profit is the liquidity traders' expected trading costs. Half of the insider's information is revealed after one trading round, that is, the new variance of the true value of the stock conditional on X is only half of the original unconditional variance.

Kyle (1985) extends this static model to a series of discrete call markets in a sequential auction setting. In this dynamic setting, the insider faces the following trade-off: if he takes on a larger position in the early periods his early profits increase but prices in the later trading rounds worsen. The dynamic considerations of the insider and other important extensions of this seminal paper are covered in more detail in Section 4.5.

Some Robustness Results

The assumed normal distribution of u and v plays an important role in simplifying Kyle's (1985) analysis. Its continuous unbounded support makes sure that the market maker can never detect a deviation by the insider. Any aggregate order flow $X = x + u$ is possible in equilibrium. Any change in X can always be attributed to a different realization of u. Therefore, no out-of-equilibrium beliefs need to be specified. This also implies that the insider can always take the equilibrium λ as given, even when he deviates from his equilibrium strategy.

In contrast, for discrete distributions of u and v, a deviation might lead to an aggregate order flow that would never arise in equilibrium. In this case, out-of-equilibrium beliefs determine the market maker's reaction to an insider's deviation. These out-of-equilibrium beliefs and the associated change of the market maker's λ determine whether a deviation is profitable for the insider or not. In other words, the existence of a specific equilibrium depends on its out-of-equilibrium beliefs. Biais and Rochet (1997) demonstrate that multiple equilibria exist in this discrete setting.

Rochet and Vila (1994) alter Kyle's (1985) static setting such that the insider observes the amount of noise trading u in addition to v. In other words, the insider knows the exact execution price. A low realization of u leads to a lower execution price and, therefore, the insider buys more shares. In short, the insider provides some additional liquidity to the market. Interestingly, although the insider knows the realization of u, his expected profits stay the same. Hence, the liquidity trader's average trading costs are also not affected. Rochet and Vila (1994) show that the equilibrium outcome in the adjusted Kyle (1985) setting coincides with the equilibrium in a setting where a single risk neutral insider submits whole demand schedules as in Kyle (1989). Rochet and Vila's (1994) main objective is to check the robustness and uniqueness of the equilibrium for any continuous distribution of u and v. The authors show that the BNE is unique and has the property that it minimizes the expected gains of the insider under incentive compatibility constraints. However, this uniqueness result typically does not carry over to the case where the insider does not observe u.

Like in any signaling model, the informed trader in Kyle (1985) moves before the uninformed market maker. However, the Kyle (1985) setup is robust to a change in the order of moves. The fact that the market maker cannot detect any deviation by the insider makes the analysis also applicable to an alternative setting where the insider and market maker choose their strategies simultaneously. For example, a market clearing process, where a competitive risk neutral market making sector submits demand schedules based on public information and the informed trader simultaneoulsy submits market orders, is equivalent to the classical Kyle (1985) setup (Vives 1995b). A setting where the market maker first commits to a linear price schedule for the net order flow $P(X)$, before the insider and the liquidity traders submit their order flow, provides a third alternative setting. Nonoptimizing behavior by the liquidity traders and the assumed competitive behavior of the market maker make this reversal in the order of moves nonproblematic. Given the possibility that the sequence of moves can be easily reversed without changing the nature of the outcome in a Kyle (1985) setting, it might be too restrictive to classify it only as a signaling model.

Bagnoli, Viswanathan, and Holden (1994) provide a comprehensive overview of the existence of linear equilibria in static Kyle (1985)-type models and sequential trade models à la Glosten and Milgrom (1985) for various distributions of u and v.

Information Inefficiency without Liquidity Traders

Laffont and Maskin (1990) develop a different signaling model in which the risk neutral insider's transactions with many small traders are directly observable. The aim of their paper is to illustrate that strategic behavior leads to informational inefficiencies even without exogenously assumed noise traders. In their setting, a continuum of risk averse small traders initially own the stocks and would like to unload their risky position. The value of the stock is given by $v = \delta + \epsilon$, where δ is either high, δ_H, or low, δ_L. A single, risk neutral, large trader knows the realization of δ. He offers to take on a fraction of the risky stock from the small traders. Since he is a monopsonist, he chooses the purchase price by choosing the quantity.

The authors show that a separating equilibrium always exists. In a separating equilibrium, the insider's information is revealed to the small traders and the profit of the monopsonist results from taking on the risk from the continuum of small traders. A pooling equilibrium also exists, as long as the difference $(v_H - v_L)$ is sufficiently small. In a pooling equilibrium, the insider's information is not revealed. The insider is better off in the pooling equilibrium since he does not face the quantity restriction imposed by the incentive constraint of the separating equilibrium.

Summary
In this chapter, we classified static market microstructure models into simultaneous move models and sequential move models. The latter set of models were further subdivided into screening and signaling models. Almost all existing static models in the literature can be grouped into these categories. As mentioned in the beginning of this chapter, there are alternative ways to classify these models.

Note that this chapter only covered a small fraction of the growing literature on market microstructure. More exciting research output can be expected, especially extensions of the more recent analysis of limit order books in screening models. Many issues like market transparency, optimal market design, the role of the market maker's inventory positions, disclosure rules, competition among exchanges, and optimal opening procedures of exchanges are not incorporated in this survey. The focus of this chapter is solely on the interaction between information and prices. For a broader coverage of the market microstructure literature we refer the interested reader to the leading book by O'Hara (1995) and the more recent survey by Madhavan (2000). Lyons (2000) also illustrates the usefulness of market microstructure models in explaining exchange rate movements in the international finance literature.

Most models covered in this chapter share the common feature that the price adjusts instantaneously to public information but only gradually to private information. This gradualism is caused by the noisy asset supply and/or strategic behavior of informed traders, or it is exogenously given by assuming a sequential trading mechanism where traders are restrained to trade only a certain quantity. The different market microstructure models surveyed in this chapter place varying levels of emphasis on these three factors. These static models form the basis for the dynamic models that are presented in the next chapter.

4

Dynamic Trading Models, Technical Analysis, and the Role of Trading Volume

In the previous chapter we discussed closed-form solution models in which each individual trader optimized his trades only at one period in time. Traders had no opportunity to resell their acquired positions in later trading rounds. In most cases the stock was liquidated and the liquidation value of the stock was paid out before re-trade could occur. In this chapter we consider models in which individual traders are active in the market place in multiple trading rounds. This both enriches and complicates the analysis. Models in Section 4.1 illustrate how traders try to learn additional information from past prices. Technical analysis has positive value and allows traders to make better investment decisions. They are able to better interpret new information if they make use of information reflected in past prices. Furthermore, technical analysis gives them a better idea about the true value of the underlying asset. Learning from past prices alters their trading strategy and thus also affects the price process. Section 4.2 illustrates how learning induces serial correlation in the price process. The section also highlights the infinite regress problem which might arise if traders try to forecast others' forecasts by inferring information from endogenous variables. Section 4.3 covers multiperiod competitive REE models starting with two models in which information is hierarchical, that is, the information of one group of traders encompasses the others' information. The first model is set in continuous time whereas the second model is in discrete time and incorporates the role of trading volume. Both models also illustrate that it is rational for uninformed traders to follow the trend. In the last multiperiod model in Section 4.3, information is dispersed among many traders. The model in Section 4.4 analyzes the informational content of past trading volume data. The final section departs from competitive REE models and considers models with strategic traders who take into account the fact that their trading activity affects the price. Traders know that if they trade more aggressively today, the price will reveal more of their private information thereby depleting their future trading opportunities.

4.1. Technical Analysis – Inferring Information from Past Prices

When one talks about technical analysis one immediately thinks of chart analysis with its head and shoulder formation, candle sticks, and numerous other rules of thumb. It would be too ambitious to capture all the different rules of thumb and street wisdom in a tractable theoretical model. Therefore, the theoretical literature simply defines technical analysis as the inference of information from past prices (Brown and Jennings 1989).

Past prices always provide information in a setting with asymmetric information. The crucial question, however, is whether the information inferred from past prices is useful. Only then would technical analysis have positive value. Technical analysis is useful if it (1) improves the traders' portfolio choice, and (2) adds to the information already revealed by the current price. In a setting where traders can trade conditional on the current price, the current price might already reveal all relevant information. This is the case for (strong-form) informationally efficient equilibria where the current price reveals a sufficient statistic for all private information in the economy. In that case there is no need to incorporate past prices in current trading decisions.

The early literature jumped to the biased conclusion that technical analysis provides no useful information as long as the market is weak-form informationally efficient. Technical analysis was therefore considered to be irrational. The reasoning was that if there was a possibility to profitably exploit information inferred from past prices, other traders would have already exploited it. However, this simple argument overlooks the fact that different traders may value the same income stream differently. Their evaluation depends on their marginal rate of substitution (MRS^i) at a certain allocation. Traders might also differ in their degree of risk aversion, endowment, and so on. Consequently, they typically do not face the same portfolio selection problem. A certain risky dividend stream might be attractive to one trader, yet it might not be considered as profitable by other traders, given their risk aversion and endowment. The models presented after Section 4.1.1 show that in a more general setting, past prices carry useful information for deriving the optimal stock holding and the future price path.

However, the simple original argument holds in economies with competitive risk neutral traders. Risk neutral traders would have already exploited any expected profit opportunity based on information inferred from past prices. Therefore, these opportunities cannot arise in equilibrium and thus technical analysis has no value. Another special example in which technical analysis has no value involves a setting in which there is a group of competitive risk neutral traders who observe the public limit order book. In this case, no risk premium is paid and the price is driven by the information of this competitive fringe which already incorporates information reflected by past prices. Section 4.1.2 also illustrates the impact of the competitive fringe on the value of technical analysis.

The main focus of technical analysis is to get a better prediction of the underlying value of the stock. Technical analysis is, however, also valuable for evaluating new information. Quite often when one receives new information, one does not know whether it is already reflected in the price or not. Looking at past price movements might help answer this question. The next section is devoted to this aspect of technical analysis.

4.1.1. Technical Analysis – Evaluating New Information

A trader who receives a piece of information faces a problem if he wants to exploit it in the stock market. Before he determines his optimal trade, he has to figure out whether this information is already reflected in the current price or not. In other words, he has to find out whether the information is really new or whether other traders have already received the same or related information, traded on it, and thus already moved the price. The trader can get a better idea of whether the information is already reflected in the price or not if he analyzes the past price movements.

This problem has been captured by models wherein traders receive information in random order. Treynor and Ferguson (1985) analyze the decision problem of a single trader i who receives a piece of information. In their setting, the event E is either first known to an individual trader i or to all other traders, that is, to the market. Since the information arrival is random, trader i does not know whether the other traders have already received the same piece of information before he received the information. More formally, Treynor and Ferguson (1985) introduce the following notation. An event occurs at t_E. It gets known to trader i at t_i and to all other traders, that is, to the market, at t_M. All time variables are discrete and random and thus unknown to the individual i. Trader i's trades alone do not move the market price. The stock price only jumps when all other traders hear the news and act on it. The authors assume that once some event occurs, the event becomes public very fast. This guarantees that the event E_j gets known to trader i as well as to all other traders before a new event E_{j+1} occurs.

Investor i is only interested in knowing whether the event E is already reflected in the price, that is, whether he got the news before the other traders or not. He, therefore, is concerned about the probability of $t_i > t_M$ versus $t_i \leq t_M$. He derives these probabilities by making use of his knowledge of

(1) the prior distribution of the information dissemination process, and
(2) the observed price process, combined with his knowledge about:
    (a) the underlying stochastic process of the price path, and
    (b) the price impact of information at t_M.

In Treynor and Ferguson (1985) event E can occur in δ time periods. The prior probability that an event occurred in t_E is $(1/\delta)$, that is, the prior is uniformly distributed. γ is the probability that all other traders will receive the information in the next period, provided they have not received it so far. Similarly, α is the probability that investor i will receive the information in the next period. This determines the transition probabilities for the Markov process with the following four possible states: ω_1 nobody, ω_2 only trader i, ω_3 only all other traders, and ω_4 all traders, received this signal.

Investor i makes use of his knowledge about the underlying price process governed by $P_t = (1 + \tilde{r}_t)P_{t-1}$, where all $\tilde{r}_t$ are independently identically normally distributed with mean zero and variance σ^2. At time t_M, when the event becomes public, the expected mean return is V instead of zero. If t_i and t_M are known, the density of possible price paths is given by

$$\Pr(\underline{r}_{t_i}|t_M, t_i) = \prod_{t=0}^{t_i} \left\{ \frac{1}{\sqrt{2\pi}\sigma} \exp\left[\frac{-(r_t - 1_{t=t_M}V)^2}{2\sigma^2} \right] \right\},$$

where the indicator function is

$$1_{t=t_M} = \begin{cases} 1 & \text{if } t = t_M \\ 0 & \text{if } t \neq t_M. \end{cases}$$

$\underline{r}_{t_i}$ denotes the whole process of returns $r_t = (P_t - P_{t-1})/P_{t-1}$ up to and including t_i.

By Bayes' rule the probability distribution $\Pr(t_M | \underline{r}_{t_i}, t_i)$ is

$$\Pr(t_M | \underline{r}_{t_i}, t_i) = \frac{\Pr(t_M | t_i) \Pr(\underline{r}_{t_i} | t_M, t_i)}{\sum_{t_M = -\infty}^{\infty} \Pr(t_M | t_i) \Pr(\underline{r}_{t_i} | t_M, t_i)}.$$

All terms on the right-hand side are known except the $\Pr(t_M | t_i)$ term. The latter terms are given by

$$\Pr(t_M | t_i) = \sum_{t_E} \Pr(t_M | t_i, t_E) \Pr(t_E | t_i),$$

where $\Pr(t_M | t_i, t_E) = \Pr(t_M | t_E)$ since, given an event occurred, the probability that all other agents get the information only at t_M is independent of when agent i received the information. All these probabilities can be directly derived from the given prior information structure.

Treynor and Ferguson (1985) provide a numerical example where the trader i infers from the past price process that, with a probability of 70 percent, all other traders have not yet received the same information.

In the last section, the authors derive an optimal portfolio strategy which allows the investor i to capitalize on his information. Their paper shows that technical analysis, that is, inferring information from past prices, helps in the evaluation of new private information.

Even if a trader knows that a piece of his newly acquired information is already partially reflected in the current price, he would still like to know the extent to which it already moved the price. This is also true in the case of a public announcement. The newly informed public would like to know the extent to which the information is already reflected in the price. Brunnermeier (1998) illustrates how the public looks at past price movements to improve their knowledge. This model makes clear that the argument presented earlier only holds as long as the past price still carries information even after the public announcement. The information content of past prices has to be about the true value of the asset and/or about the execution price. The latter is only of use for traders who can only submit market orders. The author employs a strategic market order model similar to Kyle (1985). The focus of Brunnermeier (1998) is on the characterization of the trading strategy of insiders who receive an imprecise signal prior to the public announcement. The analysis shows that the early informed insider tries to manipulate the price prior to the public announcement in order to tamper with the other traders' technical analysis after the public announcement. This activity is often characterized as signal jamming. In addition, the insider's trading strategy exhibits a speculative feature. He "buys on (positive) rumors and sells on news."

The discussion thus far indicates that technical analysis to evaluate new information helps us avoid the possibility of considering the same information twice. Therefore, it helps us get a better estimate of the true underlying value of the asset. Hence, this form of technical analysis is just an indirect way of gathering more information about the fundamental value of the stock. Inferring information about the value of the stock remains the ultimate goal of technical analysis.

4.1.2. Technical Analysis about Fundamental Value

Grundy and McNichols (1989) and Brown and Jennings (1989) are two tractable competitive call auction REE models in which not only the current price, but also the past price is useful in predicting the value of the asset. In other words, technical analysis has a positive value. Whereas Grundy and McNichols (1989) follows the static model setup developed by Diamond and Verrecchia (1981), the model of Brown and Jennings (1989) is a two-period dynamic version of Hellwig (1980).

Private Information Prior to First Trading Rounds

In Grundy and McNichols (1989) traders receive private information only at the beginning of both trading rounds in $t = 1$ and $t = 2$. For most of the paper the aggregate random supply in $t = 1$, u_1, is kept equal to u_2, that is, the aggregate random supply is perfectly correlated in the two periods. More specifically, as in Diamond and Verrecchia (1981) the exogenous random supply of a single risky asset is given by endowment shocks for each individual trader. These shocks are independently identically normally distributed with $\mathcal{N}(\mu_{u_1}, \sigma_{u_1}^2 I)$. As the number of market participants I goes to infinity, the average per capita supply shock, u_1, is still random with $\mathcal{N}(\mu_{u_1}, \sigma_{u_1}^2)$ since the variance of individual endowments depends on the number of traders I. Note also that the overall variance of the total supply shocks goes to infinity and thus the law of large numbers cannot be applied. In the limit $I \to \infty$ and the individual endowment shock gives no indication of the average per capita supply. Therefore, the only private signal trader i receives is

$$S_1^i = v + \omega + \epsilon_{S,1}^i,$$

with a common error term ω and an idiosyncratic error term $\epsilon_{S,1}^i$. Both error terms are independently normally distributed with mean zero and variance σ_ω^2 and $\sigma_{\epsilon_{S,1}}^2$. The average signal is given by $\bar{S}_1 := \lim_{I \to \infty} (\sum S_1^i / I) = v + \omega$. Traders maximize their expected exponential utility functions. The constant absolute risk aversion coefficient of trader i is given by $\rho^i \in [\rho_L, \rho_U] \subset (0, \infty)$.

As a first step, Grundy and McNichols (1989) derive a one-period reference model. In this model traders conjecture a linear price relation

$$P_1 = \alpha_{0,1} + \alpha_{S,1}\bar{S}_1 + \alpha_{u,1}X,$$

where X is the aggregate demand in equilibrium. The optimal stock holding of trader i is therefore[1]

$$x_1^i = \frac{E_1[v|\mathcal{F}_1^i] - P_1}{\rho^i \text{Var}[v|\mathcal{F}_1^i]},$$

where $E_1[v|\mathcal{F}_A^i]$ is linear in P_1 and S_1^i by the projection theorem. Notice, that $\text{Var}[v|\mathcal{F}_1^i]$ is the same for all traders. Let us simplify the notation to $\text{Var}_1[v]$. This conditional variance increases with the variance of the common error term. Averaging over all traders gives the average per capita demand

$$X = \frac{1}{\bar{\rho}\text{Var}_1[v]}[\beta_{0,1} + \beta_{P,1}P_1 + \beta_{S,1}\bar{S}_1]$$

where $\bar{\rho}$ is the harmonic mean of all traders' risk aversion coefficients, that is $I/\sum_i(1/\rho_i)$. The β terms follow directly from the projection theorem. Rearranging the traders' price conjecture gives

$$X = -\frac{\alpha_{0,1}}{\alpha_{u,1}} + \frac{1}{\alpha_{u,1}}P_1 - \frac{\alpha_{S,1}}{\alpha_{u,1}}\bar{S}_1 = u_1.$$

As outlined in Section 1.2, the REE can be obtained by equating the undetermined coefficients.

The aggregate supply u_1, given by the exogenous sum of the individual endowment shocks, is vertical, while the aggregate demand is downward sloping in P_1, since $\alpha_{u,1} < 0$. The important coefficient is $(\alpha_{S,1}/\alpha_{u,1})$. Changes in $\bar{S}_1$ lead to a parallel shift of the demand curve, whereas changes in u_1 shift the vertical supply curve. The size of the demand curve shift as $\bar{S}_1$ changes is measured by $\alpha_{S,1}$, whereas the size of the supply curve shift caused by a different u_1 is captured by $\alpha_{u,1}$. Traders cannot make out whether a price change is due to a demand shift or a supply shift ($\bar{S}_1$ or u_1 change). The simultaneous equation problem is measured by $\alpha_{S,1}/\alpha_{u,1}$.

---

[1] Let us normalize the risk-free interest rate $r = 0$, that is $R = 1$.

The Effects of a Second Trading Round

Grundy and McNichols (1989) then extend their basic model to a two-period model where, in the second round, no new private information is released and the random supply u_2 is the same as in period one. One might expect that no trader will change his stock holding since no new information has arrived. The authors show that the no-trade outcome is indeed an equilibrium. There is, however, a second equilibrium, where the average signal $\bar{S}_1$ is fully revealed. If all traders rationally conjecture

$$P_1 = \alpha_{0,1} + \alpha_{S,1}\bar{S}_1 + \alpha_{u,1}u_1$$

$$P_2 = \alpha_{0,2} + \alpha_{S,2}\bar{S}_1 + \alpha_{u,2}u_2,$$

where $u_1 = u_2$, $\bar{S}_1$ can be revealed provided both equations are linearly independent. This is the case if

$$\frac{\alpha_{S,1}}{\alpha_{u,1}} \neq \frac{\alpha_{S,2}}{\alpha_{u,2}}$$

since we then have two linearly independent equations with two unknowns.

Grundy and McNichols (1989) prove that an informationally efficient linear REE which fully reveals $\bar{S}_1$ exists as long as the variance of ω is not too large. Their proof proceeds backwards in two steps. First, given the price conjecture for the first trading round, the authors demonstrate the existence of a $\bar{S}_1$-revealing equilibrium in the second trading round. Second, it is proven that traders rationally foresee the existence of a $\bar{S}_1$-revealing equilibrium in round 2, as long as the variance of ω, σ_ω^2 is not too large. Indeed there are two $\bar{S}_1$-revealing REE if $0 < \sigma_\omega^2 < \bar{\sigma}_\omega^2$. In these equilibria, there are two sources of uncertainty in the first round: x_2^i and P_2. These equilibria show that even when no new information arrives, prices and stock holdings can change if the additional price P_2 reveals more of the private information. For the case of $\sigma_\omega^2 = 0$, both equilibria, the $\bar{S}_1$-revealing and the non-$\bar{S}_1$-revealing, are identical for the first trading round.

In the $\bar{S}_1$-revealing REE, trade occurs in period two, even though the only new public information is P_2. Grundy and McNichols (1989) also check whether this result is in line with the no-trade (speculation) theorem of Milgrom and Stokey (1982). The no-trade theorem predicts a zero trade outcome in period 2 if the allocation after trade in period 1 is interim Pareto optimal and the beliefs about the signals in $t = 2$ are concordant before the signal becomes known.[2] Beliefs are concordant if traders agree on the conditional likelihood of any given realization of the signal, that is,

$$\Pr[S_2^i = s | v = v^{\text{realized}}, \mathcal{F}_1^i] = \Pr[S_2^i = s | v = v^{\text{realized}}, \mathcal{F}_1^1] \quad \forall i, S, v^{\text{realized}}.$$

Intuitively, beliefs are concordant if traders agree about everything except the probability of payoff-relevant states. The only new signal in $t = 2$ is P_2. Since P_2 is a public signal, it is sufficient that the beliefs about P_2 are "essentially concordant," that is,

$$\frac{\Pr[S_2^i = s | v = v^{\text{realized}}, \mathcal{F}_1^i]}{\Pr[S_2^i = s | v = v^{\text{realized}\prime}, \mathcal{F}_1^i]} = \frac{\Pr[S_2^i = s | v = v^{\text{realized}}, \mathcal{F}_1^1]}{\Pr[S_2^i = s | v = v^{\text{realized}\prime}, \mathcal{F}_1^1]} \quad \forall i, S, v^{\text{realized}}.$$

A Pareto optimal allocation after the first trading round is reached if the marginal rate of substitution for consumption across any two states is the same for all investors. Grundy and McNichols show that if the investors behave *myopically* they reach a Pareto optimal allocation after the first round. However, when P_2 becomes known this allocation is no longer Pareto efficient since traders' beliefs about P_2 are not "essentially concordant" at the end of the first round. Therefore, trade will occur. If traders apply dynamic trading strategies, that is, if they do *not* behave *myopically*, trade can also occur in period 2. This is the case when $\sigma_\omega^2 > 0$, that is, when there is a common unknown noise term in the signal. The trading outcome in round 1 is neither Pareto efficient given information $\mathcal{F}_1^i$, nor are the beliefs about the public signal P_2 concordant. When $\sigma_\omega^2 = 0$, the true liquidation value v can be inferred from P_2 (in fact it is equal to P_2) and round 1 allocation is Pareto efficient and beliefs about P_2 are concordant. In this case the no-speculation theorem applies and the only trade which occurs is a swapping of two riskless assets.

Additional Public Signal Prior to Second Trading Round

Grundy and McNichols (1989) extend their model by introducing an additional publicly observable signal in $t = 2$

$$S_2^{\text{public}} = v + \epsilon_{S_2^{\text{public}}}.$$

---

[2] This is simply a restatement of the common prior assumption specified for the second period.

In this case a $\bar{S}_1$-revealing REE with trade in $t = 2$ also exists unless a particular set of parameter restrictions is satisfied. Those parameter restrictions are given in Theorem 4 of the paper. Where those parameter restrictions are satisfied, no linear REE exists, $\bar{S}_1$-revealing or otherwise. The authors also provide necessary and sufficient conditions for the existence of non-$\bar{S}_1$-revealing REE in which no trade occurs in the second round. Finally, they consider the case where the random supply (u_1, u_2) is not the same in both periods. Instead u_1 and u_2 are correlated as in Brown and Jennings (1989). Both types of equilibria exist in this generalized setting. In the non-$\bar{S}_1$-revealing type equilibrium, no informational trade will occur; the whole trading volume is determined by the additional noisy supply. In the second type of equilibrium, the sequence of prices $\{P_1, P_2\}$ only partially reveal $\bar{S}_1$ since the supply shocks are no longer perfectly correlated. However, the sequence of prices reveals more about $\bar{S}_1$ than P_1 does alone. This implies that technical analysis has positive value and that trading can be self-generating.

Additional Private Signals Prior to Second Trading Round

Brown and Jennings (1989) extend a model similar to Hellwig (1980) to two periods. In their model there are infinitely many a priori identical investors denoted by $i \in \mathbb{I} = \{1, 2, 3, \dots\}$ who are endowed with B_0 units of the riskless bond. B_0 can be normalized without loss of generality to zero since all investors have CARA utility functions. All investors start with the same information set, $\mathcal{F}_0$, with beliefs about the liquidation value of $\mathcal{N}(\mu_{v,0}, \sigma_{v,0}^2)$. At $t = 1$ and $t = 2$ each investor gets a private signal in $t = 1$ and $t = 2$ about what the liquidation value, v, of the risky asset will be in $T = 3$, that is,

$$S_t^i = v + \epsilon_{S,t}^i,$$

where $\epsilon_{S,t}^i$ is normally i.i.d. with $\mathcal{N}(0, \sigma_{S,t}^2)$. As the signals are unbiased, by the law of large numbers, the average signal $S_t = \lim_{I \to \infty} I^{-1} \sum_{i=1}^{I} S_t^i$ equals v with probability one in each t. Trader i's information set is given by $\mathcal{F}_1^i = \{\mathcal{F}_0, S_1^i, P_1\}$ in $t = 1$ and $\mathcal{F}_2^i = \{\mathcal{F}_1^i, S_2^i, P_2\}$ in $t = 2$. The information sets contain the current price P_t since traders can trade conditional on the price of the stock P_t. Let trader i's stock holding in t be denoted by x_t^i. His final wealth in period $T = 3$ is then given by

$$W_3^i = B_0 + x_1^i(P_2 - P_1) + x_2^i(v - P_2)$$

where B_0 is normalized to zero. The traders' expected utility functions are given by

$$E[-\exp(-\rho W_3^i)|\mathcal{F}_t^i],$$

where the constant absolute risk aversion measure ρ is the same for all traders. Each trader maximizes his expected utility, given his information set and his price conjecture. Backward induction allows us to break up this optimization process into two steps. Given a certain x_1^i the maximum utility value at $t = 2$ is given by

$$V_2^i(x_1^i) = \max_{x_2^i} E\{-\exp[\rho(x_1^i(P_2 - P_1) + x_2^i(v - P_2))]|\mathcal{F}_2^i\}.$$

At $t = 1$ the problem is

$$V_1^i = \max_{x_1^i} E\{V_2^i(x_1^i)|\mathcal{F}_1^i\}.$$

A REE is then given by (1) the optimal stock holding (x_1^i, x_2^i) for each investor i, and (2) the equilibrium price mappings P_1 and P_2 which have to coincide with the traders' price conjectures. The market clearing condition guarantees that demand equals supply in both periods. Whereas the average per capita demand for the risky asset is given by $x_t = \lim_{I\to\infty} \sum_{i=1}^{I} x_t^i/I$, the per capita supply is assumed to be random in this noisy REE. The random supply is given by u_1 in $t = 1$ and u_2 in $t = 2$, where $u_2 = u_1 + \Delta u_2$.[3] Brown and Jennings assume that u_1 and Δu_2 are normally distributed

$$(u_1, \Delta u_2) \sim \mathcal{N}\left[(0,0), \begin{pmatrix} \sigma_{u_1}^2 & \varrho\sigma_{u_1}\sigma_{\Delta u_2} \\ \varrho\sigma_{u_1}\sigma_{\Delta u_2} & \sigma_{\Delta u_2}^2 \end{pmatrix}\right].$$

where ϱ is the correlation between the supply increments u_1 and Δu_2. Technical analysis, that is, conditioning trade in $t = 2$ on P_1, has positive value for two reasons. First, $P_1 = L[v, u_1]$ provides a useful second signal about the true payoff v. $L[\cdot]$ is a linear operator. This effect is most pronounced in the case where u_1 is independent of u_2. Second, if u_1 and u_2 are correlated, the price P_1 in $t = 1$ helps traders get a better prediction of u_1. In other words, u_1, in turn, is useful in predicting u_2. A better prediction of u_2 reduces the noise in $t = 2$ and thus allows P_2 to reveal more about the liquidation value v. The argument also applies the other way around. Knowing P_2 allows traders to get a better prediction

---

[3] Note, that x_t denotes holdings rather than additional trading demand, whereas u_1 and Δu_2 refer to additional supply.

of u_1. Thus a joint estimation using both price conjectures P_1 and P_2 enhances information revelation. Grundy and McNichols (1989) show that for the case of perfect correlation, that is, $\Delta u_2 = 0$, P_1 and P_2 perfectly reveal v. In short, due to the two reasons described above P_1 still has predictive value in $t = 2$. Note that even if $\varrho = 0$, u_1 and u_2 are still correlated since ϱ is defined as the correlation coefficient between u_1 and Δu_2. In this case u_t follows a random walk and the prediction of u_1 using P_1 provides the expectation of u_2.

Nonmyopic REE

We are now ready to outline the derivations of the nonmyopic REE. Since all random variables in this type of model are normally distributed, one makes extensive use of the projection theorem. According to the projection theorem all conditional expected values, like $E_1^i[v]$, $E_1^i[u_1]$, $E_1^i[u_2] = \varrho \sigma_{\Delta u_2}^2 / \sigma_{u_1}^2$, $E_1^i[P_2]$, $E_2^i[v]$, are linear in their unconditional expected values and the signal surprise component, $S^i - E[S^i]$. $E_t^i[\cdot]$ is a simplified notation for $E[\cdot | \mathcal{F}_t^i]$ and $\mathrm{Var}_t^i[\cdot]$ denotes $\mathrm{Var}[\cdot | \mathcal{F}_t^i]$. The normal distribution has the nice feature that the covariance matrices $\mathrm{Var}_1^i[v, S_2^i, P_2]$ and $\mathrm{Var}_2^i[v]$ are constants on $\mathcal{F}_0$.

The optimal stock holding can be derived using backward induction. The value function in $t = 2$ given stock holding x_1^i in $t = 1$ is

$$V_2^i(x_1^i) = \max_{x_2^i} E_2^i \{ -\exp[-\rho[x_1^i(P_2 - P_1) + x_2^i(v - P_2)]]\}.$$

The optimal x_2^i in $t = 2$ is

$$x_2^i = \frac{E_2^i[v] - P_2}{\rho \, \mathrm{Var}_2^i[v]}$$

as in Hellwig (1980). Therefore

$$V_2^i(x_1^i) = E_2^i \left\{ -\exp \left[-\rho \left[x_1^i(P_2 - P_1) + \frac{E_2^i[v] - P_2}{\rho \, \mathrm{Var}_2^i[v]} (v - P_2) \right] \right] \right\}.$$

The only random variable at $t = 2$ is v, which is normally distributed. Therefore, the expectation is given by

$$V_2^i(x_1^i) = -\exp \left[-\rho[x_1^i(P_2 - P_1)] - \frac{(1/2)(E_2^i[v] - P_2)^2}{\mathrm{Var}_2^i[v]} \right].$$

The value function for $t = 1$ can then be rewritten as

$$V_1^i = \max_{x_1^i} E_1^i \left\{ -\exp \left[-\rho[x_1^i(P_2 - P_1)] - \frac{(1/2)(E_2^i[v] - P_2)^2}{\mathrm{Var}_2^i[v]} \right] \right\}.$$

$E_2^i[v]$ and P_2 are normally distributed random variables with respect to the information set, $\mathcal{F}_1^i$. In order to take expectations, we complete the squares and rewrite the equation given above in matrix form:[4]

$$V_1^i = \max_{x_1^i} E_1^i \left\{ -\exp\left[\rho x_1^i P_1 + \underbrace{(-\rho x_1^i, 0)}_{:=L^{i\prime}} \underbrace{\begin{pmatrix} P_2 \\ E_2^i[v] \end{pmatrix}}_{:=M^i} \right.\right.$$

$$\left.\left. + \underbrace{(P_2, E_2^i[v])}_{=M^{i\prime}} \frac{1}{2} \underbrace{\begin{pmatrix} +1/\mathrm{Var}_2^i z[v] & -1/\mathrm{Var}_2^i[v] \\ -1/\mathrm{Var}_2^i[v] & +1/\mathrm{Var}_2^i[v] \end{pmatrix}}_{:=N} \underbrace{\begin{pmatrix} P_2 \\ E_2^i[v] \end{pmatrix}}_{=M^i} \right]\right\}.$$

Furthermore, let Q_i be the expected value conditional on $\mathcal{F}_1^i$ of the multinomial random variable M^i and its conditional covariance matrix W, that is, $Q^i := E_1^i[M^{i\prime}]$, $\mathbf{W} := V_1^i[M^{i\prime}]$.

Taking expectations yields

$$V_1^i = \max_{x_1^i} \{ -|\mathbf{W}|^{-(1/2)} |2\mathbf{N} + \mathbf{W}^{-1}|^{-(1/2)} \exp[\rho x_1^i P_1 + L^{i\prime} Q^i$$

$$- Q^{i\prime} \mathbf{N} Q^i + (1/2)(L^{i\prime} - 2Q^{i\prime}\mathbf{N}) \underbrace{(2\mathbf{N} + \mathbf{W}^{-1})^{-1}}_{:=G} (L^i - 2\mathbf{N}Q^i)] \}.$$

The first-order condition with respect to x_1^i is given by

$$x_1^i = \frac{E_1^i[P_2] - P_1}{\rho G_{11}} + \frac{E_1^i[x_2^i](G_{12} - G_{11})}{\rho G_{11}},$$

where G_{ij} are the elements of the matrix G, and

$$x_2^i = \frac{E_2^i[v] - P_2}{\rho \, \mathrm{Var}_2^i[v]}.$$

Given the price conjectures of the trader, $x_1^i = L[\mu_{v,0}, S_1^i, P_1]$ and $x_2^i = L[\mu_{v,0}, S_1^i, S_2^i, P_1, P_2]$, where $L[\cdot]$ denotes a linear operator. This allows us to derive the market clearing price as a linear function:

$$P_2 = L[\mu_{v,0}, v, u_1, u_2], \qquad P_1 = L[\mu_{v,0}, v, u_1].$$

[4] See also Anderson (1984, Chapter 2).

Brown and Jennings (1989) show that technical analysis has value as long as P_2 also depends on u_1. This is consistent with the intuition provided earlier.

He and Wang (1995) analyze a multiperiod version of Brown and Jennings (1989), which we cover at the end of Section 4.3.

Myopic REE

Brown and Jennings (1989) can demonstrate the existence of a nonmyopic dynamic REE for the special cases where P_2 or P_2 together with P_1 are informationally efficient. They continue their analysis for myopic investor economies. Singleton (1987) was the first to analyze myopic dynamic REE models.

In a myopic investor economy[5] the first-period stock holding simplifies to

$$x_1^i = \frac{E_1^i[P_2] - P_1}{\rho \operatorname{Var}_1[P_2]}.$$

The second-period stock holding is, as before,

$$x_2^i = \frac{E_2^i[v] - P_2}{\rho \operatorname{Var}_2[v]}.$$

Brown and Jennings (1989) show that technical analysis has strictly positive value under certain parameter restrictions. As mentioned above, technical analysis has value if u_1 helps to predict u_2, and u_2 has an impact on the information revelation of P_2 and/or $P_1 = L[v, u_1]$ provides a second noisy observation of v. The authors provide three equivalent conditions under which technical analysis has no value: when individual demand in $t = 2$ is independent of P_1, or equivalently P_2 is independent of u_1, or equivalently $\operatorname{Cov}[v, P_1|P_2, S_1^i, S_2^i, \mathcal{F}_0^i] = 0$.

No Technical Analysis in a Setting with
a Risk Neutral Competitive Fringe

Vives (1995) adds a risk neutral competitive market maker sector. This enables the author to derive a closed-form solution for the case $\varrho = 0$ even if investors act nonmyopically. Vives' focus is on contrasting the informativeness of the price process in an economy with myopic investors with an economy where investors have long horizons. The risk

---

[5] Interpreting myopic investor economies as OLG models can be misleading since the agents in $t = 2$ still condition their demand on their signal in $t = 1$.

neutral competitive fringe of scalpers, floor brokers, and so on always drives the price equal to the conditional expectation of the liquidation value v given their information. They observe the limit order book in each period, that is, the aggregate demand. Introducing this competitive risk neutral fringe changes the model quite dramatically. Vives (1995) shows that the current limit order book (or equivalently the current price) is a sufficient statistic for all data from the past limit order books. Since there are no public announcements, prices are even (semi-strong) informationally efficient and, hence, technical analysis has no value.

The importance of the competitive market maker sector can be illustrated for the case where private information is only released at $t = 1$. A buy and hold strategy is optimal for the informed traders in this case. At $t = 1$ informed traders buy assets as in the static Hellwig model, and hold it until T. The aggregate demand (limit order book) in $t = 1$ contains the demand of the insiders and the demand of the noise traders, u_1. Market makers set the price equal to the conditional expectation of v given the aggregate demand. The holding of informed traders does not change in $t = 2$. Therefore, the limit order books contain only the additional noise trader demand Δu_2. Since $\varrho = 0$, Δu_2 contains no additional information and thus market makers set $P_2 = P_1$ and absorb the additional noise demand. In contrast, in a model without a competitive fringe, like in Brown and Jennings (1989), informed traders have to take on the position of the additional noise trading in $t = 2$. Since each demand function of the informed traders depends on his signal, more information is revealed by P_2. In a model with a competitive fringe, the only motive for other traders to trade is to exploit their informational advantage. They do not try to insure each other since the competitive fringe is willing to bear all the risk. This simplifies the analysis and allows Vives (1995) to derive a closed-form solution even for the case where private information arrives in every period. He shows that the net trading intensity of insiders in period t depends directly on the precision of period t signals.

Two-Period Models with Higher-Order Uncertainty

Romer (1993) introduces higher-order uncertainity in a two-period REE model. In his model asymmetric information is only partially revealed in the first period, but in contrast to Grundy and McNichols (1989) it incorporates uncertainty about the quality of other investors' signals, that is, higher-order uncertainty. Romer's analysis provides a rationale for large price movements without news. He shows that a small commonly known supply shift in the second period can lead to large price movements. The aim of his paper is to give a rational explanation for the stock market crash of 1987. This model is discussed in more detail in Section 6.1 which focuses on stock market crashes.

Slow Information Revelation due to Technical Analysis

Vives (1993) shows that in a dynamic setting information revelation through current and past prices (technical analysis) can become a victim of its own success. As the price process becomes more and more informative, less information is incorporated in the current price. This slows down the *speed of convergence* to the fully revealing outcome. In his model agents receive a conditionally independent signal S^i before they repeatedly interact in the market place in $t = 1, 2, 3, \ldots$. The author finds that in the case where information is dispersed among the traders, the speed of convergence to the fully revealing outcome is only $1/\sqrt{t^{1/3}}$. This is much slower than the standard rate of convergence of $1/\sqrt{t}$ in learning of REE. This faster rate of convergence also emerges in the case where a mass of agents know the true value. However, when information is dispersed among the market participants the rate is much slower. The intuition behind the result is the following. As time goes by and periods accumulate, the price process becomes more informative. This has the side effect that each individual trader bases his beliefs more on past and present prices and less on his own private signal. Therefore, less private information is incorporated in the current price. In fact as the price process converges to the fully revealing outcome, each individual market participant puts zero weight on his private signal. A faster rate of convergence would prevail if agents take into account the fact that a positive information externality is generated for other agents if they rely more on their own private signal. Section 5.2 analyzes the role of informational externalities in sequential decision making in more detail. Note that a slower speed of learning is, however, not necessarily welfare reducing. As Vives (1992) illustrates, slow learning is optimal in certain models.

4.2. Serial Correlation Induced by Learning and the Infinite Regress Problem

Learning from past and current prices affects investors' behavior and thus the endogenous price path. Townsend's (1983) seminal paper entitled *Forecasting the Forecast of Others* illustrates in an infinite horizon setting that learning can convert serially uncorrelated shocks into serially correlated movements in economic decision variables. Since agents may respond to variables generated by the decisions of others, time series can display certain cross-correlation and may appear more volatile. In the case of disparate but rational expectations, decision makers forecast the forecasts of others. This can lead to relatively rapid oscillations and can make forecasts, as well as forecast errors, serially correlated.

This paper also addresses the infinite regress problem. This problem arises in dynamic settings where traders try to infer each other's information which is nested, that is, nonhierarchial. This is for example the case if the information is dispersed among the market participants.

Townsend's Macroeconomic Model Setup

The author analyzes the behavior of time series in a dynamic model with a continuum of identical firms in each of two markets. The demand schedule in each market (island) i is given by

$$P^i_t = -\beta_1 Y^i_t + \xi^i_t.$$

P^i_t is the price in market i, Y^i_t is the aggregate output of all individual production functions $y^i_t = f_0 k^i_t$, and ξ^i_t is a demand shock. This shock consists of (1) a "persistent" economy-wide component u_t, and (2) a "transitory" market-specific shock ϵ^i_t, that is,

$$\xi^i_t = u_t + \epsilon^i_t,$$

where the economy-wide shock component u_t follows an AR(1) process:

$$u_t = a_u u_{t-1} + v_t \qquad -1 < a_u < 1,$$

where ϵ^i_t and v_t are jointly normal and independent. Firms can infer ξ^i_ts, but they do not know exactly which part stems from a persistent economy-wide shock u_t and which part is market-specific and transitory ξ^i_t. Twonsend (1983) derives the linear REE in the following steps. After stating the firm's maximization problem, Townsend derives the first-order conditions using the certainty equivalence theorem. He defines the dynamic *linear* rational expectations equilibrium in terms of laws of motion. Following Sargent (1979) one can derive the law of motion for the aggregate capital stock $\underline{K}_t$ in each market without directly calculating the firm-specific laws of motion. The aggregate laws of motion have the advantage that they can be computed without being specific about information sets and forecasting. In Townsend's (1983) setting the equilibrium can be found by identifying the statistically correct forecasts.

Serial Correlation Induced by Learning

Townsend (1983) addresses the inference problem in two parts. In the first part, firms in market 1 cannot observe the price in market 2, whereas market 2 firms observe both prices. Townsend calls this a hierarchical information structure. In the second part, firms in both markets can make inferences from the prices in both markets. This more general setting will lead to the infinite regress problem.

As long as firms in market 1 do not observe the price in market 2, their information set is $\mathcal{F}_t^1 = \{\underline{K}_t^1, \underline{P}_t^1, \underline{M}_t^1\}$. They observe the aggregate capital process in market 1, $\underline{K}_t^1$, up to time t and the price process in market 1, $\underline{P}_t^1$. They also know the common mean forecast of u_t by market 1. The process of the mean forecast is denoted by $\underline{M}_t$. Note that the notation $\underline{Z}_t$ denotes a stochastic process up to and including time t. This information set allows firms to exactly infer the total shock to the economy $\underline{\xi}_t^1$ even if they only make use of the observations in t. The inference problem for firms in market 2 is similar, except that their information set also contains the price in market 1, that is, $\mathcal{F}_t^2 = \{\underline{K}_t^2, \underline{P}_t^2, \underline{M}_t^2, \underline{P}_t^1\}$. The price in market 1 provides additional information on the extent to which the shock is permanent since the permanent component of the shock is countrywide. Therefore, firms in market 2 make use of P_1 in forecasting the shock components. However, the components u_t and ϵ_t of shock ξ^i cannot be inferred precisely even though past data can be used to estimate a better forecast. Typically the inference problem of the firms can be solved in two ways. One can either use the projection theorem or one can apply Kalman filtering which derives from the projection theorem. Applying the projection theorem directly has the disadvantage that the state space increases with the history of time. Kalman filtering is a steady state approach and exploits a recursive algorithm. To make sure that the economy is in a steady state, one often assumes that the initial date is $t = -\infty$. It is important to notice that Kalman filtering can only be applied if the state vector[6] in the state space form is of finite dimension. Both methods illustrate that $\hat{\underline{v}}_t := E(v_t|\mathcal{F}_t^i)$, the forecast of $\underline{v}_t$ is a linear combination of $\underline{v}_t$, and $\underline{\epsilon}_t^i$. It now becomes obvious that the learning mechanism causes some persistence. Although v_t and ϵ_t^i are uncorrelated, their forecasts are correlated since both forecasts $E(v_t|\mathcal{F}_t^i)$ and $E(v_{t-1}|\mathcal{F}_{t-1}^i)$ are based on $\underline{v}_{t-1}$. In other words, all past $\underline{v}_{t-1}$ influence the prediction of v_t. Similarly $E(u_t|\mathcal{F}_t^i)$ and $E(u_{t-1}|\mathcal{F}_{t-1}^i)$,

---

[6] A state in this recursive setup differs from the earlier state-date description. In this setting, a state does not describe a whole history. It is only a description of the current situation in the economy.

as well as the forecast errors $[E(u_t|\mathcal{F}_t^i) - u]$, are serially correlated. As time goes by and more and more observations are available, the forecast error for past u_s (for $s < t$) decreases.

The Infinite Regress Problem

So far only market 2 firms were forming inferences about the components of the demand shock from the endogenous time series of the price in market 1. The price in the first market depends on the average beliefs in this market, $\underline{M}_t^1$, that is, on market 1's expectations. These expectations are well defined and can be expressed in terms of a finite number of states. Therefore, the Kalman filter can be applied. In the second part of the paper, Townsend (1983) departs from the simple hierarchical information structure. Firms in market 1 can also draw inferences from P_t^2. Since P_t^2 depends on the common market 2 forecasts, M_t^2, firms in market 1 must have expectations about M_t^2, that is $E_t^1(M_t^2)$. But firms in market 2 also observe P_t^1. So a firm in market 2 must have expectations on M_t^1, that is $E_t^2(M_t^1)$. Thus, firms in market 1 need to know the expectations $E_t^1(M_t^2)$ and $E_t^1(E_t^2(M_t^1))$. This chain of reasoning can be continued ad infinitum. This leads to an infinite regress problem. One needs infinitely many state variables in the space of mean beliefs. This prevents us from applying the standard Kalman filter formulas. Notice that the infinite regress problem arises even though the depth of knowledge is only zero. The infinite regress problem is not due to a high depth of knowledge but due to inference from endogenous variables. Townsend (1983) then goes on to discuss a related but different infinite regress problem in which he analyzes the case of infinitely many markets.

New methods in convergence of least squares learning to REE, developed by Marcet and Sargent (1989a,b), allow us to tackle the infinite regress problem differently. Sargent (1991) shows that a solution can be found in self-referential models by defining the state variables in a different way. The idea is to model agents as forecasting by fitting vector *ARMA* models for whatever information they have available. The state vector for the system as a whole is defined to include the variables and the innovation in the vector *ARMA* models fit by each class of agents in the model. This is in contrast to the former formulation in Townsend (1983) where the state covers a system of infinitely many orders of expectations about exogenous hidden state variables. Most of the literature in finance avoids the infinite regress problem by assuming a hierarchical information structure as in Wang (1993, 1994). The problem is elegantly by-passed in existing models with differential information. This is the case in He and Wang (1995) and Vives (1995), wherein a competitive model is used, and in Foster and Viswanathan (1996), wherein a strategic model is used.

4.3. Competitive Multiperiod Models

Continuous Time Trading Model with
Hierarchical Information Structure

Wang (1993) avoids the infinite regress problem by assuming a hierarchical information structure.[7] In his model the information of the informed investors statistically dominates the information of the uninformed investors. In other words, informed traders also know all the variables that are observable by the uninformed investors. The main focus of Wang (1993) is the impact of information asymmetries on the time series of prices, risk premiums, price volatility, and the negative autocorrelation in returns, that is, the mean reverting behavior of stock prices. The author also shows that it can be optimal for less informed traders to "chase the trend." He uses a dynamic asset pricing model in continuous time to analyze these questions. In his economy, investors derive utility from a continuous consumption stream, that is, they maximize $E[\int u(c(\tau), \tau)) \, d\tau | \cdot]$, where $u(c(\tau), \tau)) = -e^{-\rho t - c(\tau)}$. They can invest either in a riskless bond with constant rate of return $(1 + r)$, or in equity which generates a flow of dividends at an instantaneous stochastic growth rate D. D is determined by the following diffusion process:

$$dD = (\Pi - kD)dt + \mathbf{b}_D d\mathbf{w},$$

where the state variable[8] Π follows an Ornstein–Uhlenbeck process,

$$d\Pi = a_\Pi(\bar{\Pi} - \Pi)dt + \mathbf{b}_\Pi d\mathbf{w},$$

and $\mathbf{w}$ is a (3×1) vector of standard Wiener processes, $a_\Pi(> 0)$, $\bar{\Pi}$, $k(\geq 0)$ are constants and $\mathbf{b}_D$, $\mathbf{b}_\Pi$ are (1×3) constant matrices (vectors).

A fraction w of informed traders observe $\underline{\Pi}_t$ in addition to $\underline{D}_t$, and $\underline{P}_t$, while the uninformed traders only observe $\underline{D}_t$ and $\underline{P}_t$, that is, $\mathcal{F}^{in}(t) = \{D_\tau, P_\tau, \Pi_\tau: \tau \leq t\}$ and $\mathcal{F}^{un}(t) = \{D_\tau, P_\tau: \tau \leq t\}$.[9] Obviously, the informed traders then also know the expected growth rate $(\Pi - kD)$.

---

[7] We changed the notation to $u_t = \Theta_t$ and $\alpha_x = p_x$ for ease of exposition.
[8] Note that the state variable Π differs from the definition of the state of the world ω.
[9] The notation $\underline{Z}_t$ represents a (continuous) process up to and including t.

When $k = 0$, Π is simply the dividend growth rate. When $k > 0$, Π/k can be interpreted as the short-run steady state level of the dividend rate D, which fluctuates around a long-run steady state level $\bar{\Pi}/k$.

Without additional noise, the REE would fully reveal Π to the uninformed investors. Although the price would adjust, no trading would occur. Wang introduces an additional state variable by assuming a stochastic quantity of stock supply. The total amount of stocks $(1 + u)$ is governed by the stochastic differential equation

$$du = -a_u u dt + \mathbf{b}_u d\mathbf{w},$$

where $\mathbf{b}_u$ is a constant (1×3) matrix (vector) and $\mathbf{w}$ are the Wiener processes mentioned above. In this environment the uninformed investors face the problem that they cannot distinguish whether a change in (P_t, D_t) is due to a change in the dividend growth rate Π_t or due to a change in noisy supply u_t.

Wang first analyses the benchmark perfect information case in which all investors are informed. The equilibrium price takes on the form:

$$P^* = \Phi + (\alpha_0^* + \alpha_u^* u),$$

where Φ represents the net present value of expected future cash flows discounted at the risk-free rate r and the second term reflects the risk premium. He shows that the expected "excess return to one share" is independent of the variance of the noisy supply. In other words, volatility in prices caused by temporary shocks in supply do not change the risk premium in the symmetric information setting. This is in contrast to a setting where investors have finite horizons and they face additional risk since the remaining trading periods in which they can unwind their positions are becoming fewer. He and Wang (1995) also consider a finite horizon model in which the variance of u affects the risk premium.

We outline all of the major steps for the asymmetric information case since they are useful for the analysis of later papers. Wang (1993) uses the following steps to determine a linear REE.

Step 1: First, he defines the primary state variables consisting of all known variables for the informed traders. The state space also covers "induced state variables" reflecting the estimates of the uninformed investors. The actual state description should incorporate all signals that the investors receive. Wang simplifies the state space by equivalently using the estimates of uninformed investors.

Step 2: He proposes a linear REE price:

$$P = (\phi + \alpha_0) + \alpha_D^* D + \underbrace{\alpha_\Pi \Pi + \alpha_u u}_{:= \xi} + \alpha_\Delta \hat{\Pi}$$

$$= \Phi + (\alpha_0 + \alpha_u u) + \alpha_\Delta \Delta,$$

where $\hat{\Pi}(t) := E[\Pi | \mathcal{F}_t^{un}]$ is defined as the uninformed investors' estimate of $\Pi(t)$. $\hat{\Pi}(t)$ depends on the whole history of dividends and prices. The equilibrium price reveals to the uninformed traders the sum $\xi :=$ $\alpha_\Pi \Pi + \alpha_u u$. Therefore, $\mathcal{F}_t^{D,P} = \mathcal{F}_t^{D,\xi}$. Note that the equilibrium price does not depend on $\hat{u} := E[u | \mathcal{F}_t^{un}]$ since $\alpha_\Pi \hat{\Pi} + \alpha_u \hat{u} = \alpha_\Pi \Pi + \alpha_u u =: \xi$. The uninformed investors can derive ξ but do not know exactly whether the price change is due to a change in Π or u.

Step 3: The estimates, $\hat{\Pi}$, and $\hat{u}$ can be derived using the proposed price conjecture. Focusing on a steady state analysis, the uninformed investors apply the Kalman filter on all past data of dividends D and prices P to infer their estimates $\hat{\Pi}$ and $\hat{u}$.[10] Their joint estimation of Π and u based on both D and P generates the *induced correlation* between the estimates of $\hat{\Pi}$ and $\hat{u}$.

Step 4: The process for the estimation error $\Delta := \hat{\Pi} - \Pi$ is derived next. Note that the estimation error for u is given by $\alpha_\Pi / \alpha_u (\Pi - \hat{\Pi})$. It follows that:

$$d\Delta = -a_\Delta \Delta dt + \mathbf{b}_\Delta d\mathbf{w}.$$

This estimation error is mean-reverting to zero and thus is only temporary. This is the case since the uninformed investors constantly update their estimates, as in Townsend (1983).

Step 5: One derives the instantaneous excess return process $dQ :=$ $(D - rP)dt + dP$. As in the static models, the traders' demand functions depend on the excess returns.

Step 6: Then the uninformed investors' optimization problem is solved. As in the static case, one can exploit the CARA utility to derive a mathematically tractable form of expected utility for the Bellman equation. The estimators, $\hat{\Pi}_t$ and $\hat{u}_t$, provide a sufficient statistic for $\mathcal{F}^{un}(t)$. Therefore, by the separation principle, $\hat{\Pi}_t$ and $\hat{u}_t$ can be estimated at the first stage and then the control problem can be dealt with in a second stage.[11] The optimal control problem is then solved in a similar manner for the informed investors.

---

[10] For a more detailed discussion see Lipster and Shiryayev (1977).
[11] One might also consult Fleming and Rishel (1975).

Step 7: Finally the market clearing conditions are imposed and the price equation proposed above is obtained.

Using simulations, Wang (1993) shows the impact of this information structure on stock prices, the risk premium, price volatility, and negative serial correlation in returns. Wang also states some comparative static results. Increasing the number of uninformed traders affects the price volatility in two ways. First, there is less information in the market and prices become less variable. Second, there exists more uncertainty about future dividend payments. Investors will demand a higher risk premium and, therefore, prices become more sensitive to supply shocks. Asymmetry in information among investors can cause price volatility to increase because the adverse selection problem becomes more severe.

The existence of uninformed investors also affects the required risk premium in equilibrium. The risk premium only depends on the fundamental risk of the asset perceived by the investors. When the fraction of uninformed investors increases, the price contains less information about future dividend growth. The author also shows that the strong mean reversion in $u(t)$ generates negative serial correlation in stock returns even in the case of symmetric information. This correlation can be enhanced as the fraction of uninformed investors increases.

Finally it is shown that the optimal investment strategy of the informed investors depends not only on the value of the underlying true state variables but also on the reaction of uninformed investors. In other words, the informed investors make use of the estimation errors of the uninformed investors. Wang (1993) also finds that the trading strategy for less informed investors appears to be a *trend chasing strategy*, that is, these investors rationally buy when the price rises and sell when the price drops.

Discrete Time Trading Model with
Hierarchical Information Structure – Analysis of Trading Volume
In a similar but discrete time version, Wang (1994) analyzes the behavior of volume. The other major difference from the continuous time model is that, although no exogenous noise is introduced, the price is only partially revealing. This is due to the incompleteness of the markets assumed in the model. If markets are incomplete and investors are heterogeneous, prices are not only affected by aggregate risk but also by individual risk. Volume can be informative in such an environment. This paper tries to show the link between volume and heterogeneity of investors. Investors differ in their information as well as in their private

investment opportunities. In order to avoid the infinite regress problem, informed investors have a strictly statistically dominant information set in comparison to uninformed traders. Markets are incomplete since only informed investors have an additional private investment opportunity besides stocks and bonds whose rate of return is $R = (1 + r)$. The dividend of a stock consists of a persistent component F_t and an idiosyncratic component $\epsilon_{D,t}$. F_t is only observable by informed investors and follows an AR(1) process:

$$D_t = F_t + \epsilon_{D,t}$$
$$F_t = a_F F_{t-1} + \epsilon_{F,t}, \quad 0 \le a_F \le 1.$$

While informed investors can observe F_t, the uninformed traders only observe the same noisy signal S_t about F_t:[12]

$$S_t = F_t + \epsilon_{S,t}.$$

Define, for later reference, the excess *share* return as $Q_t := P_t + D_t - RP_{t-1}$. Informed traders can also invest in their private investment opportunity which yields a stochastic excess rate of return of

$$q_t = Z_{t-1} + \epsilon_{q,t},$$

where Z_t follows an AR(1) process

$$Z_t = a_Z Z_{t-1} + \epsilon_{Z,t}, \quad 0 \le a_Z \le 1.$$

Similar to the stock return, the process $\underline{Z}_t$ is only known to the informed traders.

Besides making use of their information advantage, the only incentive for informed traders is to hedge the risk reflected by $\epsilon_{q,t}$. All ϵ-terms are normally i.i.d. with the exception that $\epsilon_{D,t}$ and $\epsilon_{q,t}$ can be positively correlated. Wang (1994) shows in the case of symmetric information that if $\epsilon_{D,t}$ and $\epsilon_{q,t}$ are uncorrelated, a change in expected returns on the private investment will not alter the investors' stock holdings. This result changes if there is a positive correlation between $\epsilon_{D,t}$ and $\epsilon_{q,t}$ since the stock and the private investment become substitutes. Given a positive correlation between $\epsilon_{D,t}$ and $\epsilon_{q,t}$, informed traders also want to trade to rebalance their portfolio because of a change in the profitability of their private investment opportunity. In the asymmetric information

---

[12] To avoid the infinite regress problem, informed traders also observe this signal.

case, informed traders also want to trade for informational reasons. Uninformed traders face an adverse selection problem since they cannot sort out whether a price increase is due to informed trading, that is, an increase in F_t, or due to uninformed trading.

The analysis of the equilibrium follows the same steps as in Wang (1993). First, the states of the economy $F_t, Z_t, \hat{F}_t = E[F_t|\mathcal{F}_t^{un}]$ are defined. Second, the linear pricing rule

$$P_t = -\alpha_0 + (a - \alpha_F)\hat{F}_t + \alpha_F F_t - \alpha_Z Z_t$$

is proposed. Third, from this equation it is obvious that uninformed traders can infer the sum $\xi_t = \alpha_F F_t - \alpha_Z Z_t$, thus $\xi_t = \alpha_F \hat{F}_t - \alpha_Z \hat{Z}_t$. This explains why $\hat{Z}_t$ is redundant in the state description within the class of linear equilibria. Fourth, using Kalman filtering one derives $\hat{F}_t$, $\hat{Z}_t$ and the estimation errors $\hat{F}_t - F_t =: \Delta_t$.[13] It can be shown that the estimation error u_t follows an AR(1) process, that is,

$$\Delta_t = a_\Delta \Delta_{t-1} + \epsilon_{\Delta,t}, \quad 0 \le a_\Delta < 1.$$

The unconditional variance of the estimation error, $\mathrm{Var}(\Delta_t) =: \epsilon$, reflects the degree of asymmetry of information. The strict inequality $a_\Delta < 1$ implies that the forecast error is mean reverting. The uninformed traders will learn the "old" F_s, Z_s better and better as time passes by but new F_t, Z_t appear in every period. Thus, uninformed investors are "chasing a moving target."

It is useful to derive the expected excess returns for informed and uninformed traders so that we can determine the optimal stock demand. The optimal portfolio for each group of investors is a composition of a mean–variance efficient portfolio and a hedging portfolio. Investors want to hedge since expected returns on both the stock and the private investment technology change over time. Since returns on the stock are correlated with changes in expected future returns, it provides a vehicle to hedge against changes in future investment opportunities. Given the optimal portfolios, the trading strategies for the informed and uninformed investors can be written as:

$$x_t^{in} = \beta_0^{in} + \beta_Z^{in} Z_t + \beta_\Delta^{in} \Delta_t$$
$$x_t^{un} = \beta_0^{un} + \beta_Z^{un} \hat{Z}_t.$$

---

[13] Note that $\hat{Z}_t - Z_t$ is determined by $\xi_t = \alpha_F F_t - \alpha_Z Z_t = \alpha_F \hat{F}_t - \alpha_Z \hat{Z}_t$.

This shows that the optimal stock holding of the uninformed traders only changes when their expectation about the others' private investment opportunities changes, that is, $x_t^{un} - x_{t-1}^{un} = \beta_Z^{un}(\hat{Z}_t - \hat{Z}_{t-1})$, where

$$\hat{Z}_t - \hat{Z}_{t-1} = E_t^{un}[Z_t] - E_{t-1}^{un}[Z_{t-1}].$$

This can be decomposed into

$$\{E_t^{un}[Z_{t-1}] - E_{t-1}^{un}[Z_{t-1}]\} + \{E_t^{un}[Z_t] - E_t^{un}[Z_{t-1}]\}.$$

The first component reflects the corrections of the forecast errors of previous periods and the second component induces new positions due to a change in Z_t.

Trading volume results only from changes in stock holdings between the informed and uninformed traders. Therefore, trading volume can be characterized as:

$$V_t = (1 - w)|x_t^{un} - x_{t-1}^{un}| = (1 - w)|\beta_t^{un}| \, |\hat{Z}_t - \hat{Z}_{t-1}|$$

$$E[V_t] = 2(1 - w)|\beta_Z^{un}|\sqrt{2/\pi}.$$

The effects of asymmetric information on volume can be analyzed, given these formulae. As $\text{Var}(\epsilon_{S,t})$ increases, the signal of the uninformed becomes less precise, the asymmetry of information increases, and the adverse selection problem becomes more severe. This reduces the trading volume. This need not be the case if a nonhierarchical information structure is assumed as in Pfleiderer (1984) or He and Wang (1995). Trading volume is always accompanied by price changes since investors are risk averse. If informed traders face high excess return in their private investments, they try to rebalance their portfolio by selling stocks. The price has to decline in order to make stocks more attractive to uninformed investors. This explains why the trading volume is positively correlated with absolute price changes. The price reduction mentioned above has to be even larger if the adverse selection problem is more severe. Consequently, the correlation between trading volume and price changes increases with information asymmetry. Volume is also positively correlated with absolute dividend changes. In the case of symmetric information, a public news announcement about dividends only changes the current price but not the expected return or trading volume. In the case of asymmetric information, different investors update their expectations differently. They respond to public information differently since they interpret it differently. Uninformed investors change their estimates for $\underline{F}_{t-1}$ and $\underline{Z}_{t-1}$ and trade to correct previous errors and establish new positions. Volume in conjunction with current change in dividends or returns can also be used to improve the forecast for expected future excess returns. Under symmetric information, public news (like an announcement about a dividend increase) is immediately reflected in the price. Under asymmetric information, public news can lead to corrections of previous trading mistakes. Wang (1994) shows that an increase in dividends accompanied by high volume implies high future returns. High volume indicates that the change in dividend was unanticipated. A dividend increase should, therefore, increase prices. The second component of excess returns, the price change, is different because it provides information about noninformational trading as well as the stock's future dividends. Under symmetric information, agents only trade to rebalance portfolios and it is always accompanied by changes in the current price in the opposite direction. In the case of asymmetric information, uninformed investors trade for two reasons: to correct previous errors and to take on new positions if the price adjusts to noninformational trading by the informed investors. The correlation between the current volume and the current returns and expected future returns is ambiguous.

One inconsistency in Wang's (1994) analysis is that even though volume can help predict future returns, uninformed investors in this model do make use of it. A model in which investors also take the informational content of volume into account is presented by Blume, Easley, and O'Hara (1994), which we will discuss in Section 4.4. First we will present a model with a generalized information structure as provided by He and Wang (1995).

Multiperiod Finite Horizon Model with Differential Information
In the dynamic models discussed in this section so far, information asymmetry is strictly hierarchical. This unrealistic assumption is relaxed by He and Wang (1995).[14] The authors develop a model in which different pieces of information are dispersed among many market participants. Their model can be viewed as a multiperiod generalization of Grundy and McNichols (1989) and Brown and Jennings (1989). The main economic focus of their model is the relationship between the pattern of volume and the flow and nature of information. He and Wang (1995) also analyze the link between volume and price volatility. They find that the high volume generated by exogenous private or public information

---

[14] We adjust the notation to $v = \Pi$, $u_t = \Theta_t$, $S_t^{\text{public}} = Y_t$, $\lambda_t = \alpha_t$, $\alpha_{x,t} = p_{x,t}$, and $\beta_{x,t} = d_{x,t}$ for ease of exposition.

is accompanied by high volatility in prices, whereas the high volume generated by endogenous information (like prices) is not accompanied by high volatility.

In contrast to Wang (1993, 1994), He and Wang (1995) present a finite horizon setup in which investors only consume in the terminal period T. There are infinitely many investors $i \in \{1, 2, 3, \dots\} =: \mathbb{I}$. Each investor can either invest in a bond with a certain gross return rate $R = 1$ or in a stock with a liquidation value $v + \delta$ at the final date T. The stock pays off $v + \delta$ only at the final period T and otherwise pays no dividend. Each investor $i \in \mathbb{I}$ receives a *private* signal S_t^i about the first component of the stock's liquidation value, v, at each point in time:

$$S_t^i = v + \epsilon_{S,t}^i,$$

where $\epsilon_{S,t}^i$ is normally i.i.d. with $\mathcal{N}(0, \sigma_{\epsilon,S,t}^2)$ for all investors. Investors also observe a public signal S_t^{public} about v:

$$S_t^{\text{public}} = v + \epsilon_{S\text{public},t},$$

where $\epsilon_{S\text{public},t} \sim \mathcal{N}(0, \sigma_{\epsilon,S\text{public},t}^2)$. All traders also observe the price P_t. The second component of the liquidation value, δ, is also normally distributed with mean zero and is never revealed before the terminal date T.

The true value of v would be revealed immediately in $t = 1$ if the supply was not noisy. To make the model interesting, the supply of asset is 1 plus a noise term u_t. This noise term follows a Gaussian AR(1) process:

$$u_t = a_u u_{t-1} + \epsilon_{u,t}, \quad -1 < a_u < 1.$$

This paper provides a way to characterize a linear equilibrium of the above economy in a mathematically tractable way. The vector of state variables of the economy is given by $\Phi_t = (v; \underline{u}_t; \underline{S}_t^{\text{public}}; \{\underline{S}_t^i\}_{i \in \mathbb{I}})$ where an underlined capital letter stands for the whole stochastic process up to and including time t.

The first step is to simplify the state space.[15] Before one characterizes the equilibrium price, it is useful to derive expected values for v_t and u_t conditional on different information sets. $\hat{v}_t^c$ and $\hat{u}_t^c$ are based on publicly available information, while $\hat{v}_t^{p,i}$ and $\hat{u}_t^{p,i}$ are the expected values

---

[15] In contrast to the Wang papers discussed earlier, we have included the signals directly in the state space and not the expected values of v.

based *only* on private information. Furthermore $\hat{v}_t^i$ and $\hat{u}_t^i$ represent the expected values taking all available private and public information of investor i into account. Alternatively, we also write $E_t^c[\cdot]$, $E_t^{p,i}[\cdot]$, $E_t^i[\cdot]$, instead of the hat, $\hat{\cdot}$. The different conditional variances are denoted by $\text{Var}_t^c[\cdot]$, $\text{Var}_t^{p,i}[\cdot]$, and $\text{Var}_t^i[\cdot]$. He and Wang (1995) focus on linear REE. Thus $P_t = L[\Phi_t] = L[v; \underline{u}_t; \underline{S}_t^{\text{public}}; \{\underline{S}_t^i\}_{i \in \mathbb{I}}]$, where $L[\cdot]$ expresses a linear functional relationship.

Lemma 1 of He and Wang (1995) reduces the necessary state space to $(v; \underline{u}_t; \underline{S}_t^{\text{public}})$, that is, $P_t = L[v; \underline{u}_t; \underline{S}_t^{\text{public}}]$. This can be shown by using the law of large numbers since the mean of infinitely many signals converges with probability 1 to v.[16] Furthermore, one can replace $\underline{u}_{t-1}$ by $\underline{P}_{t-1}$ if one exploits the linear relationship described above. We, therefore, have $P_t = L[v, u_t, S_t^{\text{public}}, \underline{P}_{t-1}, \underline{S}_{t-1}^{\text{public}}]$. This can be rewritten as:

$$P_t = a_t \underbrace{(v - \mu_t u_t)}_{=:\xi_t} + \underbrace{b_t S_t^{\text{public}} + L[\underline{P}_{t-1}, \underline{S}_{t-1}^{\text{public}}]}_{=L[\hat{v}_t^c]}.$$

The sum $\xi_t := v - \mu_t u_t$ can be inferred by every investor. Therefore, the following information sets are equivalent

$$\mathcal{F}^c = \{\mathcal{F}_0, \underline{P}_t, \underline{S}_t^{\text{public}}\} \Leftrightarrow \{\mathcal{F}_0, \underline{\xi}_t, \underline{S}_t^{\text{public}}\}$$

in a linear REE. He and Wang (1995) then demonstrate that the second term $b_t S_t^{\text{public}} + L[\underline{P}_{t-1}, \underline{S}_{t-1}^{\text{public}}]$ can be rewritten as $L[\hat{v}_t^c]$, that is, it satisfies a specific structure. This implies that the equilibrium is determined by v, u_t, and $\hat{v}_t^c$. One makes use of the equivalence between $\mathcal{F}^c = \{\mathcal{F}_0, \underline{P}_t, \underline{S}_t^{\text{public}}\}$ and $\{\mathcal{F}_0, \underline{\xi}_t, \underline{S}_t^{\text{public}}\}$ to derive the specific linear coefficients of $L[\cdot]$.

The *first-order* expectations $\hat{v}^c$, $\hat{u}^c$, that is, the expectations conditional on public information $(\underline{\xi}_t, \underline{S}_t^{\text{public}})$, and $\hat{v}^i$, $\hat{u}^i$, that is, the expectations conditional on all information $(\underline{\xi}_t, \underline{S}_t^{\text{public}}, \underline{S}_t^i)$, are derived by means of Kalman filtering. The stochastic difference equations are given by He and Wang's Lemma 2. It is easy to show that $\{\hat{v}_t^i, \hat{u}_t^i, \hat{v}_t^c, \hat{u}_t^c\}$ follows a Gaussian Markov process under filtration $\{\mathcal{F}_t^i\}$. Since information is differential in this model, investor i's trading strategy can also depend on *higher-order* expectations, that is, expectations about the expectations of others, and so on. Does this mean that an infinite

---

[16] Recall that there are infinitely many investors in set $\mathbb{I}$. He and Wang make use of charge spaces. For more details on charge spaces see Feldman and Gilles (1985) and Rao and Rao (1983).

regress problem à la Townsend (1983) will arise? He and Wang (1995) show this is not the case since higher-order expectations can be reduced to first-order expectations. The following steps illustrate the proof for the second-order expectations. First, one shows that $\hat{v}_t^i$ is a weighted average of $\hat{v}_t^c$ and $\hat{v}_t^{p,i}$, that is, $\hat{v}_t^i = \lambda_t \hat{v}_t^c + (1 - \lambda_t)\hat{v}_t^{p,i}$. $\hat{v}_t^c$ is given by Lemma 2 using Kalman filtering and $\hat{v}_t^{p,i}$ can be derived using the projection theorem. The weights λ_t and $(1 - \lambda_t)$ are independent of i; and λ_t is given by the ratio $V_t^{p,i}[v_t]/V_t^i[v_t]$. The second-order expectations are then derived by integrating $\lambda_t \hat{v}_t^c + (1 - \lambda_t)\hat{v}_t^{p,i}$ over i and by taking conditional expectations. This shows that the second-order expectation of v is a weighted average of two first-order expectations. This reasoning can be generalized for i's higher-order expectations as well, that is, i's higher-order expectations can be expressed as a linear function of his first-order expectations. Therefore, it is sufficient if i's optimal trading strategy depends only on his first-order expectations.[17]

For deriving the optimal stock demand, it is useful to define the excess return on one share of stock as $Q_{t+1} := P_{t+1} - P_t$. For the time being, He and Wang assume that Q_t and $\Psi_t^i =: E_t^i[\Psi]$, where Ψ_t^i is a simplified state space, follow the Gaussian process:

$$Q_{t+1} = A_{Q,t+1}\Psi_t^i + B_{Q,t+1}\epsilon_{t+1}^i$$
$$\Psi_{t+1}^i = A_{\Psi,t+1}\Psi_t^i + B_{\Psi,t+1}\epsilon_{t+1}^i.$$

This (temporary) assumption allows He and Wang in Lemma 4 to solve the investors' dynamic optimization problem. The authors state the Bellman equation, exploit the property of exponential utility function in forming expected utility for the next period, and derive the optimal stock demand function which is linear in Ψ_t^i. Finally, they verify that Q_t and Ψ_t^i follow this Gaussian process.

After imposing the market clearing condition, the equilibrium price is determined by

$$P_t = [(1 - \alpha_{v,t})\hat{v}_t^c + \alpha_{v,t}v] - \alpha_{u,t}u_t = (1 - \alpha_{v,t}\hat{v}_t^c) + \alpha_{v,t}\xi_t.$$

The stock price depends only on v, u_t, and $\hat{v}_t^c$, so $L[\hat{v}_t^c]$ summarizes the whole history. The price P_t also follows a Gaussian Markov process.

P_t is only determined implicitly since $\hat{v}_t^c$ depends on P_t. However, the derivation of the explicit solution is trivial since $\hat{v}_t^c$ is linear in P_t. Given

---

[17] The infinite regress problem can also be avoided by introducing a competitive risk neutral market making sector, as illustrated in Vives (1995). Past prices carry no additional information in such a setting.

the price, one can derive the expected excess return $E_t^i[Q_{t+1}]$ from which it follows that the investor's optimal stock demand is given by

$$x_t^i = \beta_{u,t}\hat{u}^i + \beta_{\Delta,t}\underbrace{(\hat{v}_t^i - \hat{v}_t^c)}_{:=\Delta}.$$

Given the market clearing condition

$$\beta_{u,t} = 1$$

$$\beta_{\Delta,t} = \frac{\lambda_t}{y_t(1 - \lambda_t)}.$$

He and Wang (1995) employ a recursive procedure to simulate the equilibrium values. Starting with a guesstimate for the conditional variance of v in $T - 1$, they derive coefficients $\alpha_{v,T-1}$, $\alpha_{u,T-1}$, demand, equilibrium price, and other parameters. As they proceed backwards they check whether the initial guess of the variance of v was correct. If not, they restart the procedure with a new initial guess.

Having derived the equilibrium, He and Wang then examine different patterns of trading volume and explain how private information is gradually incorporated into the price. In the benchmark case with *homogeneous information*, that is, $\sigma_{\epsilon,S,1}^2 = 0$, the true value $v = \hat{v}_t^c = \hat{v}_t^i$ is known immediately and the only remaining risk lies in δ. The equilibrium price in this case is given by $P_t = v - \alpha_{u,t}u_t$ where the second term represents the risk premium. $1/\alpha_{u,t}$ measures the market liquidity in the sense of Kyle (1985). The risk premium increases with the variance of δ and over time. The latter increase is due to the fact that the number of trading periods left to unwind speculative positions is decreasing. Furthermore, with only few periods remaining and with $|u|$ large it becomes less likely that the mean reverting AR(1) process of u_t will reach a value of zero. The volume of trade, V^*, in this benchmark case is totally determined by noise trading, which is defined by

$$V^* = \int_i |u_t - u_{t-1}| = |u_t - u_{t-1}|$$

with

$$E[V^*] = \sqrt{2/\pi \operatorname{Var}[\Delta u_t]}.$$

In the case of *differential information* the equilibrium price is given by

$$P_t = [(1 - \alpha_{v,t})\hat{v}_t^c + \alpha_{v,t}v] - \alpha_{u,t}u_t.$$

The second component, $\alpha_{u,t}u_t$, is associated with the risk premium as in the homogeneous information case. The first component reflects investors' expectations about the stock's future payoff. This is not simply proportional to the average of investors' expectations: $\lambda_t \hat{v}_t^c + (1 - \lambda_t)v_t$. This is because dynamic trading strategies generate equilibrium prices that differ from those generated by static/myopic strategies since current state variables depend on the history of the economy. This distinction between dynamic and myopic strategies also appeared in Brown and Jennings (1989) and in Grundy and McNichols (1989). In particular, the current state depends on past prices. As investors continue to trade, the sequence of prices reveals more information. This tends to decrease $\alpha_{u,t}$, whereas the reduction in the number of remaining trading rounds tends to increase $\alpha_{u,t}$.

The optimal trading strategy $x_t^i = \beta_{u,t}\hat{u}^i + \beta_{\Delta,t}(\hat{v}_t^i - \hat{v}_t^c)$ consists of two parts. The first represents the supply shock, the second investors' speculative positions. The trading activity generated by differential information is *not* the simple sum of each investor's speculative investments. This is because, in the case of heterogeneous information, noninformational trade by one investor could be viewed as an informational trade by another investor. It is also possible that investors on both sides of the trade think that their trades are noninformational, but the trading is purely due to differential information.[18] He and Wang (1995) focus on the *additional* trading volume generated by differential information. They define

$$V_t^{\text{ex}} := V_t - V_t^*.$$

Its expected value is given by

$$E[V_t^{\text{ex}}] = \frac{1}{\sqrt{2\pi}}\left(\sqrt{\text{Var}[\Delta u_t] + \text{Var}[\Delta x_t^i]} - \sqrt{\text{Var}[\Delta u_t]}\right),$$

where $\Delta x_t^i := x_t^i - x_{t-1}^i$ and $\Delta u_t := u_t - u_{t-1}$ are the changes in stock holdings. In Corollary 2, the authors provide a closed-form solution for the equilibrium volume for the special case where $\sigma_\delta = 0$. The corollary states that informational trading occurs only as long as investors receive new private information. In this case, the individual trader does not know whether the other investors trade because of new information or because of liquidity reasons. It is not common knowledge whether the allocation is Pareto efficient. This is the reason why the dynamic version of the no-trade (speculation) theorem given in Geanakoplos (1994) does

---

[18] For example there is no additional noise in t, but half of the traders think $u_t = +0.1$ and the other half think $u_t = -0.1$.

not apply in this case.[19] If on the other hand, investors receive only private information in $t = 1$, the prices will adjust but no informational trade will occur. For $a_u = 1$, this result is in line with the no-trade equilibrium outcome that arises in Grundy and McNichols (1989) when $\sigma_\omega^2 = 0$.

He and Wang (1995) then go on to analyze the behavior of trading volume after $t = 2$ for the case where $\sigma_\delta > 0$ and only the signal in $t = 1$ is informative. The main findings are that trading persists throughout the whole trading horizon. This is due to the fact that investors establish their speculative position when they receive their private information in $t = 1$ and then gradually try to unwind these positions. This generates peaks in the volume of trade in the middle of the trading horizon. In the case of public announcements, investors increase their positions right before and close them right after the announcement. Therefore, the volume and total amount of information revealed through trading depends on the timing of the announcement. Market liquidity drops right before the announcement and bounces back afterwards. They also find that new information, private or public, generates both high volume and large price changes, while existing private information can generate high volume with little price changes. He and Wang (1995) conclude their paper with further comments and possible generalizations. One conclusion is that the whole economy can be reduced to an effective two-person setup even if all investors have different risk aversion coefficients.

4.4. Inferring Information from Trading Volume in a Competitive Market Order Model

All the models discussed so far have the drawback that investors do not extract the predictive power of trading volume. In Blume, Easley, and O'Hara (1994) a group of traders make explicit use of volume data to improve their prediction of the liquidation value of an asset.

The authors consider a more general signal structure which incorporates asymmetry in second-order information, as in Romer (1993). As in the previous models, traders hold asymmetric information about the fundamentals, that is, about payoff-relevant events. They receive a private signal about the liquidation value v. In addition, traders are

---

[19] As in Grundy and McNichols (1989), the beliefs about future signals need not be concordant when $\sigma_\delta > 0$.

asymmetrically informed about the precision of the other traders' signals. In other words, in contrast to most other models the precision of the private signals is not common knowledge. Each investor knows the quality of his signal, but only a subset of investors, those in group 1, know the precision of all signals. In the sense of Morris, Postlewaite, and Shin (1995) this model exhibits a higher depth of knowledge by one degree.[20] The higher-order uncertainty about the precision of other investors' signals is the source of noise in their model and provides the basis for the predictive power of volume and technical analysis.

Difficulties in Modeling Informative Trading Volume

Blume, Easley, and O'Hara (1994) start their analysis by showing why the models in Brown and Jennings (1989) and Grundy and McNichols (1989) are not appropriate for analyzing the role of volume in predicting the value of an asset. While in Brown and Jennings (1989), trading volume leads to informationally efficient REE, in a setting à la Grundy and McNichols (1989) no inference can be drawn from volume.

In the framework of Brown and Jennings (1989) there always exists an informationally efficient REE if agents can submit demand schedules conditional on price and volume. Hence, trader i's information set is $\mathcal{F}_t^i = \{P_t, S_t^i, V_t, \chi_t\}$, where χ_t^i is an indicator function indicating whether the trader i is a buyer or seller and V_t is the per capita average trading volume

$$V_t = \frac{1}{2}\frac{1}{I}\left[\sum_{i=1}^{I} |x_t^i| + |u_t|\right].$$

The term $\frac{1}{2}$ reflects the fact that one unit of trading volume consists of one buy order as well as one sell order.

In an informationally efficient REE all traders completely rely on the price signal and volume signal and disregard their own signal. Consequently, they submit the same demand function conditional on price and volume as well as χ_t and end up with the same asset holding $x_t^i = x_t^j =: x_t$. They can infer the noisy supply term u_t by making use of the market clearing condition $x_t = I^{-1}u_t$, and χ_t^i. The average signal $\bar{S}_t$ can be inferred from the equilibrium price as it depends only

---

[20] The connection to higher-order knowledge becomes obvious in the case where the variance of the signal's noise term is either zero or infinite. An agent who receives the signal with a zero variance term knows the true value of the stock and also knows that he knows it, while the other agents who do not know the precision of the signal do not know whether the agent who received the signal knows the true value or not.

on u_t and $\bar{S}_t$. Thus, in each period t, the tuple (P_t, V_t) fully reveals $\bar{S}_t$ and u_t. This also implies that technical analysis has no value.

In Grundy and McNichols (1989) each individual is endowed with an i.i.d. random number of risky assets. The variance of this random endowment, u_t^i, is given by $\mathrm{Var}[u_t^i] = I\sigma_u^2$. In the limit economy with infinitely many traders, that is $I \to \infty$, each individual endowment itself has no informational content and the variance of the endowments is also infinite. The expected per capita trading volume $V_t = \frac{1}{2}\lim_{I\to\infty} I^{-1} \sum_{i=1}^{I} |x_t^i - u_t^i|$ is infinite as I goes to infinity. Consequently, no inference can be drawn from trading volume.

Static Market Order REE with a Generalized Information Structure

In contrast to Brown and Jennings (1989) and Grundy and McNichols (1989), Blume, Easley, and O'Hara (1994) develop a market order model with a generalized information structure. Market order models in a competitive setting were first developed by Hellwig (1982). The distinguishing feature of these models is that the information set of each trader i in market order models contains the whole price and volume process up to but *excluding* the current time t.

Blume Easley, and O'Hara (1994) assume the following information structure. The common priors for all traders about the liquidation value are $v \sim \mathcal{N}(\mu_{v,0}, \sigma_{v,0}^2)$. Each trader in group 1 receives a signal

$$S_t^i = v + \omega_t + e_t^i,$$

where the common error term $\omega_t \sim \mathcal{N}(0, \sigma_\omega^2)$ and the individual error term $e_t^i \sim \mathcal{N}(0, \sigma_{e,t}^2)$ are normally and independently distributed. Note that the variance of the error term of group 1's signal $\sigma_{e,t}^2$ varies over time.

Each trader in group 2 receives a signal

$$S_t^i = v + \omega_t + \epsilon_t^i,$$

where all ϵ_t^i are i.i.d. $\mathcal{N}(0, \sigma_\epsilon^2)$. It is common knowledge that a fraction v of I traders, that is, $I_1 = vI$ traders, are in group 1 and $I_2 = (1 - v)I$ traders are in group 2. Traders in group 1 and group 2 are also asymmetrically informed about the precision of the signals. That is, there is asymmetry in second-order information. Traders in group 1 know the precision of group 1 signals, $(1/\sigma_{e,t}^2)$, in each t. In addition, they know the precision of the signals received by group 2 traders, $(1/\sigma_\epsilon^2)$. Group 2 traders only know the signal precision of their own group.

The precision of group 1 signals, $\sigma_{e,t}^2$, varies randomly over time. This makes it impossible for group 2 traders to learn over time the group 1 signal precision.

The distribution of the signals is, therefore, given by:

- for group 1 signals: $S_t^i \sim \mathcal{N}(v, \sigma_{S_1,t}^2)$, where $\sigma_{S_1,t}^2 = \sigma_\omega^2 \sigma_{e,t}^2 [1/\sigma_\omega^2 + 1/\sigma_{e,t}^2] =: \mathrm{Var}[S_{1,t}]$

- for group 2 signals: $S_t^i \sim \mathcal{N}(v, \sigma_{S_2}^2)$, where $\sigma_{S_2}^2 = \sigma_\omega^2 \sigma_\epsilon^2 [1/\sigma_\omega^2 + 1/\sigma_\epsilon^2] =: \mathrm{Var}[S_2]$.

It is obvious from the strong law of large numbers that the average of the signals in each group, $\bar{S}_{1,t}$ and $\bar{S}_{2,t}$, converges almost surely to $v + \omega_t =: \theta_t$.

Blume, Easley, and O'Hara (1994) restrict their analysis to myopic REE. The individual demand for traders with a constant absolute risk aversion coefficient of unity, that is, $\rho = 1$, is approximated by: group 1 traders:

$$x_{1,t}^i = \frac{E_{t-1}^{i,1}[v] - P_t}{\mathrm{Var}_{t-1}[v]} + \frac{S_{1,t}^i - P_t}{\mathrm{Var}_{t-1}[S_{1,t}]};$$

group 2 traders:

$$x_{2,t}^i = \frac{E_{t-1}^{i,2}[v] - P_t}{\mathrm{Var}_{t-1}[v]} + \frac{S_{2,t}^i - P_t}{\mathrm{Var}_{t-1}[S_2]}.$$

In contrast to the standard REE where all traders submit demand schedules, there is an additional second term and the expectations are taken with respect to $\mathcal{F}_{t-1}^i$. The equilibrium price is derived by adding up all individual demand functions and imposing the market clearing condition. For the limit economy, P_1 is:

$$P_1 = \frac{(1/\sigma_{v,0}^2)\mu_{v,0} + [v(1/\sigma_{S_1,1}^2) + (1-v)(1/\sigma_{S_2}^2)]\theta_1}{(1/\sigma_{v,0}^2) + v(1/\sigma_{S_1,1}^2) + (1-v)(1/\sigma_{S_2}^2)}.$$

Group 1 traders can infer θ_1 from P_1 since they know $\sigma_{S_1,1}^2$ and $\sigma_{S_2}^2$. P_1, however, does not reveal θ_1 for group 2 traders since they do not know $\sigma_{S_1,1}^2$. Note that the conditional distribution of θ_1 given P_1 is not normal. Traders in group 2 can infer more information about θ_1 if they include trading volume in their inference calculation. The per capita trading volume in $t = 1$ is:

$$V_1 = \frac{1}{2}\frac{1}{I}\left(\sum_{i=1}^{I_1} |x^i_{1,t}| + \sum_{i=I_1}^{I} |x^i_{2,t}|\right).$$

Volume is not normally distributed. It is the sum of the absolute amount of normally distributed random variables. Blume, Easley, and O'Hara (1994) explicitly characterize the expected per capita volume V_1 in their Proposition 1:

$$V_1 = V_1(\theta_1 - P_1, \sigma^2_{S_1,1}, \sigma^2_{S_2}, \ldots).$$

Using the above equilibrium price relation, one can substitute for

$$(\theta_1 - P_1) = \frac{(1/\sigma^2_{v,0})(P_1 - \mu_{v,0})}{v(1/\sigma^2_{S_1,1}) + (1 - v)(1/\sigma^2_{S_2})}$$

a term depending on the signal precisions. The resulting equation links volume V, price P_1, and precision $(1/\sigma^2_{S_1,1})$. Hence, it shows that volume conveys information about the signal quality of group 1 traders, $(1/\sigma^2_{S_1,1})$.

Plotting the derived expression for V_1 with P_1 on the abscissa yields a V-shaped relationship between price and volume, for any given $(1/\sigma^2_{S_1,1})$. The minimum volume is reached at a price level $P_1 = \mu_{v,0}$. At the minimum volume level, the average traders' posterior means coincide with the prior mean. As P_1 deviates from $\mu_{v,0}$, the posterior means differ and the first term of the individual demand functions x^i_t on average increases the trading volume. This results in a strong correlation between volume and price change. The V-shape is very robust. As the signal precision (information quality of group 1 signals) decreases, the V-shape becomes more pronounced. The same is true when the quantity of information, that is, fraction of group 1 traders, decreases.

Keeping the price fixed and differentiating expected per capita volume with respect to the precision of trader 1 signals, $(1/\sigma^2_{S_1,1})$, yields the result that volume is increasing in the precision of group 1's signals if $(1/\sigma^2_{S_1,1}) < (1/\sigma^2_\omega)$ and decreasing if $(1/\sigma^2_{S_1,1}) > (1/\sigma^2_\omega)$ (provided $(1/\sigma^2_{S_1,1}) > (1/\sigma^2_{S_2})$). Intuitively, if group 1's signals are very imprecise, their signals are very dispersed and the traders place little confidence in their signal. They do not trade very aggressively and thus the expected trading volume is low. If on the other hand the signals are very precise, all group 1 traders receive highly correlated signals and thus the trading volume is low again since trade occurs only between the groups. There-fore, low volume can be a signal for very precise signals as well as for very imprecise signals. Volume is first increasing and then decreasing in the signal precision for a given price P_1. Hence, for an observed price volume pair (P_t, V_t) two outcomes, high or low precision, are feasible. In other words, the functional relationship is not invertible. There-fore, Blume, Easley, and O'Hara (1994) restrict their analysis to the increasing branch of $V(\cdot|P_1)$, that is, $1/\sigma^2_{S_{1,1}} \in (1/\sigma^2_{S_2}; 1/\sigma^2_\omega)$. If this is the case, the tuple (P_t, V_t) is revealing $(\theta_1, \sigma^2_{S_{1,1}})$. Since all signals incor-porate the common error term ω_t, the liquidation value $v = \theta_1 - \omega_1$ is not known.

Myopic REE in a Dynamic Setting – Technical Analysis and Trading Volume

In a dynamic setting more realizations of $\theta_t = v + \omega_t$ can be inferred and, therefore, a better estimate about the true liquidation value, v, can be made. In each period the precision of the signals for traders in group 1 is drawn randomly and the analysis is similar to the static case. One difference is that priors in period t are not exogenous, but derived from the market statistics up to time $t - 1$. Second, the volume expression is slightly different since traders' endowments in t are the equilibrium demands in $t - 1$. By the strong law of large numbers, the equilibrium price converges almost surely to v since traders can infer a new θ_t in each period. However, the trading volume does not vanish as time proceeds. Although traders' beliefs are converging, their precision is diverging at the same rate. Intuitively, agents trade in the early trading round because their beliefs are widely dispersed. However, they trade less aggressively on their information. In the later trading rounds, the beliefs are much closer to each other but traders are more confident of their own information and, hence, they take on larger positions. Blume, Easley, and O'Hara (1994) use simulations to illustrate that both effects offset each other and, therefore, volume does not decline with the number of trading rounds.

In the last section Blume, Easley, and O'Hara (1994) compare the utility of a trader who makes use of past market statistics in interpreting the current market statistics with a trader who bases his trading activity only on current market statistics and his priors in $t = 0$. The value of technical analysis is then defined by the amount of money the latter trader, who forgets all past market data, would be willing to pay to recall the forgotten past market statistics. Past market data have value because of the common error term ω_t in the signals. Blume, Easley, and O'Hara (1994) show that the value of technical analysis is decreasing in σ_ω^2 and increasing in $\sigma_{v,0}^2$. They conclude that technical analysis has higher value for small, less widely followed stocks.

Relation to No-Trade Theorem

Note that all traders trade purely for informational reasons in Blume, Easley, and O'Hara (1994). Nobody faces liquidity shocks and there are no noise traders. There are no gains from trade since agents' endowments and preferences are identical. The initial allocation is ex-ante Pareto efficient. One might think that the no-trade theorem described in Chapter 2 should apply. The no-trade theorem requires that rationality of all agents is at least higher-order mutual knowledge. The no-speculation theorem need not hold if rationality of all traders is not common knowledge. In contrast to a game theoretic equilibrium concept, the REE concept does not specify the cognitive capacity that an agent assumes his opponent players have. Blume, Easley, and O'Hara (1994) apply the REE concept. In a REE each agent is only assumed to know the mapping from traders' information onto prices. In particular, REE does not require common knowledge of rationality. In Blume, Easley, and O'Hara (1994) all traders behave rationally, but they might not be sure whether their opponents are rational. This higher-order uncertainty about traders' rationality can justify the trading outcome illustrated in Blume, Easley, and O'Hara (1994).

4.5. Strategic Multiperiod Market Order Models with a Market Maker

Market Order Models with Short-Lived Information – Intraday Trading Pattern

Admati and Pfleiderer (1988) analyze a strategic dynamic market order model.[21] Their model is essentially a dynamic repetition of a generalized version of the static model in Kyle (1985). However, their focus is on intraday price and volume patterns. They attempt to explain the U-shape of the trading volume and price changes, that is, the abnormal high trading volume and return variability at the beginning and at the end of a trading day. In their model the value of a single risky asset follows the

---

[21] To be consistent with our notation we denote: $v = F$, $\bar{v} = \bar{F}$, $I_t = n_t$, $J_t = m_t$, $X_t = \omega_t$, $u_t = z_t$, and $\sigma_\epsilon^2 = \phi_t$.

exogenous process

$$v = \bar{v} + \sum_{t=1}^{T} \delta_t,$$

where δ_t are independently identically normally distributed random variables whose realization becomes common knowledge only at t. As usual there are two motives for trading: information and liquidity. All I_t informed traders observe the same signal

$$S_t = \delta_{t+1} + \epsilon_t$$

at time t, where $\epsilon \sim \mathcal{N}(0, \sigma_\epsilon^2)$. In other words, informed traders observe a noisy version of the public information one period in advance. Since δ_{t+1} is known publicly in $t+1$ the informational advantage is only *short-lived*. Informed traders, therefore, have no incentive to restrict their trading in order to have a larger informational advantage in the next period. This simplifies the analysis on the one hand, but also neglects interesting aspects on the other.

In Admati and Pfleiderer (1988) there are two types of liquidity traders whose demand depends neither on the price nor on their information. Whereas J_t *discretionary liquidity traders* can choose a period within $[T', T'']$ in which to trade, *nondiscretionary liquidity traders* must trade a given amount at a specific time. For simplicity, it is assumed that the market maker as well as all traders are risk neutral. As in Kyle (1985) the market maker observes the total net order flow X_t, in addition to $\underline{\delta}_t := (\delta_0, \delta_1, \ldots, \delta_t)$. The total net order flow in t is given by

$$X_t = \sum_{i=1}^{I_t} x_t^i + \sum_{j=1}^{J_t} y_t^j + u_t,$$

where the first term represents the aggregated demand from informed traders, the second term the aggregated demand from discretionary liquidity traders, and the third term the aggregated demand from nondiscretionary liquidity traders. The variance of total liquidity trading, $\Psi_t = \text{Var}(\sum_{j=1}^{J_t} y_t^j + u_t)$, is endogenously determined in contrast to Kyle (1985), as it depends on the strategic decision of the discretionary traders.

The market maker tries to infer the information of the insiders from X_t. As in Kyle (1985), the zero profit condition together with risk neutrality implies that the market maker sets the price equal to his expected value. Since all random variables are normally distributed, the projection theorem implies the following linear pricing rule:

$$P_t = \bar{v} + \sum_{\tau=1}^{t} \delta_\tau + \lambda_t X_t,$$

where

$$\lambda_t = \frac{\text{Cov}[\delta_{t+1}, X_t]}{\text{Var}[X_t]}.$$

Note that $1/\lambda_t$ measures the market depth.

Each insider maximizes his capital gain in each period, given the market maker's pricing rule and the other insiders' trading strategy. The equilibrium market order size of an individual insider is given by $x_t^i = \beta_t^i S_t$, where S_t is the signal about δ_{t+1} and β_t, the trading intensity, is given by

$$\beta_t^i = \frac{1}{\lambda(I_t + 1)} \frac{\text{Var}[\delta_{t+1}]}{\text{Var}[\delta_{t+1}] + \text{Var}[\epsilon_t]}.$$

The equilibrium values for β_t^i and λ_t are then given by

$$\beta_t^i = \sqrt{\frac{\Psi_t}{I_t \text{Var}[S_t]}}$$

and

$$\lambda_t = \frac{\text{Var}[\delta_{t+1}]}{I + 1} \sqrt{\frac{I_t}{\Psi_t(\text{Var}[S_t])}}.$$

Some comparative static results for λ_t follow immediately. (1) As the number of informed traders I_t increases, the market becomes more liquid. This seems counterintuitive at first thought. As the number of informed traders increases, they compete their informational advantage away and the aggregate order flow becomes more informative. Therefore, one would think that λ_t should increase. However, the order flow of all informed traders together also increases and thus the price adjustment for each individual order is lower. This effect reduces the size of λ_t and dominates the first effect. (2) The market depth $1/\lambda_t$ is increasing with Ψ, the variance in liquidity traders demand. This is like in Kyle (1985).

The costs of trading for the liquidity traders, which equals the profit for insiders, is the difference between what the liquidity traders pay and the expected value, that is, $E[(P_t(\underline{\delta}_t, \underline{X}_t) - v)(\sum_{j=1}^{J_t} y_t)|\underline{\delta}_t, \underline{X}_{t-1}, \sum_{j=1}^{J_t} y_t]$ which is equal to $\lambda_t(\sum_{j=1}^{J_t} y_t)^2$. Therefore, discretionary liquidity traders would trade when λ_t is smallest, that is, when the market is deepest. This is the case when Ψ_t is high and thus it is optimal for these traders to "clump" together. This increases Ψ_t even more. High variance in noise trading, Ψ_t, allows insiders to hide more of their trade behind noise trade. Their demand in equilibrium is given by $x_t^i = \beta_t^i S_t$, where S_t is the signal about δ_{t+1} and the trading intensity β_t is linear in $\sqrt{\Psi_t / \mathrm{Var}(S_t)}$. Thus, at times when liquidity traders clump together, informed traders also trade more aggressively. This increases the overall trading volume in this trading period. Admati and Pfleiderer (1988) demonstrate the existence of equilibria in which discretionary traders clump together. In equilibrium, discretionary traders have to coordinate when to trade. The problem is that many equilibria can arise. It is plausible that the convention arose that these traders all trade at the beginning and at the end of the trading day. The authors also apply a refinement criterion that shows that these equilibria are the only ones that are robust to small perturbations in the vector of variances of the discretionary liquidity demands. As in Kyle (1985), the amount of information revelation by prices is independent of the total variance of liquidity trading. More noise trade would suggest less informative prices. On the other hand, more noise allows insiders to be more aggressive in their trade. This makes the price more informative. The aggressiveness of the insiders is such that both effects will balance out.

Admati and Pfleiderer (1988) also extend the analysis to incorporate endogenous information acquisition. Traders can buy the signal S_t at a fixed cost c. This makes the number of informed traders, I_t, endogenous. The authors apply two different models of entry. In their second approach, the number of insiders, I_t, is known in equilibrium. When I_t is high, more insiders compete with each other and, therefore, their profits will be lower, or equivalently, the trading costs for liquidity traders will be lower. At times when discretionary traders clump together, Ψ_t is high and, therefore, many insiders will enter the market. This reduces the trading costs for liquidity traders even more since more insiders are competing against each other. Thus, endogenous information acquisition intensifies the effects explained above and one would expect large trading volume at certain times.[22]

---

[22] Pagano (1989a) provides a model which illustrates the negative correlation between trading volume and market thinness as well as volatility. In this model risk averse investors value the stock for hedging reasons differently and have to pay a fixed transaction cost to enter the market. Each additional trader who enters the market reduces the market thinness and thus the volatility. This generates a positive externality for the other risk averse traders. Pagano (1989a) shows that there are multiple "bootstrap"

Market Order Models with Long-Lived Information

In Admati and Pfleiderer's model information is only private for one period, that is, it is only short-lived. As in the static Kyle (1985) model, insiders restrain the market order size in order to have a better execution price. In a model with long-run information, aggressive trading can not only worsen the execution price for the current trading round but also for all future trading rounds. Kyle's (1985) article also captures the dynamic setting which is modeled as a series of discrete call markets (a sequential auction). The insider holds long-run private information and faces the trade-off that taking on a larger position in early periods increases early profits but worsens prices in later trading rounds. He tries not to trade his informational advantage away. Therefore, he exploits his information across time by hiding behind noise trading. Kyle (1985) derives a dynamic linear recursive equilibrium. The author solves the insider's dynamic programming problem by proposing an ad hoc value function which he verifies at a later stage. The author also analyzes the insider's problem in continuous time by letting the time intervals converge to zero. In the continuous auction equilibrium, noise trading follows a Brownian motion and the informed trader continuously pushes the price towards his price valuation. The speed of price adjustment is equal to the difference between his price valuation and the current price divided by the remaining trading time. The market depth, $1/\lambda$, is constant over time and the market is "infinitely tight," that is, it is extremely costly to turnover a position in a very short period of time. This is the case because the insider can break up his informational trade into many small pieces. The price follows a Brownian motion (which is a martingale process).

Back (1992) extends Kyle's continuous time model by modeling strategy spaces and information directly in continuous time. In Holden and Subrahmanyam (1992) there are many informed traders who compete against each other. This speeds up information revelation through prices. As in the Cournot case, insiders who have the same information are more aggressive and, therefore, trade more of their insider information away. The information is revealed immediately as time becomes continuous. The insiders are risk averse in Holden and Subrahmanyam (1994). This further speeds up information revelation. Risk averse

equilibria, some with low trading volume and high price volatility, and others with high trading volume and low volatility. The latter are Pareto superior. Pagano (1989*b*) shows that traders may be unable to coordinate on a single market in the presence of different transaction costs.

agents trade more aggressively in early periods since future prices are more uncertain.

Foster and Viswanathan (1996) allow for a more general information structure where the signals are only correlated. Their model captures the most general setting with I risk neutral informed investors and a general signal structure.[23] Each investor gets a long-lived individual private signal at $t = 0$. In contrast to Admati and Pfleiderer (1988), there are no discretionary liquidity traders. (Nondiscretionary) liquidity traders demand $u_t \sim \mathcal{N}(0, \sigma_u^2)$ shares in period $t \in [1, \ldots, T]$. As in Kyle (1985), the market maker only observes the total net order flow $X_t = \sum_{i=1}^{I} x_t^i + u_t$ and sets the price at time t according to

$$P_t = E[v | \underline{X}_t],$$

where his prior distribution of v is given by $\mathcal{N}(P_0, \sigma_v^2)$ and $\underline{X}_t$ denotes the whole process $(X_1, \ldots, X_t)$. Informed traders $i \in \mathbb{I} = \{1, 2, \ldots, I\}$ have to submit their market orders x_t^i before X_t becomes known. Since each trader i knows his individual demand, $\underline{x}_t^i$ and the whole history of $\underline{X}_{t-1}$ he can infer the net order flow of *all other* traders $\underline{z}_{t-1} = \underline{X}_{t-1} - \underline{x}_{t-1}^i$. Each informed trader receives an individual signal S_0^i at the start of trading. The joint distribution of all individual signals with the asset's true value is given by

$$(v, (S_0^1, \ldots, S_0^I)) \sim \mathcal{N}\left[(P_0, \vec{0}), \begin{pmatrix} \sigma_v^2 & \Delta_0 \\ \Delta_0 & \Psi_0 \end{pmatrix} \right],$$

where Δ_0 is a vector with I identical elements, that is, $\Delta_0' = (c_0, c_0, \ldots, c_0)$ and Ψ_0 is the variance–covariance matrix of the signals given by

$$\Psi_0 = \begin{pmatrix} \Lambda_0 & \Omega_0 & \ldots & \Omega_0 \\ \Omega_0 & \Lambda_0 & \ldots & \Omega_0 \\ \ldots & \ldots & \ldots & \ldots \\ \Omega_0 & \Omega_0 & \ldots & \Lambda_0 \end{pmatrix}.$$

This signal structure imposes a strong symmetry assumption since (1) all signals have the same covariance c_0 with the true asset value,

---

[23] For consistency we adjust the notation to $I = M$, $t = n$, $X_t = y_n$, $v = v$, $S_0^i = s_{i,0}$, $\bar{S} = \hat{v}$, $P_t = p_n$, $\hat{S}_{0,t}^i = t_{in}$, $S_t^i = s_{in}$, and $\hat{\cdot}^i = \cdot^i$.

(2) all signals have the same variance Λ_0, and (3) the cross-variance between signals is Ω_0 for all signals. It also covers the special cases $\Omega_0 = \Lambda_0$ where all insiders get the same signal, and $\Omega_0 = 0$ where all signals are independent.

By applying the projection theorem one gets

$$E[v - P_0 | S_0^1, \ldots, S_0^I] = \Delta_0'[\Psi_0]^{-1} \begin{pmatrix} S_0^i \\ \cdots \\ S_0^I \end{pmatrix}.$$

By the imposed symmetry assumptions, all elements of the vector $\Delta_0'[\Psi_0]^{-1}$ are identical, say to κ. Therefore, the inner product can be rewritten as

$$E[v - P_0 | S_0^1, \ldots, S_0^I] = \underbrace{\kappa I}_{:=\theta} \underbrace{\frac{1}{I} \sum_{i=1}^{I} S_0^i}_{:=\bar{S}} = \theta \bar{S}.$$

$\bar{S}$, the average of all signals S_0^i, is a sufficient statistic for all signals. It follows that the market maker and the informed traders need not infer each individual signal S_0^i but only the average signal $\bar{S}$. This allows us to simplify the sufficient state description dramatically.

The market maker's estimate of S_0^i at t is given by

$$\hat{S}_{0,t}^i := E[S_0^i | X_1, \ldots, X_t] = E[S_0^i | \underline{X}_t].$$

The market maker sets a competitive price $P_t = E[v | \underline{X}_t]$. Since $(S_0^1, \ldots, S_0^I)$ is a sufficient statistic for X_t and[24]

$$P_t = E[E[v | S_0^1, \ldots, S_0^I] | X_t] = \theta E[\bar{S} | \underline{X}_t] = \theta \frac{1}{I} \sum_{i=1}^{I} \hat{S}_{0,t}^i + P_0$$

the informational advantage of informed trader i in period t is the difference

$$S_t^i := S_0^i - \hat{S}_{0,t}^i.$$

---

[24] A typo slipped into equation (5) of Foster and Viswanathan (1996). The last term $+P_0$ is missing.

Foster and Viswanathan (1996) further define the following conditional variances and covariances

$$\Sigma_t := \text{Var}(\theta\bar{S}|\underline{X}_t) = \text{Var}(\theta\bar{S} - P_t) = \text{Var}(E[v|S_0^1,\ldots,S_0^I]|\underline{X}_t),$$

$$\Lambda_t := \text{Var}(S_0^i|\underline{X}_t) = \text{Var}(S_t^i),$$

$$\Omega_t := \text{Cov}(S_0^i, S_0^j|\underline{X}_t) = \text{Cov}(S_t^i, S_t^j),$$

and derive the following relationships using the projection theorem:

$$\Sigma_t = \frac{\theta^2}{I}[\Lambda_t + (I - 1)\Omega_t],$$

which implies

$$\Lambda_{t-1} - \Lambda_t = \Omega_{t-1} - \Omega_t,$$

$$\Sigma_{t-1} - \Sigma_t = \theta^2[\Lambda_{t-1} - \Lambda_t],$$

and therefore

$$\Lambda_t - \Omega_t = \chi \quad \forall t.$$

Since the market maker will learn the average signal $\bar{S}$ much faster than any individual signal, the correlation between the informational advantage of insiders, Ω_t, must become negative after a sufficient number of trading rounds. This negative correlation between S_t^i and the fact that the insider learns faster from the aggregate order flow than the market maker will lead to the waiting game explained below. Foster and Viswanathan (1996) use a BNE concept given the price setting behavior of the market maker. They restrict their analysis to linear Markov equilibria. The equilibrium is represented by a tuple $(\mathbf{X}^1,\ldots,\mathbf{X}^I,\mathbf{P})$ where $\mathbf{X}^i$ is a vector of demand correspondences for trader i for each date, t, that is,

$$\mathbf{X}^i = (x_1^i,\ldots,x_T^i), \quad \text{where } x_t^i = x_t^i(S_0^i, \underline{X}_{t-1}^i, \underline{z}_{t-1}^i),$$

and $\mathbf{P}$ is a vector of price setting functions for each t, that is,

$$P_t = P_t(\underline{X}_t) = E[v|\underline{X}_t].$$

$x_t^i(\cdot)$ is the stock holding of trader i at time t which maximizes his profits from time t until T. $\mathbf{X}^i(\cdot)$ is optimal by backward induction. The authors impose a Markov perfect refinement criterion on the possible set of equilibria. How restrictive this criterion is depends on which state space the (trade) strategies can be based on. There are, therefore, two different state spaces: the first state space is given by the choice of nature, whereas the second covers events of the original state space on which traders can base their trading strategies. The smaller the latter state space is, the more restrictive is the Markov perfect refinement criterion. The state space given by the choice of nature is $(v, \{S_0^i\}_{i \in I}, \underline{u}_T)$. Incorporating the choice of each trader, one can consider the following extended state space $(v, \{S_0^i\}_{i \in I}, \{\underline{x}_T, \underline{u}_T\}_{i \in I})$. Since $u_t = \sum_{i=1}^I x_t^i - X_t$, the state space can be also written as $(v, \{S_0^i\}_{i \in I}, \{\underline{x}_T, \underline{X}_T\}_{i \in I})$. An equivalent representation of the state space is $(v, \{\underline{S}_T^i\}_{i \in I}, \{\hat{\underline{S}}_{0,T}^i\}_{i \in I}, \{\underline{x}_T, \underline{X}_T\}_{i \in I})$, as $S_t^i = S_0^i - \hat{S}_{0,t}^i$. All strategies have to satisfy the measurability condition, that is, traders can condition their strategies only on states they can distinguish, that is, on partitions. The authors focus on linear recursive Markov perfect equilibria which satisfy the following conditions:

$$x_t^i = \beta_t S_{t-1}^i,$$

$$\hat{S}_{0,t}^i = \hat{S}_{0,t-1}^i + \zeta_t X_t,$$

$$P_t = P_{t-1} + \lambda_t X_t,$$

where $X_t = \sum_i^I x_t^i + u_t$. It is shown that $\lambda_t = \theta \zeta_t$ and $\hat{S}_{0,t}^i = \hat{S}_{0,t-1}^i + \zeta_t X_t$ is necessary to guarantee that the forecasts of the others' forecasts is linear.

Foster and Viswanathan (1996) also show how the infinite regress problem discussed in Townsend (1983) can be avoided. The dimensionality of the state space can be reduced since a sufficient statistic for the past can be found for this equilibrium concept. Trader i bases his strategy on his information set $(S_0^i, \underline{X}_{t-1}, \underline{x}_{t-1}^i)$. Since his optimal demand is given by $x_\tau^i = x_\tau^i(S_0^i, \underline{X}_{\tau-1})$ $\forall \tau$ in equilibrium, his information set can be simplified to $(S_0^i, \underline{X}_{t-1})$. This also illustrates the fact that trader i can only manipulate trader j's beliefs about the true value, v, via $\underline{X}_t$. The authors show that S_{t-1}^i, the information advantage at $t-1$, is a sufficient statistic for trader i to predict $E[v - P_{t-1} | \mathcal{F}_{t-1}^i] = \eta_t S_{t-1}^i$ since P_{t-1} is common knowledge and all random variables are normal. η and ϕ are constant regression coefficients. As this is true for all traders, it is also sufficient for trader i to forecast S_{t-1}^j in order to forecast the forecasts of others, that is, $E[S_{t-1}^j | \mathcal{F}_{t-1}^i] = \phi_t S_{t-1}^i$. The tth order forecast, the forecast of trader i about the forecast of trader j about the forecast of trader i, and so on, is also a linear function of S^i_{t-1} by induction. This also shows that the hierarchy of forecasts is not history dependent and that the infinite regress problem, discussed in detail in Section 4.2, is avoided. Their analysis shows that, in equilibrium, the dimensionality issue can be resolved.

In order to check whether this is really a BNE, one has to show that no trader has an incentive to deviate from his equilibrium strategy. A larger state space is needed for analyzing deviation. Thus, the dimensionality issue arises again. Suppose only trader i deviates from the equilibrium strategy and submits arbitrary market orders $(x^i_1, \ldots, x^i_t)$ in the first t periods. All other traders cannot detect trader i's deviation and thus still play their equilibrium strategies. Let $X^{i'}_t, P'_t, \hat{S}^{i,i'}_{0,t}$, and $S^{j,i'}_t$ with the additional superscript $^{i'}$, be the corresponding variables when traders play the equilibrium strategies. By construction $S^{i,i'}_t$, the informational advantage, is orthogonal to $(\underline{X}^{i'}_{t-1})$. Note that $(\underline{X}^{i'}_{t-1})$ is in i's information set because i also knows the strategy he would have followed in equilibrium and thus he can also derive the change in other traders' expectations caused by his strategy change. Therefore, trader i's information set also captures $S^{i,i'}_{t-1}$, $P^{i'}_{t-1}$, and $S^{j,i'}_{0,t-1}$. A sufficient statistic for his information set is given by $S^{i,i'}_{t-1}$ together with the deviation from the equilibrium price $(P^{i'}_{t-1} - P_{t-1})$. Therefore, $E[v - P_{t-1}|\mathcal{F}^i_{t-1}] = E[v - P^{i'}_{t-1}|S^{i,i'}_{t-1}] + (P^{i'}_{t-1} - P_{t-1})$. Foster and Viswanathan conjecture the value function for trader i as:

$$V^i[S^{i,i'}_{t-1}, P^{i'}_{t-1} - P_{t-1}] = \alpha_{t-1}(S^{i,i'}_{t-1})^2 + \psi_{t-1}S^{i,i'}_{t-1}(P^{i'}_{t-1} - P_{t-1})$$
$$- \mu_{t-1}(P^{i'}_{t-1} - P_{t-1})^2 + \delta_{t-1}$$

and derive the optimal market order size for a certain time period. The resulting conditions for the Markov perfect linear recursive equilibrium allow them to verify that the proposed value function was indeed correct. Finally, the authors relate their results to less general models, like Kyle (1985), Holden and Subrahmanyam (1992), and others.

For calculating numerical examples, Foster and Viswanathan (1996) apply a backward induction algorithm for the case of three traders and four trading rounds. They compare four different correlations between the initial signals S^i_0; very high, low positive, zero, and low negative correlation. The major findings are that (1) the lower the signal correlation, the less informative is the price process, (2) the profit for insiders is lowest with identical information and highest with positive but not perfect correlation, (3) λ_t, the market maker's sensitivity falls over time, if the signal correlation is positive, and rises over time if the correlation is negative, and (4) the conditional correlation of the remaining information advantage S_t^i is decreasing over time and becomes negative provided there are enough trading rounds.

These results are the outcome of two effects. First, the competitive pressure is reduced under heterogeneous signals since each trader has some monopoly power. Second, traders play a waiting game when the S_t^i's become negatively correlated. This is driven by the fact that the market maker learns more about the average signal than about the individual signals. With negatively correlated S_t^i, traders are more cautious and more reluctant to take on large positions early. If traders have different private information, more aggressive trading reveals even more information to the competing insiders than to the market maker. Foster and Viswanathan then go on to analyze the effects of increasing the number of trading rounds keeping the total liquidity variance, $T\sigma_v^2$, constant. With more trading rounds, the speed of information revelation is higher and a U-shape pattern of λ_t arises and becomes more pronounced. This U-shape of the market maker's sensitivity results from the waiting game. Their analysis suggests that dynamic competition with heterogeneously informed traders can be quite distinct. Whereas insiders with identical information trade very aggressively, that is, they are in a "rat race", insiders with heterogeneous information trade less aggressively since they play a waiting game.

Back, Cao, and Willard (1997) conduct the same analysis in continuous time. They prove that there is a unique linear equilibrium when signals are imperfectly correlated and derive a "closed-form" expression for the equilibrium. However, a linear equilibrium does not exist when signals are perfectly correlated.

Vayanos (1996) studies a strategic dynamic continuous share auction model à la Kyle (1989). He shows that the foregone gains from trade lost due to strategic behavior increase as the time between trades shrinks.

In summary, both strategic and competitive dynamic models illustrate how traders can partially leave each others' signal by observing current and past prices and trading volumes. Often traders can even observe the past actions of individual players and infer information from these actions. The next chapter illustrates how this might lead to herding behavior.

5

Herding and Informational Cascades

It is important to understand crowd and group dynamics in order to understand many economic phenomena. The literature on social learning gives rational and plausible explanations for herding behavior and information cascades.

Herding behavior is often associated with people blindly following the decisions of others. Imitating somebody's action can be rational if the predecessor's action affects one's (1) payoff structure such that imitation leads to a higher payoff (*payoff externality*) and/or (2) his probability assessment of the state of the world such that it dominates the private signal (*informational externality*). A mixture of both externalities is present in most economic settings. Herding models due to *reputational effects* in a principal–agent setting are one example. In these models the payoff externalities are endogenous since they depend on the beliefs of the evaluator.

Imitation is only feasible if players move sequentially. The literature distinguishes between *exogenous sequencing* where the order of moves is pre-specified, and *endogenous sequencing* where the decision makers decide when to move and whether to move first or not. In endogenous sequencing models, it is possible that every individual (that is, the whole herd) moves at the same time. For example, all agents can move immediately after the leader has made a decision. It might even be the case that everybody decides to move simultaneously. In this case the decision maker has to follow the action he believes the others will take. These different types of herding models are described below in greater detail.

5.1. Herding due to Payoff Externalities

In almost any game, the payoff structure of an agent is affected by the other players' actions. Payoff externalities are often exogenously specified by the payoff structure of the game. These externalities might, however, also arise endogenously. For example, in a multiple agent setting, the wage a principal pays to one agent might depend on the other agent's action. Whether agents choose the same or different actions depends on the payoff structure of the game. If the players' strategies are "strategic complements" in the sense of Bulow, Geankoplos, and Klemperer (1985), then each player's incentive to act in a certain way increases as the others act this way as well. In other words, the marginal utility of increasing one's strategy increases in one's rival's strategy. In that case, players have an incentive to act alike. On the other hand, if one's marginal utility is increasing with a decline in one's rival's strategy, then the strategies are "strategic substitutes" and the players do not act alike.

In most games it can make a large difference whether the agents decide sequentially or simultaneously. Endogenous sequencing significantly enlarges the strategy space of each player. When agents can decide when to move, they often act simultaneously in equilibrium.

There are many examples of models where agents act alike due to the payoff structure. One famous group of games where agents "act alike" in pure strategy equilibria are coordination failure games. Unfortunately they have multiple equilibria and, hence, an equilibrium selection problem arises. Investigative herding, that is, herding in information acquisition, often occurs due to payoff externalities. Bank runs are another popular example of herding models due to payoff externalities. Most of these models exogenously specify that all agents run at the same time. However, runs often occur simultaneously even in models with endogenous sequencing. The behavior of discretionary liquidity traders in Admati and Pfleiderer (1988) described in Section 4.6 can also be viewed as herding. All discretionary liquidity traders try to trade at the same time, that is, they herd together.

5.2. Herding and Cascades due to Information Externalities

A successor will try to infer his predecessors' information from their actions provided these predecessors based their actions on their signals and the decisions have a common value component. This positive information externality can be so strong that the successor ignores his own signal (or does not give it the appropriate weight). *Herding due to informational externalities* occurs if an agent imitates the decision of his predecessor even though his own signal might advise him to take a different action. This herding can also lead to *informational cascades*. In an informational cascade, individuals' actions do not reveal any information to successors and thus it prevents information aggregation. In other words, there is no state of the world or possible signal realization in which a successor's beliefs depend on his immediate predecessor's action. Some authors use the term *partial informational cascade* if there are some states or extreme signal realizations which can break the herding behavior. Informational cascades can occur if a successor can only partially infer the predecessors' information from their actions. Any pre-play communication between predecessors and successors is ruled out in these models.

5.2.1. Exogenous Sequencing

This strand of literature was independently initiated by Banerjee (1992) and Bikhchandani, Hirshleifer, and Welch (1992) as well as Welch (1992).

Herding due to Two-Dimensional Signal Space

In Banerjee (1992) I risk neutral agents choose an asset $j \in [0, 1]$ on an interval of the real line. The payoffs of all assets are zero, with the exception of asset j^*, which has a certain payoff of v. All agents have uniform priors. An agent gets a signal with probability $\alpha < 1$. If an agent receives a signal, it is true with probability β and false with probability $(1 - \beta)$. If the signal is fake, then it is uniformly distributed on the interval $[0, 1]$. Agents make their decision sequentially. Successors can observe the predecessors' decisions, but not their signals.

Banerjee (1992) derives the following BNE after assuming three tie-breaking rules which disfavor a herding outcome. If the first agent receives a signal, he follows it. If he does not receive a signal, he chooses $j = 0$ by assumption. Agent 2 only follows the first agent if he has not received a signal. If he has received a signal he follows his own signal. His action can be identical to agent 1's action. For agent 3 it is always optimal to follow his two predecessors if they have chosen the same action $j' \neq 0$, regardless of his own signal. Both predecessors only choose the same asset $j' \neq 0$ if (1) either agent 1 got signal j' and agent 2 got no signal and followed agent 1, or (2) agent 1 and agent 2 both got the same signal j'. In the former case, which occurs with conditional probability $(1 - \alpha)$, agent 3 is indifferent between following the predecessors' decisions and his own signal. In the latter case, which occurs with conditional probability α, j' is the optimal action j^* with probability one. The event that agent 1 and agent 2 get the same wrong signal j' occurs with zero probability. Therefore, agent 3 will follow his predecessors and ignore his own signal. Agent 4 knows that agent 3's decision carries no information about his own signal. Thus, he faces exactly the same situation as agent 3 and he will choose the same asset as the first two decision makers. Agent 5, 6, ... face exactly the same situation and, hence, herding will occur.

Herding also leads to an informational cascade in this setting. It is quite likely that all agents chose the wrong action. This is the case when agent 1 receives a wrong signal and agent 2 receives no signal. Agent 2 follows agent 1 and consequently the whole crowd runs in the wrong direction. This happens, even though the optimal asset j^* could be found with probability one, if a large enough number of agents could communicate with each other. This inefficiency in information aggregation only occurs (in sequential decision making) if the predecessors' actions are not a sufficient statistic for their information, that is, the successors can only partially infer the information of the predecessors. In Banerjee (1992) the one-dimensional action space on $[0, 1]$ cannot reflect the signal since it is two-dimensional. One dimension of the signal is on the interval $[0, 1]$ and the second dimension is binary $\{0, 1\}$ indicating whether the predecessor received a signal or not.

Herding due to Discrete Action Space

In contrast to Banerjee (1992), in Bikhchandani, Hirshleifer, and Welch (1992) every agent receives a noisy signal for sure, that is, the signal space is one-dimensional and the action space is discrete: adopt or reject. An agent can adopt the new project (technology) at a cost of $c = \frac{1}{2}$. The project pays off either $v^h = 1$ or $v^l = 0$ with equal probability $\frac{1}{2}$. Each agent receives a binary signal, $S^i \in \{S_H, S_L\}$. Its realization, high S_H or low S_L, reveals the correct state of the world $\{h, l\}$ with probability $q > \frac{1}{2}$. Although the signal in their basic example is also only binary $\{S_H, S_L\}$, the discrete action space $\{$adopt, reject$\}$ cannot capture the whole information of a later decision maker.[1] This information consists of one's own signal and of information derived from his predecessors' actions.[2] Agent 1 adopts the project only if he receives a high signal. Everybody can perfectly infer the first agent's signal from his action since the priors are common knowledge. If agent 2 gets a different signal as compared to agent 1, he is indifferent between adopting and rejecting the project. Let us assume that an agent follows his own signal if he is

---

[1] In their generalized version, the signals can take on finitely many discrete values.
[2] A continuous action space could reveal the posterior of an immediate predecessor which is a sufficient statistic for all past signals. No herding occurs in this case.

indifferent. Given this tie-breaking rule, everybody can infer agent 2's signal too. If both agents 1 and 2 have chosen the same action, agent 3 will choose the same action regardless of his own signal. Agent 4 can no longer infer agent 3's signal. All the decision makers that follow agent 3 know that he ignored his own signal. Thus, they do not try to infer any information from his action. They face the same problem as agent 3 and, therefore, join the crowd. Everybody ends up in an information cascade, thereby preventing the aggregation of information. Therefore, convergence to the correct action need not occur. If the first two agents accidentally receive the wrong signal, everybody will end up choosing the wrong action. Note that the informational cascade would not have arisen if all agents would take into account the fact that their decision generates a positive externality for all their successors.

In their section "Fashion Leaders," the authors demonstrate that if agent 1 receives a signal with higher precision, informationally ineffi-cient cascades occur sooner and also become more likely. In this case, it is more likely that agent 2 follows agent 1. Zhang's (1997) model shows formally that the agent with the highest precision signal will move first in equilibrium in a setting with an endogenous decision sequence. Zhang's (1997) model is discussed in more detail in the next section. Public information can also have a large impact on informational cascades. Information which is made public prior to agent 1's decision can make inefficient cascades even more likely. On the other hand, public infor-mation that is released after a cascade has already begun will always be socially beneficial. A small amount of public information can shatter a long-lasting cascade. As explained above, a cascade is created by the decision of the first two agents and, thus, the public information need only lift out their information.

Introducing a Continuous Signal Space and Partial Cascades

Gale (1996) provides an example with a continuous *signal space* $S^i \in [-1; +1]$ while the action space is still binary $\{a_H, a_L\}$ as in Bikhchandani, Hirshleifer, and Welch (1992). Welch's (1992) herd-ing model also considers a setting with continuous signal space. In Gale (1996) partial cascades arise which can be shattered by extreme signals.

There are at least I identical investment opportunities. The payoff of each investment project is given by the average of all signals, that is, $v = I^{-1} \sum_{i=1}^{I} S^i$. Given that the signals are uniformly distributed over $[-1, +1]$, the first best solution is achieved if all agents invest if and only if $v = I^{-1} \sum_{i=1}^{I} S^i > 0$. In sequential decision making, agent 1 invests if $S^1 > 0$ and agent 2 if $S^2 + E[S^1|\text{action}^1] > 0$, and so on. If agent 2 observes that agent 1 has invested, he will invest if $S^2 + E[S^1|S^1 > 0] = S^2 + \frac{1}{2} > 0$. If agent 2 also invests, agent 3 will invest if $S^3 + \frac{3}{4} > 0$, and so forth. In other words, if agents 1 and 2 have invested then agent 3 needs to receive a really bad signal $S^3 < -\frac{3}{4}$ in order to not invest, that is, not to follow his predecessors. This means that the *partial informational cascade* becomes more and more stable over time. That is, the signal necessary to break up a cascade has to be more and more extreme. Although herding behavior will occur, a full informational cascade can never occur in Gale's (1996) setting.

Role of Discreteness of the Action Space

Lee (1993) shows how crucial the discreteness of the *action space* is. Discreteness plays a dual role: (1) it prevents somebody's actions from fully revealing his posteriors, and (2) it prevents each agent from fully using his information. In Lee's model the likelihood of an inefficient cascade decreases as the action space grows. He also claims that Banerjee's model is an exceptional case since signals are two-dimensional and the (degenerated) payoff structure in Banerjee (1992) does not distinguish between small and large errors.

Confounded Learning when Agents' Preferences Differ

Smith and Sørensen (2000) not only consider a continuous signal space but also allow agents' preferences to differ. If agents' preferences differ, the successor does not know whether a predecessor's action is due to a different signal realization or due to a different preference ordering. Incorporating diversity in taste can also lead to situations of "confounded learning." In such situations the observed history does not provide additional information for decision making and the decision of each type of agent might forever split between two actions.

Information Externalities Reduce Speed of Learning

Information cascades typically do not arise in a continuous action space, and a one-dimensional signal space. A one-dimensional action space can fully reflect a one-dimensional signal or posterior as long as all agents have identical preferences. In the market setting in Vives (1993), noise prevents immediate information revelation of the sufficient statistic of all the individuals' signals. In Vives (1993) the market participants do not see the (previous) actions of the participants directly, but they can act conditionally on past and current prices. In this model, *noise* in the prices plays the same role as discreteness does in the models discussed earlier. As explained in Section 4.1.2, each market participant acts based on his private signal and the information he infers from current and past prices. The more emphasis he puts on his private signal instead of the publicly observable price signals, the more information he reveals to the others. In other words, actions that are based more on private signals generate a positive informational externality. Vives (1993) shows that since the market participants do not take this informational externality into account, the market is not only less informationally efficient in the current trading round but the rate of convergence to the full information outcome in a repeated market interaction setting is also extremely slow.

Relation to Experimentation

A natural extension to the herding literature would be to allow agents to act more than once and/or to revise their decisions. This leads us to models of experimentation. Experimentation can be viewed as a special form of costly information. The *experimentation* literature stems from Rothschild's (1974) two-armed bandit analysis. Smith and Sørensen (1997) relate the literature of experimentation to herding models. Herding models correspond to the experimentation problem faced by a single myopic experimenter who forgets his formal signal but remembers his past actions. The incorrect herding outcomes correspond to the familiar failure of complete learning in an optimal experimentation problem. If there is a confounding action and the agent is impatient, beliefs need not converge to the true value or functional relationship. Nonconvergence to the true value is common in many experimentation models. See for example Bergemann and Välimäki (1996), Bolton and Harris (1999), Leach and Madhavan (1993), and Keller and Rady (1999) for different models of experimentation.

5.2.2. Endogenous Sequencing, Real Options, and Strategic Delay

In many economic situations, agents can decide when to decide. They own a *real (American)* option with a fixed exercise price but an unknown final value of the underlying asset. Holding an option gives the decision maker the right to wait for some time in order to learn something about the value of the underlying asset. Waiting incurs some costs but it allows him to make a better investment decision in a later period of time. However, there is a difference between the standard real option setting and herding models with endogenous sequencing. Whereas the amount of information released is exogenous in the standard real option settings, it depends on the investment decision of the other players in most herding models. If the other agents invest in the meantime, the agent learns more about the value of the underlying asset. Thus the benefits of waiting and consequently the value of the real option depends on the timing, that is, the equilibrium strategy of the other agents.

If each decision maker can decide when to decide, everybody would want to decide last in order to profit from the positive information externalities generated by his predecessors' decisions. Strategic delays caused by information externalities were first discussed by Chamley and Gale (1994) and Gul and Lundholm (1995).

Endogenous Sequencing in Discrete Time

In Chamley and Gale (1994) time is discrete $t = 1, 2, \ldots, \infty$ and a random number of agents have an opportunity to invest or not to invest with the option to invest later. Each investor knows whether he himself has an investment opportunity, but he does not how many other investors have this opportunity as well. In more formal terms, each agent receives a binary signal $S^i \in \{0, 1\}$. The agent has an investment opportunity and participates in the game only if $S^i = 1$. The true payoff of the identical underlying investment opportunities is increasing in $\sum_{i=1}^{I} S^i$, the number of possible investment opportunities, not in the number of investments actually undertaken. Agents who invest early reveal that they had an investment opportunity. This positive information externality allows the successors to update their beliefs about the true I. In order to prevent all agents from waiting forever, the authors assume that each agent's waiting costs are given by a common discount factor $0 < \delta < 1$. Chamley and Gale (1994) focus on *symmetric* perfect Bayesian equilibria in which agents apply behavioral strategies.[3] They show that there are three exclusive possible equilibrium continuation paths given a certain history of past investments. If beliefs about the number of people who got an investment opportunity are sufficiently optimistic, all players immediately invest and the game ends. On the other hand, if these beliefs are sufficiently pessimistic, no one will invest and hence no information is revealed. In this case the game ends as well, since the situation will not change even one period later. For intermediate beliefs, given a certain investment history, all remaining players with investment opportunity face (1) an individual incentive to invest,

---

[3] Action rules determine an action at a certain partition/decision node. A strategy is a sequence of action rules. Randomizing over different action rules at any partition is a behavioral strategy. Randomizing over *pure* strategies is a mixed strategy.

and (2) a positive option value of waiting. That is, if all the players who possess an investment option would invest then player i prefers to wait and act in the next period on the basis of more information. However, if all the players who possess an investment option would wait then player i prefers to invest because if he also waits he does not learn anything and he bears the cost of waiting. So the informational gain from waiting is a function of the symmetric investment probability. The higher that probability is, the higher is the informational gain from waiting. In a symmetric equilibrium, all other players fix their symmetric investment probability such that player i is indifferent between the two actions. He randomizes between (1) investing today and thus surrendering the option value, and (2) waiting. In a symmetric equilibrium, everybody employs the same behavioral strategy. In the next period all agents who have not invested update their beliefs about I from the random number of investments in this period. It is obvious that information aggregation is inefficient in such a setting. The authors also show that as the period length increases, the possibility of herding disappears.

In Gale (1996) agents' signals about the payoff of the identical investment opportunities are drawn from a continuous distribution, $S^i \in [-1, 1]$. The payoff of each investment project is $v = I^{-1} \sum_i^I S^i$. Gale (1996) considers only the two-agent case, $I = 2$. Given a common discount factor δ, the agent with the higher signal is more impatient to invest than the agent with the lower signal. The aim is to derive the threshold level $\bar{S}$ for the signal value required to motivate an agent to invest in period 1. Whether the agent exercises his real option early depends on the probability that he will regret in the next period that he has invested early. An investor i who invests early regrets it if the other agent $-i$ has not invested and his posterior beliefs about the payoff are negative, that is $S^i + E[S^{-i}|S^{-i} < \bar{S}] < 0$. The event that the other agent does not invest occurs with probability $\Pr(S^i < \bar{S})$. In equilibrium, an agent with signal $\bar{S}$ is indifferent between waiting and investing in the first period:

$$(1 - \delta)\bar{S} = -\delta \Pr(S^i < \bar{S}) \{\bar{S} + E[S^i|S^i < \bar{S}]\}.$$

There exists a unique equilibrium $\bar{S}$ in which information is not fully revealed and the outcome need not be efficient. For example, if both signals are $0 < S^i < \bar{S}$ nobody will invest even though it would be socially optimal. Another feature of the equilibrium is that the game ends after two periods. If nobody invested in the first two periods, investment stops forever, that is, an investment collapse can occur. Similar results carry over to a more general setting with I agents.

Endogenous Sequencing in Continuous Time,
Perfect Information Revelation, and Clustering

In contrast to Chamley and Gale (1994), in Gul and Lundholm (1995) time is assumed to be continuous. In Bikhchandani, Hirshleifer, and Welch (1992) and Banerjee (1992) agents (partially) ignore their own information. This leads to inefficient information aggregation, and even to information cascades. The timing decision of when to act as well as when *not* to act improves the information aggregation in models with endogenous sequencing. In Gul and Lundholm (1995), endogenous sequencing leads to informationally efficient *clustering*. In their model agents maximize a utility function which captures the trade-off between the accuracy of a prediction and how early the prediction is made (waiting costs). Each agent observes a signal $S^i \in [0, 1]$, which helps him to forecast $v = \sum_{i=1}^{I} S^i$. The authors show that the strategy of each player can be fully described by a function $t^i(S^i)$. The function $t^i(S^i)$ reports the latest possible time at which agent i with signal S^i will make his forecast given that the other players have not done so already. Since $t^i(S^i)$ is continuous and strictly decreasing, that is, $t^i(S^i)$ is invertible, the time when the first agent acts fully reveals his signal to the succeeding decision maker. In a two-agent setting, the second agent will make his prediction immediately afterwards. Whereas in the models with an exogenous sequencing only the succeeding decision makers profit from positive information externalities, in models with endogenous sequencing the first agent learns from the others as well. He learns from their inaction. The first agent can *partially* infer the signals of his successors by noticing that they have not acted before him. This biases his decision towards the successor's forthcoming decisions. Consequently, agents tend to cluster, that is, their forecasts are closer together in a setting with an endogenous sequencing than in a setting with exogenously ordered forecast. Gul and Lundholm (1995) call this effect *anticipation*.[4] There is a second source of clustering called *ordering*. This occurs because (1) agents with the most extreme signal realizations have higher waiting costs and thus act first, and (2) the signals of predecessors are revealed fully, whereas inaction of the successors only partially reveals their signals. More pronounced signals have a larger impact on the true value $v = \sum_{i=1}^{I} S^i$. Since more pronounced signals are fully revealed first, while signals with lower impact are fully revealed later, forecasts are "on average" closer together than in the case where the less pronounced signals would be fully revealed first.

---

[4] Note the similarity to (descending) Dutch common value auctions.

Signals with Different Precisions

The distinctive feature of Zhang's (1997) model is that the precision (quality) of the private signal, and not just its content, is private information. His model incorporates higher-order uncertainty. The signal is binary and reports with probability q^i which of the two investment projects is the good one. The quality (precision) of the signal is measured by q^i, where each q^i is drawn from a continuous probability distribution over $[\frac{1}{2}, \bar{q}]$, with $\bar{q} < 1$. The realization of the signal as well as its quality q^i is only known to agent i. The agents' action space at each point in time is either to wait (which discounts the payoffs by δ) or to invest either in investment project 1 or 2. As in Gul and Lundholm (1995), time is assumed to be continuous.

Zhang (1997) derives a unique equilibrium in pure strategies in closed form. The equilibrium exhibits an initial delay of action until the agent with the highest precision (highest q^i) invests. Given the binary investment choice and binary signal space, the second decision maker will always ignore his signal since it is of worse quality. He will immediately mimic the first mover's investment decision. Consequently, the second agent's investment choice carries no additional information and therefore all other agents will immediately follow the first mover as well. In summary, after a certain initial delay one can observe a sudden onset of investment cascades. In contrast to Gul and Lundholm (1995), the outcome is not informationally efficient since everybody's investment decision depends only on the signal with the highest precision. Moreover, the initial delay generates waiting costs, which is a source of allocative inefficiency. As the number of agents increases, the per capita efficiency loss is bounded away from zero. In this case, each player tends to wait longer since it is more likely that someone has a more precise signal and will invest before him.

Gale (1996) discusses the problems which arise in herding models in continuous time. For a more detailed discussion of the "closure problem" that arises see Harris, Stinchcombe, and Zame (1997).

5.3. Herding and Anti-herding in Reputational Principal–Agent Models

In reputational herding models the first agent's action affects the second agent's assessment about the state of the world (informational externality) as well as his payoff structure (payoff externality). In reputational principal–agent models which were initiated by Holmström (1999), there are different types of agents. For example, agents can be either "smart," that is, they receive signals with high precision, or "dumb," that is, they receive signals with low precision. The agent's payoff depends only on the principal's evaluation, that is, the principal's beliefs about his type. Consequently, the agent does not care about the chosen action per se; he only cares about it to the extent to which it affects the principal's evaluation.

These models are closely related to the *cheap talk games* à la Crawford and Sobel (1982). In standard cheap talk games, the informed agent sends a message to the receiver, that is, the principal. The principal chooses his ex-post optimal action based on the agent's message. The principal's equilibrium choice of action generally creates *endogenous signaling costs* which allow equilibria with partial sorting. In other words, although the agent does not bear a direct cost from signaling, he cares about which message he sends since it affects the principal's action and also his payoff. The agent will only send a noisy signal to the receiver if the preferences between the sender and the receiver are not completely congruent.[5]

In reputational principal–agent models the principal, rather than taking the decision on his own, delegates the decision making process to the agent. This is equivalent to a setting where the principal takes the action, but commits himself to follow a specific action after observing a certain signal. In other words, if the action is delegated to the agent, it need not be ex-post optimal for the principal. The agent's action does not affect his payoff directly. However, it affects his payoff indirectly since the principal reassesses the agent's ability after observing his actions and the realization of the physical state. In most herding models, the principal can also observe the realization of investment profitability. This is, however, not the case in the single manager setting assumed in Holmström (1999) and Prendergast and Stole (1996).

5.3.1. Exogenous Sequencing

Scharfstein and Stein (1990) developed the first herding model in a reputational principal–agent setting. In their model two risk neutral agents (managers) invest sequentially in two identical investments projects. The payoffs of investing in the project are $\{v_H > 0, v_L < 0\}$ while noninvestment yields zero return. Each agent receives a binary signal $\{S_H^i, S_L^i\}$

---

[5] Brandenburger and Polak (1996) can also be viewed as a special form of cheap talk game. Their paper will be discussed in Section 6.4.

about the true liquidation value $v \in \{v_H, v_L\}$ of the projects. The signal depends not only on the true state of the world but also on the type of the agent. Each manager is either smart or dumb. Neither the principal nor the agents themselves know their type. The signal structure in Scharfstein and Stein (1990) satisfies the following conditions:

(1) $Pr(S_H|v_H, smart) > Pr(S_H|v_L, smart)$;
(2) $Pr(S_H|v_H, dumb) = Pr(S_H|v_L, dumb)$;
(3) $Pr(S_H|smart) = Pr(S_H|dumb)$; and
(4) smart agents' signals are (perfectly) correlated.

Condition (1) states that a smart agent gets the right signal with higher probability, that is, their signal precision is higher. Condition (2) says that dumb managers get a completely uninformative signal. Condition (3) guarantees that the signal is purely about the investment project and cannot be used by a single agent to improve his knowledge about his type. Ottaviani and Sørensen (1999a) clarify the decisive role of condition (3). Condition (4) states that if both agents are smart then their forecast error is perfectly correlated.

Given these conditions, Scharfstein and Stein (1990) show that there exists a separating equilibrium in which agent 1 invests if he receives a high signal and does not otherwise. Condition (3) is sufficient (but not necessary) to guarantee a separating equilibrium for agent 1. Thus, agent 2 as well as the principal can perfectly infer agent 1's signal from his action. A separating equilibrium for agent 2 would also exist if instead of condition (4) the signals for both agents are conditionally independent, that is, their forecast errors are independent. In this case no herding would occur and the first best outcome would prevail. In the first best outcome, agent 2 makes use of the information which he inferred from agent 1's action, but he does not ignore his own signal as in the herding outcome.

Herding in reputational principal–agents models can occur for two reasons: (a) due to endogenous payoff externalities if error terms of the agents' signals are correlated, and/or (b) due to information externalities by relaxing condition (3) as highlighted by Ottaviani and Sørensen (1999a).

Payoff Externalities due to Correlated Error Terms
In Scharfstein and Stein (1990) the agent's error terms are perfectly correlated. Agent 2 cares only about his reputation with respect to the principal. That is, he wants to appear to be smart. The principal's updating rule about agent 2's type becomes a function of agent 1's

investment decision if their signals are conditionally correlated. In other words, agent 1's decision causes a payoff externality for agent 2 via the principal's beliefs. Scharfstein and Stein (1990) show that a separating equilibrium does not exist and agent 2 always employs a herding (pooling) strategy in equilibrium given out-of-equilibrium beliefs which satisfy the intuitive criterion of Cho and Kreps (1987). The intuition is the following. Since smart agents' private information is positively correlated, smart agents have a tendency to choose the same investment projects. That would not be the case for dumb agents if they followed their (independently distributed) private signal. Agents, therefore, deduce that by choosing the same action they can "look smart," which provides an incentive to ignore private information and imitate agent 1's action. Graham (1999) relaxes the perfect correlation assumption (4) to any positive correlation and derives qualitatively similar results.

Information Externalities when Agents (Partially) Know their Type

Ottaviani and Sørensen (1999a) show that both agents might also herd even if their signals are conditionally independent provided (a) one relaxes condition (3) and/or (b) one introduces a more general signal structure. In this case, agents might also herd due to informational externalities.

If condition (3) is relaxed, the one-dimensional signal provides agents information about the profitability of the investment project and also about their own type. As this signal becomes more and more informative about the agent's type, uninformative herding à la Bikhchandani, Hirshleifer, and Welch (1992) prevails. This occurs because the agents receive a separate signal about their type. Thus, the cheap talk (signaling) problem is two-dimensional.

Instead of relaxing condition (3), agents could also receive an additional signal about their type. In Trueman (1994) the agents know their type with certainty, whereas in Avery and Chevalier (1999) agents receive only a noisy signal about their type. Avery and Chevalier (1999) stick with the four conditions in Scharfstein and Stein (1990). Depending on the precision of the private "type" signal, there are three possible outcomes: (1) If the agents know relatively little about their type, the *herding equilibrium* à la Scharfstein and Stein (1990) arises. (2) For more precise "type" signals there exists an *efficient equilibrium*. In the efficient equilibrium agent 1 always follows his signal. Agent 2's action depends on his "type" signal. He follows his signal if he has received a high "type" signal and he imitates agent 1's actions if he has received a low "type" signal. In other words, only managers with a high "type" signal contradict the first managers' action. (3) If the "type" signal is sufficiently precise only an *anti-herding* (signaling) equilibrium exists. In this equilibrium, if agent 2 has a high "type" signal, he follows his signal. Conversely, if agent 2 has a low "type" signal he follows a mixed strategy between following his own signal and contradicting agent 1's action. It pays off for the "low" type agent to sometimes contradict agent 1's action since it makes him look smart in the (less likely) event that agent 1 was wrong. This equilibrium is only semi-separating because agent 1's actions only partly reveals his type.

In Trueman (1994) the agents know their types perfectly. This model analyzes herding among analysts who forecast the earnings of a company. Earnings can take on one of four values. They can be extremely negative, slightly negative, slightly positive, or extremely positive. The common prior distribution is symmetric around the mean zero where the more extreme outcomes are less likely. The prior probability for each of the moderate outcomes is $\frac{1}{4} < \pi < \frac{1}{2}$. Analysts receive a private signal about the forthcoming earnings. The signal allows each analyst to distinguish between whether the earning will be negative or positive. However, they do not know with certainty the exact earnings, that is, whether earnings are moderate or extremely high/low. As far as the exact amount of earnings is concerned, the signals of "dumb" analysts only have precision $q^{dumb} > \frac{1}{2}$, whereas the signals of "smart" analysts have precision $q^{smart} > q^{dumb}$. Each analyst's posterior is in between the moderate and extreme outcome. A high type (smart) analyst puts more weight on his signal whereas the posterior of a low type (dumb) analyst relies more on the prior.

Trueman (1994) first analyzes the case of *simultaneous forecasts* by the two analysts. Given the principal's beliefs that any other forecast different from a possible "truthful" analyst's posterior makes you look "dumb," every analyst will choose one of the possible truthful posteriors. In equilibrium the forecast of "smart" analysts always coincides with their true posterior. "Dumb" analysts do not forecast their true posterior since it would immediately reveal their type. If they receive a moderate signal, they forecast the posterior that a "smart" analyst would make with the same signal. Although they put too much emphasis on the signal, it is in line with the prior which also tends towards the moderate outcome. On the other hand, "dumb" analysts apply a mixed strategy if their signal indicates an extreme outcome. With a certain probability they forecast the posterior that a "smart" analyst would draw with the same extreme signal, that is, they put a lot of weight on the signal and less weight on the prior. To compensate for this the agents also forecast, with a certain probability, the posterior a "smart" agent would draw given a moderate signal. The randomization and, thus, the beliefs of the principal must be such that the "dumb" investors are indifferent between both of these forecasts. As the prior distribution becomes more skewed towards the moderate outcomes, "dumb" agents increase the probability of contradicting their extreme signals and following their prior.

In a scenario where both agents release their *forecast sequentially*, the equilibrium strategy for the first analyst is the same as in the simultaneous forecast scenario. This is due to the fact that the two analysts' forecast are independent conditional on realized earnings and the principal evaluates both analysts only after the earnings announcement. However, the second analyst's strategy changes since he learns something from the first announcement. In other words, the second forecaster's de facto priors are affected by the first announcement. If the second analyst is "smart," he never engages in herding behavior and he follows his own signal. If he is "dumb" and he receives a moderate signal, he still follows his signal. However, if the second forecaster observes an extreme signal, the probabilities of his mixed strategy are affected by the first agent's forecast. In the case where the first agent announces an extreme outcome, the second analyst's "de facto" priors are more inclined towards an extreme outcome and, thus, he follows his extreme signal with a higher probability. If the first analyst announces a moderate signal, the second analyst follows the first analyst with a higher probability. In other words, both forecasts are more correlated compared to the simultaneous forecast scenario. This is driven by the informational externality of the first analyst's forecast. However, compared to the efficient outcome, the weak second analyst does not take the information externality fully into account. Since the first analyst had in expectations a more precise signal, the second analyst should always follow his forecast. However, he contradicts the first analyst with a certain probability in order to look smart, that is, he *anti-herds*.

Herding on Own Earlier Decisions

In Prendergast and Stole (1996) the same individual makes a decision in each period. He receives a signal in each period and he perfectly knows his type. As in Holmström (1999) the principal can evaluate the type of the agent only based on the agent's decision since he does not observe the realized return. This is in contrast to the papers described earlier. The assumed agent's payoff in Prendergast and Stole (1996) is a linear combination of his reputation as well as of the actual outcome of his decision. The equilibrium separates low-type agents from high-type agents but involves distortions in order to satisfy the incentive compatibility constraints. Talented (high-type) managers with more precise signals follow their signals to a larger extent and put less weight on their priors. Therefore, in the beginning their decisions will be more variable than the decision the low-type managers would recommend. After a certain number of decisions, high-type managers trust their early estimate and new signals become less and less informative. Low-type managers also want to appear talented and thus mimic the talented managers. In the beginning they exaggerate their own information, that is, they act over-confidently. Although later signals still have high informational value for less talented managers, they are reluctant to update their early deci-sions in order to appear as talented. In other words, they herd on their early decisions and become conservative. The fact that they overreacted on their early signals makes their outcome even worse. The tendency not to revise early decisions explains the famous sunk cost fallacy. A similar outcome as in Prendergast and Stole (1996) might also arise in a moral hazard setting where managers pretend to experiment in the initial periods in order to collect information.

Reputational Herding due to Noncontinuous Payoff Schemes

In Zwiebel (1995) herding due to reputational effects is driven by nonlin-earities induced by the possibility of being fired. In his model managers know their type. Some managers have the option to go for a stochasti-cally dominating action instead of the less profitable "standard action." The "standard action" has a lower expected return. However, it allows the principal to better evaluate the manager's type. As in Holmström and Ricart I Costa (1986) a benchmark about the investment's returns helps the principal evaluate the manager's type. The benchmark for the "stan-dard action" is more accurate to evaluate the manager's type. Zwiebel (1995) shows that agents whose type is below a certain threshold choose the "nonstandard action" and thus take on additional personal risk. They gamble on resurrection. Those managers who are above the thresh-old become too risk averse (conservative) and they opt for the inefficient standard action. Very good managers take on the more profitable project since they do not have to worry too much about being mistaken for a bad manager.

5.3.2. Endogenous Sequencing

To my knowledge there are no papers examining reputational herding models in a setting where the agents are free to choose when to act. It is, however, easy to see that the delegation and enumeration of agents according to their reputation might alleviate the strategic delay problem discussed in Section 5.2.2. For example in Zhang (1997) the decision makers wait too long in the hope that they can profit from the positive informational externality of potential predecessors. On the other hand, if agents cared not only about the decision itself but also about their reputation, acting fast might also be beneficial. Moving early might signal that the agent received a very precise signal, that is, that he is a "smart" agent.

6

Herding in Finance, Stock Market Crashes, Frenzies, and Bank Runs

The last chapter illustrated herding and informational cascades in a general context. This chapter shows that herding can also arise in financial markets and describes how herding behavior can be used to explain interesting empirical observations in finance. For example, herding can result in stock market crashes and frenzies in auctions. The stock market might still be rising prior to a crash if bad news is hidden and not reflected in the price. A triggering event can reveal this hidden news and lead to a stock market crash. Crashes and frenzies in auctions are described in greater detail in Section 6.1.3.

Another example is the use of investigative herding models to show that traders have a strong incentive to gather the same short-run information. Trading based only on short-run information guarantees that the information is reflected in the price early enough before traders unwind their acquired positions. Section 6.2 illustrates the different reasons why traders might want to unwind their positions early and highlights the limits of arbitrage. It also throws new light on Keynes' comparison of the stock market with a beauty contest.

This short-run focus of investors not only affects the stock price but can also potentially affect corporate decision making. In Section 6.3 we cover two models which show that if investors focus on the short-run, and if corporate managers care about the stock market value, then corporate decision making also becomes short-sighted.

Finally, bank run models are closely linked to herding models. Seminal bank run papers are presented in Section 6.4. While the early papers did not appeal to herding models directly, this connection is explicitly drawn in the more recent research on bank runs. Insights from the bank run literature can also help us get a better understanding of international financial crises. For example, the financial crisis in Southeast Asia in the late 1990s is often viewed as a big bank run.

6.1. Stock Market Crashes

A stock market crash is a significant drop in asset prices. A crash often occurs even when there is no major news event. After each stock market crash, the popular literature has rushed to find a culprit. The introduction of stop loss orders combined with margin calls and forced sales caused by the decline in value of assets that served as collateral were considered to be possible causes for the crash of 1929. Early writings after the stock market crash of 1987 attributed the crash exclusively to dynamic portfolio insurance trading. A dynamic portfolio trading strategy, also called program trading, allows investors to replicate the payoff of derivatives. This strategy was often used to synthesize a call option payoff structure which provides an insurance against downward movements of the stock price. In order to dynamically replicate a call option payoff, one has to buy stocks when the price increases and sell shares when the price declines. Stop loss orders, sales triggered by the fall of value of collateral, and dynamic trading strategies were obvious candidates to blame for the 1929 and 1987 crashes, respectively, since they did not obey the law of demand and were thus believed to destabilize the market. Day traders who trade over the internet are the most likely candidates to be blamed for the next stock market crash.

Pointing fingers is easy, but more explicit theoretical models are required to fully understand the mechanism via which a stock market crash occurs. A good understanding of these mechanisms may provide some indication of how crashes can be avoided in the future. The challenge is to explain sharp price drops triggered by relatively unimportant news events. Theoretical models which explain crashes can be grouped into four categories:

(1) liquidity shortage models;
(2) multiple equilibria and sunspot models;
(3) bursting bubble models; and
(4) lumpy information aggregation models.

Each of these class of models can explain crashes even when all agents act rationally. However, they differ in their prediction of the price path after the stock market crash. Depending on the model, the crash can be a correction and the stock market can remain low for a substantial amount of time or it can immediately bounce back.

The first class of models argues that the decline in prices can be due to a temporary *liquidity shortage*. The market dries up when nobody is willing to buy stocks at a certain point in time. This can be due to unexpected selling pressure by program traders. These sales might be mistakenly interpreted as sales driven by bad news. This leads to a large price decline. In this setting, asymmetric information about the trading motive is crucial for generating a stock market crash. The model by Grossman (1988) described in the next section illustrates the informational difference between traded securities and dynamic trading strategies that replicate the payoff of derivatives. Crashes which are purely driven by liquidity shortage are of a temporary nature. In other words, if the price drop was caused by liquidity problems, one would expect a fast recovery of the stock market.

The second class of models shows that large price drops that cannot be attributed to significant news events related to the fundamental value of an asset may be triggered by *sunspots*. A sunspot is an extrinsic event, that is, a public announcement which contains no information about the underlying economy. Nevertheless, sunspots can affect the economic outcome since agents use them as a coordination device and, thus, they influence agents' beliefs. The economy might have multiple equilibria and the appearance of a sunspot might indicate a shift from the high asset price equilibrium to an equilibrium with lower prices. This leads to a large change in the fundamental value of the asset. This area of research was discussed earlier in Section 2.3 and will only be partly touched upon in this section. Note that all movement between multiple equilibria need not be associated with sunspots. Gennotte and Leland (1990) provide an example of a crash that arises even in the absence of sunspots. In their model there are multiple equilibria for a range of parameter values. The price drop in Gennotte and Leland (1990) is not caused by a sunspot. As the parameter values change slightly, the high-price equilibrium vanishes and the economy jumps discontinuously to the low-price equilibrium. This model will be described in detail in the next section.

The third class of models attributes crashes to *bursting bubbles*. In contrast to models with multiple equilibria or sunspot models, a crash which is caused by a bursting bubble may occur even when the fundamental value of the asset does not change. In this setting, there is an excessive asset price increase prior to the crash. The asset price exceeds its fundamental value and this is mutually known by all market participants, yet it is not common knowledge among them. Each trader thinks that the other traders do not know that the asset is overpriced. Therefore, each trader believes that he can sell the risky asset at a higher – even more unrealistic – price to somebody else. At one point the bubble has to burst and the prices plummet. A crash due to a bursting bubble is a correction and one would not expect prices to rebound after the crash. Although bursting bubbles provide a very plausible explanation for crashes, bubbles are hard to explain in theoretical models without introducing asymmetric information or boundedly rational behavior. The possibility of bubbles under asymmetric information is the focus of Section 2.3 of this survey and is therefore not discussed again in this section.

A sharp price drop in theoretical models can also occur even when no bubble exists. That is, it is not mutual knowledge that the asset price is too high. Often traders do not know that the asset is overpriced, but an additional price observation combined with the knowledge of the past price path makes them suddenly aware of the mispricing. Models involving this *lumpy information aggregation* are closely related to herding models. The economy might be in a partial informational cascade until the cascade is shattered by a small event. This event triggers an information revelation combined with a significant price drop. Section 6.1.2 illustrates the close link between herding models with exogenous sequencing and sequential trading models. Frenzies in descending multi-unit Dutch auctions – as covered in Section 6.1.3 – are closely related to herding outcomes in models with endogenous sequencing. The difference between these trading models and pure herding models is that herding is not only due to informational externalities. In most settings, the predecessor's action causes both an informational externality as well as a payoff externality. A stock market crash caused by lumpy informational aggregation is often preceded by a steady increase in prices. The crash itself corrects this mispricing and, hence, one does not expect a fast recovery of the stock market.

The formal analysis of crashes that follows can be conducted using different model setups. We first look at competitive REE models before we examine sequential trade models. We illustrate how temporary liquidity shortage, dynamic portfolio insurance, and lumpy information revelation by prices can explain crashes. The discussion of these models sheds light on the important role of asymmetric information in understanding stock market crashes.

6.1.1. Crashes in Competitive REE Models

In a competitive REE model, many traders simultaneously submit orders. They take prices as given and can trade any quantity of shares in each trading round. In this setting, crashes can occur because of temporary liquidity shortage, multiple equilibria due to portfolio insurance trading, and sudden information revelation by prices. We begin by looking at Grossman's (1988) model where program trading can lead to temporary liquidity shortage.

Temporary Liquidity Shortage and Portfolio Insurance Trading

Grossman (1988) was written before the stock market crash in October 1987. In his model poor information about hedging demand leads to a large price decline. The original focus of the paper was to highlight the informational difference between traded options and synthesized options. Its main conclusion is that derivative securities are not redundant, even when their payoffs can be replicated with dynamic trading strategies. This is because the price of a traded derivative reveals information, whereas a synthesized option does not.[1] In a world where investors have asymmetric information about the volatility of the underlying stock price, the price of a traded option provides valuable information about the underlying asset's future volatility. The equilibrium price path and the volatility of a risky asset are driven by news announcements about its liquidation value as well as by investors' risk aversion.

In Grossman (1988) there are three periods, $t = 1, 2, 3$. There are public announcements about the value of the stock in period $t = 2$ and in $t = 3$. After the second announcement in $t = 3$, every investor knows the final liquidation value of the stock. Each public announcement can be either good or bad, that is $S_t^{\text{public}} \in \{g, b\}$, where $t = 1, 2$. Consequently, the price in $t = 3$ can take on one of four values: P_{3bb}, if both signals are bad; P_{3bg}, if the public announcement in $t = 2$ is good but the one in $t = 3$ is bad, P_{3gb}, or P_{3gg}. The price in $t = 2$, P_{2g} or P_{2b}, depends on the investors' risk aversion. In this model, there is a fraction f of investors whose risk aversion increases significantly as their wealth declines. These investors are only willing to hold a risky asset as long as their wealth does not fall below a certain threshold. As the price of the stock declines due to a bad news announcement in $t = 2$, and with it the value of their portfolio, investors become much more risk averse and less willing to hold risky stocks. They would only be willing to hold the stock in their portfolio if the expected rate of return, $(P_3 - P_2)/P_2$, is much higher. This can only be achieved if the price in $t = 2$ drops drastically. Given their risk aversion, these traders want to insure themselves against this price decline in advance. Thus, they would like to

---

[1] Section 2.2.2 discusses the informational difference between traded securities and trading strategies at a more abstract level.

hold a position which exhibits a call option feature. To achieve this they can either buy additional put options in $t = 1$ or alternatively they can employ a dynamic hedging strategy which replicates the call option pay-off structure. This dynamic trading strategy requires the investor to sell stocks when the price is falling in $t = 2$ and buy stocks when it is rising. These sales lead to an even larger price decline. The larger the fraction f of investors with decreasing risk aversion, the larger the number of traders who either follow this dynamic trading strategy or buy a put option. Thus, the volatility of the stock price in $t = 2$ increases as f increases.

To counteract this large price decline, there are also less risk averse market timers who are willing to bear part of this risk and provide liquidity at a much lower expected rate of return. These market timers can only provide liquidity to the extent that they have not committed their funds in other investment projects in $t = 1$. Market timers have to decide in $t = 1$ how much capital M to set aside to profitably smooth out temporary price movements. The amount of capital M that market timers put aside in $t = 1$ depends on their expectations about market volatility, that is, on the expected fraction f of risk averse investors who might insure themselves with dynamic hedging strategies or by buying put options.

Grossman (1988) compares three scenarios:

1. If the extent of adoption of dynamic hedging strategies f is known to everybody in $t = 1$, then market timers reserve funds in $t = 1$ for market interventions in $t = 2$. They will do so as long as this intervention is more profitable than using these funds for other purposes. Their activity stabilizes the market and reduces the price volatility in $t = 2$.

2. If the extent of dynamic hedging strategies f is not known in $t = 1$, but put options are traded in $t = 1$, the price of the put option reveals the expected volatility in $t = 2$. The price of the put option in $t = 1$ might even fully reveal f. It provides the market timers with valuable information about how much money M to put aside. Market timers stabilize the market as in the case where f is directly observable. Note that it is only required that a liquid option market exists which reveals information about the volatility of the underlying stock. Intermediaries who write put options can hedge their position with dynamic trading strategies.

3. If the extent of hedging strategies f in the market is not known and not revealed by an option price, the market timers face uncertainty about the profitability of their price smoothing activity in $t = 2$. If they underestimate the degree of dynamic hedging activity, they do not

have enough funds in $t = 2$ to exploit the high price volatility. This makes the prices much more volatile and might explain stock market crashes. After a slightly negative news announcement in $t = 2$, the price drops dramatically since all dynamic hedgers become much more risk averse and sell their stocks. Market timers also do not have enough funds in reserve to exploit this cheap buying opportunity. The market only bounces back later when the market timers can free up money from other investment projects and provide liquidity. In Grossman (1988) the market price bounces back in $t = 3$ as all uncertainty is resolved in that period.

Note that as long as the put option price reveals f, the put option payoff can be replicated with dynamic trading strategies. However, if all traders switch to dynamic hedging strategies, the option market breaks down and thus f is not revealed to the traders. In this case the volatility of the underlying stock is not known. This makes an exact replication of the option payoff impossible.

Large price movements in Grossman (1988) are due to a lack of liquidity provision by market timers, who underestimate the extent of sales due to portfolio insurance trading. In this model, traders do not try to infer any information about the value of the underlying stock from its price. It is arguable whether dynamic hedging demand alone can trigger a price drop of over 20 percent as experienced in October 1987. Portfolio insurance trading covered only $60–90 million in assets, which represents only 2–3 percent of the outstanding equity market in the US. Although sales by portfolio insurers were considerable, they did not exceed more than 15 percent of total trading volume. Contrary to the experience of recent shocks, Grossman's model also predicts that the price would rebound immediately after the temporary liquidity shortage is overcome. Therefore, this model might better capture the "almost crash" caused by the Long Term Capital Management (LTCM) crisis during the fall of 1998 than the more long-lived crash of 1987.

Multiple Equilibria in a Static REE

While the stock market crashes in Grossman (1988) because market timers who have not put enough money aside cannot submit orders after a price drop due to sales by program trades, in Gennotte and Leland (1990) the market crashes because some other market participants incorrectly interpret this price drop as a bad signal about the fundamental value of the stock. In the latter model, traders hold asymmetric information about the value of the stock and, thus, the price of the underlying stock is also a signal about its fundamental liquidation value. Consequently, even these other market participants start selling their shares. Combining asymmetric information about the fundamental value of the stock with uncertainty about the extent of dynamic hedging strategies can lead to a larger decline in price in $t = 2$. The reason is that the traders wrongly attribute the price drop to a low fundamental value rather than to liquidity shortage. They might think that many other traders are selling because they received bad information about the fundamental value of the stock, while actually many sell orders are triggered by portfolio insurance trading.

Gennotte and Leland (1990) employ a static model even though stock market crashes or price changes occur over time. As the parameters change over time, the price equilibrium changes. The repetition of a static model can often be considered as a sufficient representation of a dynamic setting. Thus, comparative static results with respect to some parameters in a static model can be viewed as dynamic changes over time. A stock market crash – defined as a large price movement triggered by a small news announcement – occurs if a small change in the underlying information parameter causes a discontinuous drop in the equilibrium price.

The authors model this discontinuity in a static REE limit order model à la Hellwig (1980) with two different kinds of informed traders:[2]

(1) (value-)informed traders, who each receives an idiosyncratic individual signal $S^i = v + \epsilon^i$ about the liquidation value $v \sim \mathcal{N}(\mu_v, \sigma_v^2)$;
(2) (supply-)informed traders, who know better whether the limit order book is due to informed trading or uninformed noise trading.

Supply-informed traders can infer more information from the equilibrium price P_1. The aggregate supply in the limit order book is given by the normally distributed random variable $u = \bar{u} + u_S + u_L$. That is, u is divided into the part $\bar{u}$ which is known to everybody, u_S which is only known to the supply-informed traders, and the liquidity supply u_L which is not known to anybody. The individual value-informed trader's demand is, as usual, given by

$$x^i = \frac{E[v|S^i, P_1] - P_1}{\rho \, \mathrm{Var}[v|S^i, P_1]}.$$

[2] To facilitate comparison across papers, I have adjusted the notation to $S^i = p_i'$, $v = p$, $\mu_v = \bar{p}$, $\sigma_v^2 = \Sigma$, $p_1 = p_0$, $u = m$, $u_L = L$, $u_S = S$.

Similarly, the supply-informed trader's demand is given by

$$x^j = \frac{E[v|u_S, P_1] - P_1}{\rho \operatorname{Var}[v|u_S, P_1]}.$$

In addition to the informed traders' demand, there is an exogenous demand from portfolio traders who use dynamic trading strategies. Their demand $\pi(P_1)$ rises as the price increases and declines as the price falls.

As long as $\pi(P_1)$ is linear and common knowledge, the equilibrium price $P_1 = f(v - \mu_v - k_1 u_L - k_2 u_S)$ is a linear function with constants k_1 and k_2. In this linear case, the price P_1 is normally distributed. For nonlinear hedging demands $\pi(P_1)$, the argument of the price function, $f^{-1}(P_1)$, is still normally distributed and, therefore, the standard technique for deriving conditional expectations for normally distributed random variables can still be used. Discontinuity in $f(\cdot)$ makes "crashes" possible, that is, a small change in the argument of $f(\cdot)$ leads to a large price shift. $f(\cdot)$ is linear and continuous in the absence of any program trading, $\pi(P_1) = 0$. This rules out crashes.

Nevertheless, even for $\pi(P_1) = 0$ an increase in the supply can lead to a large price shift. Gennotte and Leland (1990) derive elasticities measuring the percentage change in the price relative to the percentage change in supply. This price elasticity depends crucially on how well a supply shift can be observed. The price change is small if the change in supply is common knowledge, that is, the supply change is caused by a shift in $\bar{u}$. If the supply shift is only observed by supply-informed traders, the price change is still moderate. This occurs because price-informed and supply-informed traders take on a big part of this additional supply even if the fraction of informed traders is small. Supply-informed traders know that the additional excess supply does not result from different price signals while price-informed traders can partially infer this from their signal. If, on the other hand, the additional supply is not observable to anybody, a small increase in the liquidity supply u_L can have a large impact on the price. In this case, traders are reluctant to counteract the increase in liquidity supply u_L by buying stocks since they cannot rule out the possibility that the low price is due to bad information that other traders might have received. Regardless of whether the supply shift is known to everyone, someone, or no one, the equilibrium price is still a linear continuous function of the fundamentals and thus no crash occurs.

By adding program trading demand, the price P_1 becomes even more volatile since $\pi(P_1)$ is an increasing function. Dynamic hedgers buy stocks when the price increases and sell stocks when the price declines. This violates the law of demand. As long as $\pi(P_1)$ is linear, $P_1 = f(\cdot)$ is continuous and linear. Crashes only occur when the program trading is large enough to cause a discontinuous price correspondence $f(\cdot)$. The discontinuity stems from the nonlinearity of program trading $\pi(P_1)$ and the lack of knowledge of the amount of program trading $\pi(P_1)$. Crashes are much more likely and prices are more volatile if some investors underestimate the supply due to program trading. Gennotte and Leland (1990) illustrate their point by means of an example of a put-replicating hedging strategy (synthetic put). In this example, the excess demand curve is downward sloping as long as all traders or at least the supply informed traders know the level of program trading demand. In the case where hedging demand is totally unobserved, the demand curve looks like an "inverted S." There are multiple equilibria for a certain range of aggregate supply.[3] The aggregate supply can be depicted as a vertical line. Thus as the aggregate supply shifts, the equilibrium with the high asset price vanishes and the asset price discontinuously falls to a lower equilibrium level. This is illustrated in Figure 6.1.

Gennotte and Leland's (1990) explanation of a stock market crash provides a different answer to the question of whether the market will bounce back after the crash. In contrast to Grossman (1988), the price can remain at this lower level even when the supply returns to its old

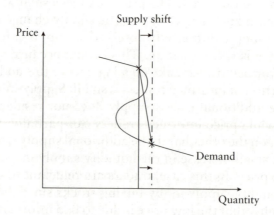

Figure 6.1. *Price crash in a multiple equilibrium setting*

[3] In this range, crashes can also be generated by sunspots. A different realization of the sunspot might induce traders to coordinate in the low-price equilibrium instead of the high-price equilibrium.

level. The economy stays in a different equilibrium with a lower asset price.

The reason why uninformed portfolio trading has a larger impact in Gennotte and Leland (1990) than in Grossman (1988) is that it affects other investors' trading activities as well. Asymmetric information about the asset's fundamental value is a crucial element of the former model. Program trading can lead to an "inverted S"-shaped excess demand curve. As a consequence, there are multiple equilibria in a certain range of parameters and the price drops discontinuously as the underlying parameter values of the economy change only slightly. It is, however, questionable whether this discontinuity in the static setup would also arise in a fully fledged dynamic model. In a dynamic model, traders would take into account the fact that a possible small parameter change can lead to a large price drop. Therefore, traders would already start selling their shares before the critical parameter values are reached. This behavior might smooth out the transition and the dynamic equilibrium will not necessarily exhibit the same discontinuity.

Delayed Sudden Information Revelation in a Dynamic REE

Romer (1993) illustrates a drastic price drop in a dynamic two-period model. In this model, a crash can occur in the second period since the price in the second trading round leads to a sudden revelation of information. It is assumed that traders do not know the other traders' signal quality. The price in the first trading round cannot reveal both the average signal about the value of the stock as well as precision of the signals, that is higher-order uncertainty. In the second trading round, a small commonly known supply shift leads to a different price which partially reveals higher-order information. This can lead to large price shocks and stock market crashes.

In Romer (1993) each investor receives one of three possible signals about the liquidation value of the single risky asset, $v \sim \mathcal{N}(\mu_v, \sigma_v^2)$:[4]

$$S^j = v + \epsilon_{S^j},$$

where $\epsilon_{S^2} = \epsilon_{S^1} + \delta^2$, $\epsilon_{S^3} = \epsilon_{S^2} + \delta^3$ and $\epsilon_{S^1}, \delta^2, \delta^3$ are independently distributed with mean of zero and variance $\sigma_{\epsilon_{S^1}}^2$, $\sigma_{\delta^2}^2$, $\sigma_{\delta^3}^2$, respectively. Thus, S^j is a sufficient statistic for S^{j+1}. There are two equally likely states of the world for the signal distribution. *Either* half of the traders receive

---

[4] The notation in the original article is: $v = \alpha, S_j = s_j, \mu_v = \mu, \sigma_v^2 = V_\alpha, u_1 = Q, \mu_{u_1} = \bar{Q}, \sigma_{u_1}^2 = V_Q$.

signal S^1 and the other half receive signal S^2 *or* half of the traders receive signal S^2 and the other half receive signal S^3. It is obvious that traders who receive signal S^1 (or S^3) can infer the relevant signal distribution since each investor knows the precision of his own signal. Only traders who receive signal S^2 do not know whether the other half of the traders have received the more precise signal S^1 or the less precise signal S^3. As usual, the random supply in period 1 is given by the independently distributed random variable $u_1 \sim \mathcal{N}(\mu_{u_1}, \sigma^2_{u_1})$.[5]

The stock holdings in equilibrium of S^1-traders, $x^1(S^1)$, can be directly derived using the projection theorem. S^1-traders do not make any inference from the price since they know that their information is sufficient for any other signal. Traders with S^3-signals face a more complex problem. They know the signal distribution precisely but they also know that they have the worst information. In addition to their signal S^3, they try to infer signal S^2 from the price P_1. The equilibrium price in $t = 1$, P_1, is determined by $x^2(S^2, P_1) + x^3(S^3, P_1) = u_1$ (assuming a unit mass of each type of investor). Since an S^3 trader knows $x^2(\cdot)$, $x^3(\cdot)$, and the joint distribution of S^2, S^3, and u_1, he can derive the distribution of S^2 conditional on S^3 and P_1. Since $x^2(S^2, P_1)$ is not linear in S^2, $x^3(S^3, P_1)$ is also nonlinear. S^2-investors do not know the signal precision of the other traders. Therefore, the $\mathrm{Var}[P_1|S^2]$ depends on the higher-order information, that is, on whether the other half of the traders are S^1- or S^3-investors. S^2-traders use P_1 to predict more precisely the true signal distribution, that is, to predict the information quality of other traders. If they observe an extreme price P_1, then it is more likely that other investors received signal S^3. On the other hand, if P_1 is close to the expected price given their own signal S^2, then it is more likely that the others are S^1-traders. S^2-investors' demand functions $x^2(S^2, P_1)$ are not linear in P_1 since P_1 changes not only the expectations about v, but also its variance. This nonlinearity forces Romer (1993) to restrict his analysis to a numerical example. His simulation shows that S^2-investors' demand functions are very responsive to price changes.

Romer's (1993) key insight is that a small shift in aggregate supply in period $t = 2$ induces a price change which allows the S^2-investors to infer the precision of the other traders' signals. A small supply change leads to the revelation of "old" information which has a significant impact

---

[5] Even without the random supply term u_1, the REE is not (strong form) informationally efficient since a single price cannot reveal two facts, the signal and the signal's quality. The structure is similar to the partially revealing REE analysis in Ausubel (1990). However, if there is no noisy supply, the no-trade theorem applies.

on prices. Note that in contrast to Grundy and McNichols (1989), discussed in Section 4.1.2, the supply shift in period $t = 2$ is common knowledge among all traders. An uncertain supply shift would prevent S^2-investors from learning the type of the other investors with certainty. Romer (1993) uses this insight to explain the October 1987 market meltdown.

In his model the stock market crash in $t = 2$ is a price correction. The revelation of information through P_2 makes investors aware of the early mispricing. Therefore, in contrast to Grossman (1988) but in line with Gennotte and Leland (1990), this model does not predict any rebounding of the price after the stock price.

In Section II of his paper, Romer (1993) develops an alternative model to explain stock market crashes. In this model, informed traders trade at most once. They can trade immediately if they pay a fee. Else, they can save the fee and but then their trade will be executed at a random time or not at all. This model is closer in spirit to the sequential trade models that are covered in the next section.

Modeling crashes within a dynamic REE setup gets complex very quickly. Even the analysis in Romers' (1993) two-period REE setup is restricted to numerical simulations. One needs models which cover a longer time horizon to really understand the dynamics of stock market crashes. The more simplistic sequential trade models provide one possible framework for a dynamic analysis.

6.1.2. Crashes in Sequential Trade Models

Sequential trade models are more tractable and, thus, allow us to focus on the dynamic aspects of crashes. The literature based on sequential trade models also analyzes the role of portfolio insurance trading and stresses the importance of asymmetric information to explain crashes.

The economic insights of the herding literature provide a basis for understanding stock market crashes. An informational cascade or a partial informational cascade can arise in trading models. If the market is in a partial cascade, the actions of predecessors need not lead to a price change for a long time. Eventually, a fragile partial cascade might burst and cause a significant price change. This is in contrast to a full information cascade which never bursts. Using Lee's (1998) terminology, an informational avalanche occurs when a partial cascade bursts.

Sequential trade models à la Glosten and Milgrom (1985) and herding models à la Bikhchandani, Hirshleifer, and Welch (1992) share some common features:

1. Traders can only buy or sell a fixed number of shares. Their action space is, therefore, discrete.
2. Agents also trade one after the other.

This replicates an exogenous sequencing model where the timing of agents' trade is exogenously specified. In descending Dutch auctions, traders can decide when to trade and thus they are closely related in spirit to herding models with endogenous sequencing. The latter class of models is discussed in the next section.

Portfolio Insurance Trading in Sequential Trade Models

As in Gennotte and Leland (1990), Jacklin, Kleidon, and Pfleiderer (1992) attribute the stock market crash in 1987 to imperfect information aggregation caused by an underestimation of the extent of dynamic portfolio insurance trading. The authors reach this conclusion after introducing dynamic program trading strategies in the sequential trade model of Glosten and Milgrom (1985). The market maker sets a competitive bid and ask price at the beginning of each trading round. Given this price schedule, a single trader has the opportunity to buy or sell a fixed number x of shares or to not trade at all. The probability that an informed trader trades in this period is μ. This trader knows the final liquidation value of the stock $v \in \{v_L, v_M, v_H\}$. An informed trader buys (sells) the stock when its value stock v is higher (lower) than the ask (bid) price and does not trade at all if v is between the bid and ask price. An uninformed trader trades in this period with probability $(1 - \mu)$. Uninformed traders are either dynamic hedgers or liquidity traders. The fraction of dynamic hedgers θ is not known and can be either θ_H or θ_L. The strategy of dynamic hedgers is exogeneously modeled in a very stylized manner and exhibits some similarity to herding behavior. Dynamic hedgers either buy or sell shares. They buy shares for two reasons: to start a new dynamic hedging strategy or to continue with an existing strategy. In the latter case, they buy shares if the trading (in)activity in the previous trading round increases their judgment about the value of the stock. In addition, dynamic hedgers sell shares with some probability. They always buy or sell shares and are never inactive in the market. This distinguishes them from informed traders and liquidity traders. Liquidity traders buy or sell x shares with the same probability r or do not trade at all with the remaining probability $1 - 2r$.

The authors illustrate the price path by means of a numerical simulation. One can rule out a stock market crash following a significant price rise as long as the fraction θ is known to the market makers. However, the price might rise sharply if the market maker underestimates the degree of dynamic portfolio trading. The market maker mistakenly interprets buy orders from dynamic hedgers as informed traders with positive information. This leads to a sharp price increase. After many trading rounds, the fact that he observes only few "no trade outcomes" makes him suspicious that the earlier order might have come from dynamic hedgers. He updates his posterior about θ and significantly corrects the price. This leads to a stock market crash. Since the crash is a price correction, one does not expect the price to bounce back.

Jacklin, Kleidon, and Pfleiderer (1992) focus solely on dynamic trading strategies and make no reference to the herding literature. However, rational hedging also generates similar behavior. The articles described next explicitly draw the connection between the herding literature and trading games and, hence, provide deeper insights.

Herding and Crashes in Sequential Trade Models

Avery and Zemsky (1998) illustrate a sequential trade model with an information structure similar to the herding model in Bikhchandani, Hirshleifer, and Welch (1992). A fraction μ of the traders are informed while $(1-\mu)$ are uninformed liquidity traders. Liquidity traders buy, sell, or stay inactive with equal probability. Each informed trader receives a noisy individual signal about the value of the stock $v \in \{0, 1\}$. The signal is correct with probability $q > \frac{1}{2}$. In a sequential trade model, the predecessor's action not only causes a *positive informational externality* as in Bikhchandani, Hirshleifer, and Welch (1992), but also a *negative payoff externality*. The price changes since the market maker also learns from the predecessor's trade. Hence, he adjusts the bid and ask schedule accordingly. This changes the payoff structure for all successors. Avery and Zemsky (1998) show that the price adjusts in such a way that it offsets the incentive to herd. This is the case because the market maker and the insiders learn at the same rate from past trading rounds. Therefore, herding will not occur given pure *value uncertainty*. In general, as long as the signals are monotonic, the herding incentives are offset by the market maker's price adjustment. Consequently, a (full) informational cascade does not arise.

Indeed, informational cascades can be ruled out even for information structures which lead to herding behavior since the authors assume that there is always a minimal amount of "useful" information. Hence, the price converges to the true asset value and the price process exhibits no "excess volatility," regardless of the assumed signal structure, due to the price process' martingale property. This implies that large mispricings followed by a stock market crash occur only with a very low probability.

Avery and Zemsky (1998) also explicitly analyze some nonmonotonic signal structures. As in Easley and O'Hara (1992), they introduce higher-order uncertainty via *event uncertainty*. Insiders receive either a perfect signal that no new information has arrived, that is, the value of stock remains $v = \frac{1}{2}$, or a noisy signal which reports the correct liquidation value $v \in \{0, 1\}$ with probability q. Viewed differently, all insiders receive either a totally useless signal whose precision is $q' = 1/2$ (no information event) or all insiders receive possibly different signals but with the same precision $q' = q \in (1/2, 1]$. The precision, q', is known to the insiders, but not to the market maker. In other words, the market maker does not know whether an information event occurred or not. This asymmetry in higher-order information between insiders and the market maker allows insiders to learn more from the price process (trading sequence) than the market maker. Since the market maker sets the price, the price adjustment is slower. Bikhchandani, Hirshleifer, and Welch (1992) can be viewed as an extreme case where prices are essentially "fixed." Slow price adjustment reduces the payoff externalities which could offset the information externality. Consequently, traders might herd in equilibrium. However, no informational cascade arises since the market maker can gather information about the occurrence of an information event. Surprisingly, herding increases the market maker's awareness of information events and does not distort the asset price. Therefore, herding in a setting with only "event uncertainty" cannot explain large mispricings or stock market crashes.

A more complex information structure is needed to simulate crashes. Avery and Zemsky (1998) consider a setting with two types of informed traders in order to explain large mispricings. One group of traders receives their signals with low precision q_L, whereas the other receives them with high precision $q_H = 1$, that is, they receive a perfect signal. The proportion of insiders with the perfect signal is either high or low and it is not known to the market maker. The authors call this information structure *composition uncertainty*. This information structure makes it difficult for the market maker to differentiate between a market composed of well-informed traders following their perfect signal from one with poorly informed traders who herd. In both situations a whole chain of informed traders follows the same trade. If the prior probability is very low that poorly informed traders are operating in the market, a chain of buy orders make the market maker think that a large fraction of traders is perfectly informed. Thus, he increases the price. If the unlikely event occurs in which only poorly informed traders herd, the asset price may exceed its liquidation value v. The market maker can infer only after many trading rounds that the uninformed traders have herded. In that case, the asset price crashes. Avery and Zemsky (1998) refer to this event as a bubble even though it is not a bubble in the sense described in Section 2.3. Bubbles only occur if traders mutually know that the price is too high yet they still hold or buy the asset. This is the case since they think that they can unwind the position at an even higher price before the liquidation value is paid out. Bubbles in a sequential trading setting à la Glosten and Milgrom (1985) can never occur since this setting does not allow agents to trade a second time. That is, traders cannot unwind their acquired position. All traders have to hold the asset until the liquidation value is paid out.

Gervais (1997) is similar to Avery and Zemsky (1998). However, it shows that uncertain information precision can lead to full informational cascades where the insider's information precision never gets fully revealed. Thus, the bid–ask spread does not reflect the true precision. In Gervais (1997) all agents receive a signal with the same precision, $q_H > q_L, q_L > \frac{1}{2}$, or $q_{no} = \frac{1}{2}$. If the signal precision is $q_{no} = \frac{1}{2}$, the signal is useless, that is, no information event occurs. In contrast to Avery and Zemsky (1998), the signals do not refer to the liquidation value of the asset, v, directly, but only to a certain aspect v_t of v. More formally, the trader who can trade in trading round t receives a noisy signal S_t about the component v_t. There is only one signal for each component v_t, which takes on a value $1/T$ or $-1/T$ with equal probability of $\frac{1}{2}$. The final liquidation value of the asset is then given by $v = \sum_{t=1}^{T} v_t$. As in Glosten and Milgrom (1985), the risk neutral market maker sets competitive quotes. If the bid–ask spread is high, insiders trade only if their signal precision is high. The trade/no-trade sequence allows the market maker to update his beliefs about the quality of the insider's signals. He can also update his beliefs about the true asset value v. Therefore, the competitive spread has to decrease over time. Note that the trading/quote history is more informative for insiders because they already know the precision of the signal. When the competitive bid–ask spread decreases below a certain level, insiders will engage in trading independent of the precision of their signal. This prevents the competitive market maker from learning more about the signals' precision, that is, the economy ends up in a cascade state with respect to the precision of the insider's signals.

In Madrigal and Scheinkman (1997) the market maker does not set a competitive bid–ask spread. Instead, he sets the bid and ask prices which maximize his profit. The price function in this one-period model displays a discontinuity in the order flow. As in Gennotte and Leland (1990), this discontinuity can be viewed as a price crash since an arbitrarily small change in the market variables leads to a large price shock.

Crashes due to Information Avalanches

Lee's (1998) model departs in many respects from the Glosten–Milgrom setting. It is still the case that in each period only a single trader receives a signal about the liquidation value $v \in \{0, 1\}$. However, in Lee (1998) the trader can decide when to trade and he can also trade more than once.[6] In particular, traders have the possibility of unwinding their position in later trading rounds. This model is, therefore, much closer in spirit to herding models with endogenous sequencing. The trades are also not restricted to a certain number of shares. However, when agents want to trade they have to pay a one-time fixed transaction fee c to open an account with a broker. There are no liquidity traders or dynamic hedgers in this model; there are only risk averse informed traders. Traders are assumed to be price takers. Prior to each trading round the market maker sets a *single* price at which all orders in this trading round will be executed. This is in contrast to the earlier models where the market maker sets a whole price schedule, or at least a bid and an ask price. The market maker's single price $p_t = E[v|\{x_t^i\}_{i \in \mathbb{I}}]$ is based on all observed individual orders in all the *previous* trading rounds. The market maker loses money on average since he cannot charge a bid-ask spread even though informed traders are better informed than he is. This "odd" assumption simplifies matters and is necessary to induce informed traders to trade. Otherwise the no-trade (speculation) theorem of Milgrom and Stokey (1982) would apply in a setting without liquidity traders.

Each informed trader receives one of N possible signals $S_n \in \{S_1, \ldots, S_N\} =: S$ which differ in their precision. The signals satisfy the monotone likelihood property and are ranked accordingly. The market maker can observe each individual order and since there are no liquidity traders he can fully infer the information of the informed trader. However, by assumption the market maker can only adjust the price for the next trading round. The price in the next trading period then fully reflects the informed trader's signal and, thus, the informed trader has no informational advantage after his trade is completed. Due to the market maker's risk neutrality, no risk premium is paid and, hence, the

---

[6] The notation departs from that in the original article: $v = Y$, $x_t^i = z_t^i$, $S_n = \theta_n$, $S = \Theta$.

risk averse insider is unwilling to hold his risky position. He will unwind his entire position immediately in the next trading round. This trading strategy of 'acquiring and unwinding in the next round' would guarantee informed traders a certain capital gain. Consequently, it would be optimal for the informed traders to trade an infinite number of stocks in the first place. In order to avoid this, Lee (1998) assumes that in each period the liquidation value v might become common knowledge with a certain probability γ. This makes the capital gains random and, thus, restrains the trading activity of the risk averse informed traders. In short, the model setup is such that the informed agents trade at most twice. After they buy the asset they unwind their position immediately in the next period. Therefore, the trader's decision is de facto to wait or to trade now and unwind the position in the next trading round. This makes the "endogenous reduced action space" of the trading game *discrete*.

As trading goes on and the price converges (maybe wrongly) to the value $v = 0$ or $v = 1$, the price impact of an individual signal and thus the capital gains for informed traders become smaller and smaller. It is possible that the expected capital gains are so small that it is not worthwhile for the informed trader to pay the transaction costs c. This is especially the case for traders with less precise signals. Consequently, all traders with less precise signals $S_n \in \hat{S} \subset S$ will opt for a "wait and see strategy." That is, all traders with signals $S_n \in \hat{S}$ herd by not trading. In Lee's words, the economy is in a *partial informational cascade*. When agents do not trade based on their information, this information is not revealed and, hence, the market accumulates a lot of hidden information which is not reflected in the current stock price. An extreme signal can shatter this partial informational cascade, as shown in Gale (1996) in Section 5.2.2. A trader with an extreme signal might trade when his signal strongly indicates that the price has converged to the wrong state. This single investor's trade not only induces some successors to trade but might also enlighten traders who received their signal earlier and did not trade so far. It might now be worthwhile for them to pay the transaction costs c and to trade based on their information. These traders are now eager to trade immediately in the same trading round as long as the market maker has committed himself to the same price. Consequently, there will be an avalanche of orders and all the hidden information will be revealed. In other words, an *informational avalanche* in the form of a stock market crash occurs. The subsequent price after the stock market crash is likely to be closer to the true liquidation value. The analysis in Lee (1998) also shows that the whole price process will eventually end up in a total informational cascade, that is, where no signal can break up the cascade.

Information avalanches in Lee (1998) hinge on the assumption that the market maker cannot adjust his quoted price within a trading round even when there are many individual orders coming in. Since the market maker is forced to execute a large order flow at a price that is much too high, he is the biggest loser in the event that a crash occurs. It would be interesting to determine the extent to which this assumption can be relaxed without eliminating the occurrence of informational avalanches. As in almost all models discussed so far, there is no reason why a crash has to be a price decline. It can also be a sharp price increase. This is a general criticism of almost all models given the empirical observations that one mostly observes sharp price declines.

In contrast to the standard sequential trade models, Lee's (1998) analysis has the nice feature that traders can choose endogenously when to trade and what amount to trade. In the standard auction theory covered in the next sections, bidders can also choose the timing of their bid. However, their quantity is fixed to a unit demand.

6.1.3. Crashes and Frenzies in Auctions and War of Attrition Games

While in the standard sequential trade models à la Glosten and Milgrom (1985) the order of trades is exogenous, auctions with ascending or descending bidding allow bidders to decide when to bid or stop bidding. Thus, these models correspond more to endogenous sequencing herding models. In contrast to pure informational herding models but like sequential trade models, the bidders' decisions cause both an information externality as well as a payoff externality. The information externality might even relate to the payoff externality. This is the case when the predecessor holds private information and his action affects the payoff structure of the successors. For example, when a bidder quits in a standard ascending auction (Japanese version), he reveals to the remaining bidders that there is one less competitor. This is a positive payoff externality for the remaining bidders. In addition, he reveals a signal about the common value of the good.

This section only covers the small part of the auction literature that focuses on crashes.[7] Due to its central role in this literature, let us first

---

[7] The auction literature was initiated by Vickrey (1961). There are several excellent overview articles that describe this literature. We refer the interested reader to Klemperer (1999, 2000), Matthews (1995), McAfee and McMillan (1987), and Milgrom (1989).

discuss the revenue equivalence theorem developed by Myerson (1981) and Riley and Samuelson (1981).

The Revenue Equivalence Theorem

The revenue equivalence theorem (RET) is the most important theorem in auction theory. It states that under certain conditions any auction mechanism that (1) assigns the good to the bidder with the highest signal and (2) grants the bidder with the lowest feasible signal a zero surplus, leads to the same expected revenue to the seller. This equivalence holds for a fixed number of risk neutral bidders and if the signals are independently drawn from a common, strictly increasing, atomless distribution, for example on $[\underline{V}, \bar{V}]$ It applies to a pure private value auction. It also extends to a pure common value auction provided the individual signals S^i are independent and the common value is a function of them, that is, $v = f(S^1, \dots, S^I)$.

Let us outline the intuitive reasoning for this result. Without loss of generality, we choose signals $S^i = v^i$ such that they coincide with the unconditional value of the asset for bidder i. Suppose the expected payoff for a bidder with private signal v^i is $U^i(v^i)$. If the v^i-bidder tries to mimic a bidder with a signal $v^i + \Delta v$, his payoff would be the payoff of a $(v^i + \Delta v)$-bidder with the difference that, in the case that he wins the object, he values it Δv less than the $(v^i + \Delta v)$-bidder. He would receive the object with probability $P(v^i + \Delta)$ if he mimics the $(v^i + \Delta v)$-bidder. In any mechanism the bidder should have no incentive to mimic somebody else, that is, $U(v^i) \geq U(v^i + \Delta v) - \Delta v \Pr(v^i + \Delta v)$. Similarly, the $(v^i + \Delta v)$-bidder should not want to mimic the v^i-bidder, that is, $U(v^i + \Delta v) \geq U(v^i) + \Delta v \Pr(v^i)$. Combining both inequalities leads to

$$Pr(v^i) \leq \frac{U^i(v^i + \Delta v) - U^i(v^i)}{\Delta v} \leq \Pr(v^i + \Delta v).$$

For very small deviations $\Delta v \to 0$, this reduces to

$$\frac{dU^i}{dv} = \Pr(v^i).$$

Integrating this expression leads to the following expected payoff function.

$$U^i(v^i) = U^i(\underline{V}) + \int_{x=\underline{V}}^{v^i} \Pr(x) \, dx.$$

This payoff function determines the expected payoff for any v^i-type bidder. The no mimic conditions are satisfied as long as the bidder's payoff function is convex, that is, the probability of winning the object increases in v^i.

The risk neutral bidder's expected payoff $U(v^i)$ is given by his expected value of the object $E[v|v^i] = v^i$ times the probability of receiving the object, minus his expected transfer payment, T, in short, by $v^i \mathrm{Pr}^i(v^i) - T$. Two different auction mechanisms lead to the same payoff for a v^i-bidder if the bidder with the lowest signals receives the same payoff $U^i(\underline{V})$ in both auction mechanisms. If in addition the probability of winning is the same, then the expected transfer payoff for any type of bidder is the same in both auctions and so is the expected revenue for the seller.

The revenue equivalence theorem is extremely useful and powerful. Instead of analyzing the more complicated actual auction mechanism, one can restrict the analysis to simpler mechanisms by appealing to the revenue equivalence theorem.

Frenzies and Crashes

Bulow and Klemperer's (1994) auction article emphasizes frenzies and crashes within a multi-unit Dutch auction. As in the real option litera-ture, a potential buyer has to decide whether to buy now or later, rather than now or never.[8] Bulow and Klemperer (1994) consider a private value setting, wherein each of $K + L$ potential buyers' *private* value for one good v^i is independently drawn from a distribution $F(v^i)$ which is strictly increasing and atomless on $[\underline{V}, \bar{V}]$. A seller offers K identical units of a good for sale to $K + L$ potential buyers. The seller can com-mit himself to a specific selling procedure. Hence, the seller receives the whole social surplus except the information rent, which goes to the bid-ders. Crashes and frenzies arise in any selling mechanism and are derived using the revenue equivalence theorem.

For concreteness, Bulow and Klemperer (1994) illustrate crashes and frenzies in a multi-unit Dutch auction. The seller starts at a high price and lowers it continuously until a purchase occurs. Then, the seller asks the remaining bidders whether somebody has changed his mind and would like to buy at this price too. If this is the case, he sells the goods to them and if some additional goods remain he asks the remaining bidders again

---

[8] The trade-off in the real option literature is that by delaying the purchase, the investor incurs waiting costs but gains the opportunity to learn something about the common value of the product.

whether their willingness to pay has changed. The authors define multiple sales at a single price as a *frenzy*. If nobody changes his mind, that is, if nobody else is willing to buy at this price, the seller continues to lower the price. If too many bidders have changed their mind and want to buy at this price, he runs a new Dutch auction among these bidders with the remaining goods. This might lead to higher prices. Therefore, the bidder is faced with a trade-off. On the one hand, if he waits, the price may be lower, but on the other hand waiting also increases the likelihood of a frenzy which could lead to a higher price or to the possibility that he walks home empty handed. In general, somebody else's purchase generates a negative externality for the remaining bidders since the number of remaining goods diminishes and with it the probability of receiving a good at this price decreases. Nevertheless, the option to wait changes the buyers "willingness to pay" in comparison to a setting where the seller commits to a single take-it-or-leave-it price.

Since the revenue equivalence theorem applies in this multi-unit setting, each bidder's expected payment must be the same for any auction design. In particular, the willingness to pay $\omega(v^i)$ for a bidder with private value v^i equals the expected price a bidder would pay in a standard multi-unit English auction. For k remaining goods and $k + l$ remaining bidders, each bidders "willingness to pay" is equal to his expectation of the $(k + 1)$st highest value out of the $k + l$ remaining values, provided this value is lower than his own valuation v. For bidders with high v^i, the willingness to pay is almost the same. To illustrate this, consider the bidder with the highest possible value, $\bar{v}$. He knows for sure that his valuation is the highest. Therefore, his estimate of the $(k + 1)$ highest valuation is the k highest of the other $(k + l - 1)$ bidders. This estimate decreases only slightly for bidders with lower v^i's as long as they are pretty sure that they are among the k bidders with the highest values. In other words, the WTP $\omega(v)$ is very flat, especially for high private values, v, compared to the standard demand curve – which represents the buyers' willingness to accept a take-it-or-leave-it final offer. Figure 6.2, which is taken from Bulow and Klemperer (1994), illustrates this point for a uniform distribution.

The WTP for the remaining bidders changes when one of the other bidders buys one of the goods. A purchase reduces the number of remaining goods available for the rest of the bidders. This increases the price each remaining bidder expects to pay (negative payoff externality) and thus shifts all other bidders' WTP functions upwards. Therefore, when the seller offers more sales at the same selling price, bidders with close enough v values might change their mind and come forward to buy at

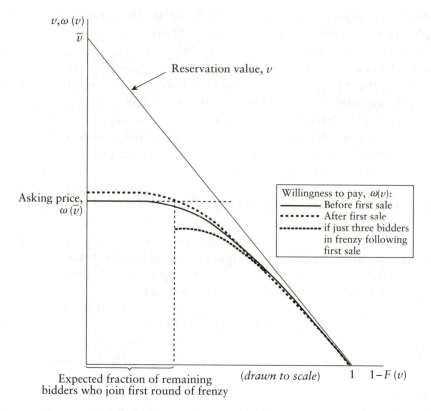

Figure 6.2. *Frenzy in an auction*

the same price. Since the WTP function $\omega(1 - F(v^i))$ is very flat, it is very likely that many bidders will come forward in the second round of sale at the same price. That is a frenzy might emerge. More specifically one of the following three scenarios can occur. (1) More bidders than expected change their mind but the demand can be satisfied. In this case the *frenzy* feeds itself since the bidders who did not buy in the second round might change their mind after observing that so many bidders have decided to buy in the second round. The seller offers the good at the same price in a third round and so on. (2) Too many bidders come forward and the seller cannot satisfy the demand. The seller then initiates a new descending multi-unit Dutch auction among these bidders by starting at the original starting price. (3) Although all WTPs increased no bidder or less than the expected number of bidders are willing to participate in the second round. In this case a "crash" occurs where it becomes common knowledge among all bidders that no purchase will occur until the price has fallen to a strictly lower level. The seller goes on lowering the price and one observes a discrete price jump. It needs to be stressed that these effects will be even stronger in a common value environment. With common values, the purchase is an additional signal for the remaining bidders that the value of the good is high. Thus, the remaining bidders' WTP increases even further.

War of Attrition Game

A *war of attrition (chicken) game* is like a sealed bid *all pay auction*. In an all pay auction, each bidder pays his own bid independently of whether he wins the object or not. In a war of attrition game the player who suffers the longest, that is, pays the most, wins the prize. Each player's strategy is like a bidding strategy, which specifies the point at which to stop suffering. The only difference between a war of attrition game and an all pay auction is that in the war of attrition game the player's payment does not go to the seller of an object, but is socially wasted. In a setting with independent private values of the object, the expected surplus of each player is the same in both games as it is in any auction, as long as the assumptions for the RET apply. This allows us to switch to the mechanism of the second price auction which is much easier to analyze.

Bulow and Klemperer (1999) use the RET to analyze a generalized war of attrition game. In Bulow and Klemperer (1999) each of $K + L$ player can win one of K objects. The player pays one unit per period as long as he stays in the race. After quitting, his costs reduce to $c \leq 1$ (possibly to zero) until L players ("losers") quit, that is, the game ends. If the players pay no costs after dropping out, that is, $c = 0$, $L - 1$ players quit immediately and the remaining $K + 1$ players play a standard multi-unit war of attrition game analyzed in Fudenberg and Tirole (1986). This result is derived by means of the RET. The expected total suffering can be calculated using a simpler standard $K + 1$ price auction because of the RET. We know from the $K + 1$ price auction that the expected total payment, or suffering in this case, of all $K + L$ players coincides with expected $K + 1$ highest evaluation. After $L - 1$ lowest types drop out, the expected total amount of suffering of the remaining $K + 1$ players is still the same. This can only be the case if the $L - 1$ lowest types drop out immediately. Bulow and Klemperer (1999) also analyze the case where each player has to suffer until the game ends, independently of whether he drops out early or not, that is, $c = 1$. In this case the drop out strategy is independent of the number of players and of other players' drop out behavior. The optimal drop out strategies for intermediate cases of $0 < c < 1$ are also characterized by Bulow and Klemperer (1999).

6.2. Keynes' Beauty Contest, Investigative Herding, and Limits of Arbitrage

In reality, traders do not receive all information for free. They have to decide whether and which information to gather prior to trading. This affects their trading behavior as well as the stock price movements. Models in this section illustrate that traders have an incentive to gather the same information and ignore long-run information.

In his famous book *The General Theory of Employment, Interest and Money*, Keynes (1936) compared the stock market with a *beauty contest*. Participating judges – rather than focusing on the relative beauty of the contestants – try to second-guess the opinion of other judges. It seems that they would rather choose the winner than the most beautiful girl. Similarly in stock markets, investors' search effort is not focused on fundamentals but on finding out the information that other traders will trade on in the near future. Their intention is to trade on information right before somebody else trades on the same information. In Keynes' words, "skilled investment today is to '*beat the gun*' ... ." This section argues that this is a rational thing to do, in particular if the investor – for whatever reason – intends to unwind the acquired position early.

In a setting where traders have to decide which information to collect, the value of a piece of information for the trader might depend on the other traders' actions. New information allows traders to update their estimate about the value of assets. Hence, in their view assets might become mispriced. Yet, private information only provides investors with a profitable trading opportunity if (1) they can acquire a position without immediately revealing their private information, *and* (2) they are able to unload their acquired position at a price which reflects their private information. In other words, as long as they acquire the position, the asset has to remain mispriced. However, when investors liquidate the required position, the price has to incorporate their information. Traders cannot exploit their knowledge if they are forced to liquidate before the asset is priced correctly. The mispricing might become even worse in the medium term. In this case, forced early liquidation leads to trading losses.

An asset is mispriced if its price does not coincide with the equilibrium price (*absolute* asset pricing). The exploitation of a mispriced asset is often referred to as *arbitrage*. Arbitrage – in the strict theoretical sense – refers only to mispricing *relative* to other assets. It involves no risk since one buys and sells assets such that future payoff streams exactly offset each other and a positive current payoff remains. In an incomplete market setting, there are often insufficient traded securities that exactly offset future payoff streams of an asset. The asset is, thus, not redundant. Therefore, mispricing of (nonredundant) assets need not lead to arbitrage opportunities in the strict sense. Practitioners often call all trading strategies which exploit mispricing "risky arbitrage trading." In contrast to riskless arbitrage trading, these trading strategies exploit mispricing even though the future payoff streams cannot be offset. Some models in this section adopt this broader definition of arbitrage, thereby essentially covering any information based trading.

Whether or not an asset's mispricing is corrected before the trader has to liquidate his position depends on whether the same information spreads to other traders. This new information is only fully reflected in the asset price when other market participants also base their trading activity on it. Brennan (1990) noted the strong interdependence of individual information acquisition decisions. In a market with many investors the value of information about a certain (latent) asset may be very small if this asset pays a low dividend and no other investor acquires the same information. If, on the other hand, many investors collect this information, the share price adjusts and rewards those traders who gathered this information first. Coordinating information collection activities can, therefore, be mutually beneficial.

There are various reasons why investors unwind their position early before the final liquidation value of the stock is known. The following sections discuss three different reasons why investors might want to unwind their position early. Traders try to unwind their position early because of:

(1) short-livedness;
(2) risk aversion in an incomplete market setting;
(3) portfolio delegation in a principal–agent setting.

If the traders liquidate their position early then they care more about future price developments than about the true fundamental value of the stock. Consequently, traders *prefer short-run information* to long-run information. They might even ignore long-run information. The future development of the asset price also depends on the information other traders gather. This explains why traders have an incentive to gather the same information, that is, why they herd in information acquisition. *Investigative herding* is the focus of Froot, Scharfstein, and Stein (1992).

6.2.1. *Unwinding due to Short Horizons*

Short-Livedness and Myopia

Short-lived agents convert their stocks and other savings into consumption latest in their last period of life. Agents with *short horizons* may live longer but they think only a few periods ahead. Their current behavior is often similar to that of short-lived individuals. In addition, myopic people's behavior is *dynamically inconsistent*. In the current period, myopic investors ignore some future payoffs. However, they will value them in some future period. The marginal rate of *temporal* substitution between consumption in two periods changes dramatically over time. Myopia is, therefore, an extreme form of hyperbolic discounting and has to be attributed to boundedly rational behavior. Myopia alters an agent's trading strategy since they do not take into account how their current trading affects their future optimal trading. However, the backwards induction argument still applies, which rules out major alterations of the price process in a setting with exogenous information acquisition. Nevertheless, there might exist additional equilibria if risk averse agents are short-lived or myopic. In these equilibria asset prices are very volatile and traders demand a higher risk premium since short-lived agents care only about the next period's price and dividend. Spiegel (1998) illustrates this in an overlapping generations (OLG) model. Similarly in DeLong, Shleifer, Summers and Waldmann (1990) short-livedness combined with risk aversion prevents arbitrageurs from driving prices back to their riskless fundamental value. The risk averse arbitrageurs care only about next period's price which is risky due to the random demand of noise traders.

Introducing Endogenous Information Acquisition

In models with endogenous information acquisition, short-livedness can also have a large impact on the price process. Brennan (1990) noticed the interdependence of agents' information acquisition decisions for low dividend paying (latent) assets. He formalizes this argument with an overlapping generations (OLG) model where agents only live for three periods. A short life span might force traders to liquidate their position before the information is reflected in the price. This is the case if the other traders did not gather the same information.

In Froot, Scharfstein, and Stein (1992) traders are also forced to unwind their acquired position in period $t = 3$ even though their information might be only reflected in the price in $t = 4$. Consequently, all traders worry only about the short-run price development since they have to unwind their position early. They can only profit from their information if it is subsequently reflected in the price. Since this is only the case if enough traders observe the same information, each trader's optimal information acquisition depends on the others' information acquisition. The resulting positive information spillover explains why traders care more about the information of others than about the fundamentals. Froot, Scharfstein, and Stein's (1992) analysis focuses on investigative herding. Herding in information acquisition would not occur in the stock market if agents only cared about the final liquidation value. In that case, information spillovers would be negative and thus, it would be better to have information that others do not have. Consequently, investors would try to collect information related to different events.

In Froot, Scharfstein, and Stein (1992) each individual can only collect one piece of information. Each trader has to decide whether to receive a signal about event A or event B. The trading game in Froot, Scharfstein, and Stein (1992) is based on Kyle (1985). The asset's liquidation value is given by the sum of two components, δ^A and δ^B,

$$v = \delta^A + \delta^B,$$

where $\delta^A \sim \mathcal{N}(0, \sigma_{\delta^A}^2)$ refers to event A and $\delta^B \sim \mathcal{N}(0, \sigma_{\delta^B}^2)$ refers to the independent event B. Each trader can decide whether to observe either δ^A or δ^B, but not both. After observing δ^A or δ^B a trader submits a market order to the market maker at $t = 1$. Half of the submitted market orders are executed at $t = 1$ and the second half at $t = 2$. The period in which an order is processed is random. Liquidity traders submit market orders of aggregate random size u_1 in each period $t = 1$ and u_2 in $t = 2$. As in Kyle (1985) the risk neutral market maker sets a competitive price in each period based on the observed total net order flow. Thus, the price only partially reveals the information collected by the informed traders. Traders acquire their position either in $t = 1$ at a price P_1 or in $t = 2$ at a price P_2, depending on when their order, which was submitted in $t = 1$, will be executed. At $t = 3$ all traders, that is, insiders and liquidity traders, unwind their position and by assumption the risk neutral market maker takes on all risky positions.

The fundamental value $v = \delta^A + \delta^B$ is publicly announced either in period $t = 3$ before the insiders have to unwind their position or in period $t = 4$ after they unwind their portfolio. With probability α, v is known in $t = 3$ and with probability $(1 - \alpha)$ it is known in $t = 4$. If the fundamentals are known to everybody in $t = 3$, the acquired positions are unloaded at a price $P_3 = \delta^A + \delta^B$. If the public announcement occurs only in $t = 4$, the price does not change in period $t = 3$, that is, $P_3 = P_2$ and the traders unwind their position at the price P_2. In this case the expected profit per share for an insider is $\frac{1}{2}(P_2 - P_1)$. The $\frac{1}{2}$ results from the fact that the insider's order is only processed early with a probability $\frac{1}{2}$. Only then does the insider receive the shares at a price of P_1, which he can later sell in $t = 3$ for $P_3 = P_2$. The trader makes no profit if his order is executed late and the fundamentals are only announced in $t = 4$. With probability α, the fundamentals δ^A and δ^B are already announced at $t = 3$, that is, $P_3 = v$. In this case a trader who submitted an order at $t = 1$ and buys a share for P_1 or P_2 with equal probability, sells it at $t = 3$ for $P_3 = v$. His expected profit in this case is given by $v - \frac{1}{2}[P_1 + P_2]$. Thus, the overall expected profit per share for an informed trader is

$$E\left\{\alpha\left[v - \frac{P_1 + P_2}{2}\right] + (1 - \alpha)\left[\frac{P_2 - P_1}{2}\right]\right\}.$$

In both cases the profit is determined by P_3, the price at which the informed trader unwinds his position; $P_3 = v$ with probability α. Thus, δ^A and δ^B are equally important, with probability α. With probability $(1 - \alpha)$, $P_3 = P_2$. Since P_2 depends on the information set of all informed traders, each insider cares about the information that the other traders are collecting.

For illustrative reasons let us consider the polar case $\alpha = 0$, that is δ^A and δ^B are only publicly announced in $t = 4$. If all other investors collect information δ^A, then information δ^B is worthless in this case since δ^B will only enter into the price in $t = 4$. In period $t = 4$ investors will have already unwound their positions. Consequently, all investors will herd to gather information δ^A and nobody will collect information δ^B.[9] Thus, the short horizons of traders creates positive informational spillovers which lead to herding in information acquisition.

In an even more extreme scenario, if all investors herd on some noise term ζ, which is totally unrelated to the fundamental value $v = \delta^A + \delta^B$, a rational investor is (weakly) better off if he also collects information ζ rather than information about fundamentals alone. If $\alpha = 0$ and all other investors are searching for ζ, the fundamentals δ^A and δ^B are only reflected in P_4. The price at which the traders have to close their position, $P_3 (= P_2)$ might depend on the "sunspot" ζ, given their strategies.

---

[9] In a (Nash) equilibrium the information that other traders are collecting is mutual knowledge.

For the more general case of $\alpha > 0$, where δ^A and δ^B might already be announced in $t = 3$, herding in information might still occur. This is still the case if α is sufficiently small. In contrast if $\alpha = 1$, each trader prefers to collect information about events that are not the main focus of the other traders' information gathering effort. In short, individuals' search efforts are "strategic substitutes" if $\alpha = 1$, and "strategic complements" if $\alpha = 0$.

The above reasoning can also be analyzed in a multiperiod overlapping generations (OLG) framework. A new generation of short-sighted traders enters the market in each period. Inefficient herding still occurs in the following OLG setting. Generation t speculators can study one of k pieces of information. At the end of period t, one of these pieces will be randomly drawn and publicly announced. In the following period $t + 1$, a new piece of information can be studied. Thus, each trader in each generation can study one of k pieces of information. For each generation it pays off to have accidentally studied the information that gets publicly announced at the end of the period. Since this only occurs with a probability $1/k$ it is more worthwhile to collect information which is also studied by other traders and thus is reflected in the price for sure. In short, herding in information acquisition may also occur in this OLG setup.

Arbitrage Chains

Dow and Gorton's (1994) "arbitrage chains" model stresses that the value of exploiting a certain piece of information depends on the likelihood that another insider will receive the same information in the next trading round and drive the price closer to its fundamental. Only then can the insider, who lives for two periods, unwind his position at a profit. If there is no agent who trades on the same information in the next trading round then the trader would have been better off by investing in a bond since he would have saved transaction costs, c. In contrast to Froot, Scharfstein, and Stein (1992), Dow and Gorton (1994) consider an infinite horizon economy $t = -\infty, \ldots, \infty$ with overlapping generations (OLG). Each agent lives only for two periods. All young people receive a fixed endowment W. Consumption takes place only in the agents' second period of life and thus agents try to save. Agents can save by buying a bond with riskless return of r or a stock which pays a dividend of either 1 or 0 in each period. The dividend payments are serially uncorrelated and a dividend of 1 is paid with (prior) probability π. Another differentiating feature of Dow and Gorton's model from Froot, Scharfstein, and Stein (1992) is that the information acquisition process

is assumed to be exogenous. The insider cannot decide *which* information to gather. A young trader receives a perfect signal about the dividend
payments in t^{div} with a certain probability $\gamma_t = \gamma_{t+1}\epsilon = \epsilon^{(t^{\text{div}}-t)}$.[10] This
probability converges smoothly to 1 as t approaches t^{div}. In addition to
the young informed trader, uninformed hedgers might also be present
in certain periods. They are active in the market place with probability
$\frac{1}{2}$. These traders have a strong incentive to trade for hedging reasons as
their wage of 0 or 1 in the next period is perfectly negatively correlated
with the dividend payments. In short, each generation consists either of
a single informed arbitrageur and/or uninformed hedgers or nobody.

The price setting is similar to Kyle (1985). A single competitive market maker sets the price after observing the order flow. In contrast to
Kyle (1985), he also observes each individual order. He can deduce the
orders from the old generations since they unwind their earlier trades.
This unwinding keeps the market maker's inventory from growing ever
larger. Although the market maker can observe each individual order
he does not know whether the orders from the young generation is due
to hedging needs or informed trading. Young uninformed hedgers try to
hedge their wage income risk by buying x_t stocks. The informed trader
might also buy x_t stocks. Given the market maker's beliefs, the informed
trader can only hide behind hedgers if he submits a buy order of the same
size x_t. Any other order size would reveal to the market maker that he
trades for informational reasons. An informed young trader will only
buy the stock if he receives a positive signal about the dividend payment
in the near future t^{div}. If the dividend payment in t^{div} is more than K
periods away, he will ignore his signal. The market maker knows that
the insider might get a signal about the dividend payment (in t^{div}). Prior
to $t^{\text{div}} - K$, the market maker always sets the price p_t equal to π/r since
nobody is trading for informational reasons. The stock price is equal to
the average dividend payment π in perpetuity, discounted at the rate r.
However, an insider might be trading in periods closer to t^{div} and thus
the market maker adjusts the price according to the observed order flow
from the young generation. If the order flow is $2x$, the market maker
knows for sure that an informed trader submitted a buy order and thus
the dividend payments in t^{div} will be 1. Therefore, he adjusts the price
to $p_t = \pi/r + (1 + r)^{-(t^{\text{div}}-t)}(1 - \pi)$. If nobody submitted an order, the
insider might have received bad news or no news. Therefore, the market
maker will lower the stock price. If he observes a single buy order x

---

[10] For consistency with the rest of the chapter, we replace the original notation δ_t
with γ_t and T with t^{div}.

then he does not know whether an informed trader or a hedger submitted it. The aggregate order flow of x might stem from the insider if he received a good signal and no hedger was active in the market place, or it might stem from the hedgers. In the latter case, the arbitrageur has received either no signal or a bad signal. Dow and Gorton's (1994) model specification is such that the market maker's belief β about the dividend payment in t^{div} is not affected in this case. The market maker adjusts the price only slightly to reflect the fact that the expected dividend payment in t^{div} of β is now one period closer and thus requires less discounting.

Given this pricing rule, the insider's profit is highest in the case where only he transacts with the market maker when he buys the stock and one period later when he sells his stock; the new generation's order flow is $2x$, as this fully reveals the private information to the market maker. Dow and Gorton (1994) show that the optimal trading strategy for an insider is to ignore any long-run information that refers to dividend payments which are more than K periods in the future. This is the result of two effects: (1) As long as t^{div} is in the distant future, it is very unlikely that the information will be reflected in the next period's price. Therefore, it is not worthwhile to pay the (round trip) transaction costs c. (2) The second effect is due to discounting. If the information refers to a positive dividend payment ($= 1$) in the distant future, its present value and thus the present capital gains will be smaller. Given that transaction costs c have to be paid immediately, short-run information is more valuable. Both effects together make it optimal for an insider to ignore any information concerning dividend payments not within a K periods' reach. In other words, an insider only trades on short-run information. A whole chain of insiders might emerge who trade on their information in this window of K periods prior to t^{div}.

In OLG models, bubbles are possible if long-run information is ignored. Consider a situation where all traders in one generation – except the market maker – know that the asset is mispriced. They might not trade on this information if the probability is low that the next generation's young traders will have the same information and also not trade on it.

Dow and Gorton (1994) depart from the standard models in two ways. (1) They introduce trading costs c and (2) they assume exogenously short livedness/horizons. But even when all traders have long horizons, transaction costs alone make very long-run information worthless. This is due to the discounting effect described above. Transaction costs cause a short-term bias in the kind of information that is incorporated in asset prices. Traders' short horizons multiply this bias. To see this, even when there is an informed insider in each trading round, that is, $\gamma = 1$, the profits of short-sighted agents are only half that of the long-horizon decision maker. The reason is that, with probability $\frac{1}{2}$, no hedger will arrive in the next period. In this case, the market maker cannot infer the insider's information even in the next period and, thus, the "unwinding" price will not fully reflect the insider's information. As the probability that an insider trades in the next trading round γ decreases, so do the expected capital gains for myopic traders. The smaller the probability γ, the higher the potential capital gain has to be in order to make up for the transaction costs c.

Dow and Gorton's OLG model can be easily extended to a setting with endogenous information acquisition. Obviously, traders will be unwilling to purchase long-run information. Herding in information acquisition might occur if traders have to choose between different short-run information referring to the same dividend payment at t^{div}, for example, between an imprecise signal $S_{t,T}^A$ and an imprecise signal $S_{t,T}^B$. On the other hand, traders with long horizons would not herd. Agents are, however, endogenously myopic if they have to pay a "cost of carry" in each period instead of the one-time transaction cost c.

6.2.2. Unwinding due to Risk Aversion in Incomplete Markets Settings

The short livedness assumed in Froot, Scharfstein, and Stein (1992) induce the traders to unwind their position early. In Hirshleifer, Subrahmanyam, and Titman (1994) and Holden and Subrahmanyam (1996) informed traders have long horizons but they want to unwind their position for risk-sharing purposes after their information is revealed. This implicitly makes them partly myopic, that is, they care about both the intermediate price and the fundamental value.

Hirshleifer, Subrahmanyam, and Titman (1994) show that herding in information acquisition occurs under certain parameter values in their competitive REE model. After they have decided which information to collect, a continuum of competitive risk averse traders receive their signal accidentally early or late. Before focusing on the information acquisition decision, Hirshleifer, Subrahmanyam, and Titman (1994) derive interesting results pertaining to the investors' trading pattern. For the time being, let us consider the case where all risk averse investors search for the *same* information δ about the liquidation value v of a single risky asset. Let

$$v = \bar{v} + \delta + \epsilon,$$

where $\bar{v}$ is known and $\delta \sim \mathcal{N}(0, \sigma_\delta^2)$ and $\epsilon \sim \mathcal{N}(0, \sigma_\epsilon^2)$ are independently distributed. Some investors, whose mass is M, receive information δ accidentally early, that is, already in $t = 1$, whereas the others, whose mass is $(N - M)$ are informed later. Both groups of traders receive the same information δ, but at different times. All traders maximize CARA utility functions of the final wealth W_3, that is, $U = -\exp(-\rho W_3)$. The demand for the risky asset by the early-informed is denoted by $x_t^e(\delta, \cdot)$, whereas that by the late-informed is $x_t^l(\cdot, \cdot)$. The aggregate demand of liquidity traders is modeled by the random variables $u_1 \sim \mathcal{N}(0, \sigma_{u_1}^2)$ in $t = 1$ and $\Delta u_2 \sim \mathcal{N}(0, \sigma_{\Delta u_2}^2)$ in $t = 2$.[11] Finally, there is also a group of risk neutral competitive market makers (such as scalpers and floor brokers) who observe the limit order book, that is, the noisy aggregate demand schedules, but not the information δ. The noisy aggregate demand function is $X_1(\cdot) = M x_1^e(\delta, \cdot) + (N - M) x_1^l(\cdot) + u_1$ in $t = 1$ and $X_2(\cdot) = M x_2^e(\delta, \cdot) + (N - M) x_2^l(\delta, \cdot) + u_1 + \Delta u_2$ in $t = 2$. Given risk neutrality and competitiveness of the market makers, the market makers set a semi-strong efficient price with respect to their information sets, that is, $P_1 = E[v \mid X_1(\cdot)]$ and $P_2 = E[v \mid X_1(\cdot), X_2(\cdot)]$.

In equilibrium, investors conjecture the following linear price relations:

$$P_2 = \bar{v} + a\delta + bu_1 + c\Delta u_2$$
$$P_1 = \bar{v} + e\delta + fu_1.$$

The equilibrium is derived by backward induction. At $t = 2$ both groups of investors, early and late informed, know δ and, therefore, their stock holding is as usual

$$x_2^e(\delta, P_2) = x_2^l(\delta, P_2) = \frac{\bar{v} + \delta - P_2}{\rho \sigma_\epsilon^2}.$$

---

[11] All demand functions are expressed in stock holdings, therefore the additional demand in $t = 2$ is given by $\Delta u_2 := u_2 - u_1$.

At $t = 1$ only the group of early-informed investors knows δ. Their stock holding is

$$x_1^e(\delta, P_1) = \frac{E[P_2|\mathcal{F}_1^e] - P_1}{\rho}\left[\frac{1}{\mathrm{Var}[P_2|\mathcal{F}_1^e]} + \frac{1}{\sigma_\epsilon^2}\right]$$
$$+ \frac{\bar{v} + \delta - E[P_2|\mathcal{F}_1^e]}{\rho\sigma_\epsilon^2}.$$

The demand of early-informed traders consists of two components. The first term captures the speculative demand due to an expected price change. The second term is the expected final stock holding which the early-informed traders try to acquire at the "on average" better price P_1. Investors who receive their signal only at $t = 2$ demand nothing at $t = 1$, that is, $x_1^l = 0$. This is due to the fact that they do not have superior information as compared to the market makers in $t = 1$. Since the market makers are risk neutral (1) no risk premium is offered and (2) the expected P_2 is unbiased. In other words, risk averse late-informed traders cannot hedge their period 2 demands already at $t = 1$.

There are five equilibrium configurations for the coefficients of the price relations in this economy. No trading occurs in the fully revealing equilibrium. In addition, there are two equilibria where prices do not move, that is, $P_1 = P_2$. Hirshleifer, Subrahmanyam, and Titman (1994) focus on the remaining two equilibria in which trading occurs and the price is not the same in both periods. In these equilibria, both price changes $(P_1 - P_0)$ and $(P_2 - P_1)$, are positively correlated with δ. On average P_2 reveals more about δ than P_1. This is due to the fact that the market makers' information set, which determines the price, improves when two noisy aggregate demand curves are observed. Both aggregate demand curves depend on information δ. Since Δu_2 is independent of u_1, the correlation between u_1 and u_2 eases the inference of δ from both demand curves. However, the price changes, $(P_1 - P_0)$ and $(P_2 - P_1)$, themselves are uncorrelated and thus prices follow a martingale process given the market makers' filtration.

The trading behavior of the early-informed investors exhibits speculative features. They take on large positions in $t = 1$ and "on average" partially unwind their position in $t = 2$ at a more favorable price P_2. More precisely, their trading in $t = 1$, x_2^e, is positively correlated with the price change $(P_2 - P_1)$ in $t = 2$. However, their trading in $t = 2$ is negatively correlated with this price change. Therefore, these investors partially unwind their position and realize capital gains "on average." The intuition for this result is as follows. No risk premium is paid since the market makers' are risk neutral. Thus, risk averse traders would be unwilling to take on any risky stock position in the absence of any informational advantage. Early-informed investors have an informational advantage since they receive the signal δ in $t = 1$ and, hence, they are willing to take on some risk. Their informational advantage, together with the existence of noise traders, compensates them for taking on the risk represented by the random variable ϵ. However, the informational advantage of early-informed traders with respect to the late-informed traders vanishes in $t = 2$ for two reasons. First, late-informed traders receive the same signal δ. Thus, early-informed traders share the risk with late-informed traders in $t = 2$, that is, $\text{Cov}(x_2^l, x_2^e) > 0$. Second, the informational advantage of the early-informed traders with respect to the market makers shrinks as well, since market makers can observe an additional limit order book at $t = 2$. This limit order book carries information for the market makers, especially since the stock holding of the noise traders is correlated in both periods. This allows the market makers to get a better idea about δ and, thus, P_2 should be "on average" closer to $\bar{v} + \delta$ than P_1. In period two, both these effects cause early-informed traders to partially unwind the position they built up in the previous period. The unwinding behavior of early-informed traders in this sequential information arrival model also stimulates trading volume.

The fact that early-informed traders on average unwind their position in $t = 2$ is in sharp contrast to models based on Kyle (1985). In these models the risk neutral insider tries to buy the stocks in small pieces in order to hide behind noise trading, that is, his stock holding over time is positively correlated. However, Brunnermeier (1998) shows in a Kyle (1985) setting with a more general information structure that speculative trading by a risk neutral insider can also arise for strategic reasons. This is in contrast to Hirshleifer, Subrahmanyam, and Titman (1994) where speculative trading is only due to investors' risk aversion.

Having analyzed the trading stage, Hirshleifer, Subrahmanyam, and Titman (1994) show that herding can occur in the information acquisition stage. At the time when they decide which information to collect, traders do not know whether they will find the information early or late. The authors derive expressions for utility levels of the early-informed and late-informed individuals. The authors then provide a numerical example in which the ex-ante utility before knowing when one receives the information is increasing in the total mass of informed traders. If this is the case, it is worthwhile for traders to concentrate on the same informational aspects, that is, gather information about the same stocks. In other words, traders will herd in information acquisition.

Whether the ex-ante utility of a higher mass of informed traders really increases depends on the parameters, especially on σ_ϵ^2. There are three main effects: (1) Increasing the mass of informed traders leads to more late-informed traders. This makes it easier for early-informed traders to unwind larger positions in $t = 2$. There are more traders in $t = 2$ that are willing to share the risk resulting from ϵ. (2) This, however, is disadvantageous for the late-informed traders since there is tougher competition among them and the extent of noise trading does not change. (3) Increasing the mass of informed traders also increases the number of early-informed traders. This decreases the utility of both early-informed and late-informed traders. In order to obtain herding, the former effect has to outweigh the latter two. This requires that σ_ϵ^2 is sufficiently high. The authors try to extend their analysis by introducing some boundedly rational elements. This extension lies outside the scope of the current literature survey.

Less Valuable Long-term Information due to Unexpected Intermediate Price Moves

In Hirshleifer, Subrahmanyam, and Titman (1994) all traders search for the *same* piece of information which they randomly receive earlier or later. In contrast, in Holden and Subrahmanyam (1996) traders can decide whether to search for *short-term* information or for *long-term information*. They choose between two signals which are reflected in value at different points in time. Holden and Subrahmanyam (1996) show that under certain conditions all risk averse traders focus exclusively on the short-term signal. Trading based on long-term information has the disadvantage that unexpected price changes can occur before the collected long-term information is fully reflected in the price.

The liquidation payoff of a single risky asset in their model is given by

$$v = \bar{v} + \delta^{\text{short}} + \eta + \delta^{\text{long}} + \epsilon,$$

where δ^{short}, η, δ^{long}, and ϵ are mutually independent normally distributed and $\bar{v}$ is normalized to zero without loss of generality. Traders who acquire short-term information observe δ^{short} at $t = 1$. At $t = 2$, δ^{short} as well as η becomes publicly known and thus they are fully reflected in the price P_2. No trader receives a signal about η in $t = 1$. δ^{long} and ϵ are made public in $t = 3$. Consequently, they are only fully incorporated in the price P_3 in $t = 3$. The long-run information signal reveals δ^{long} to the informed trader in $t = 1$. Note that the markets are incomplete since the components of v cannot be traded directly. This assumption is essential for the analysis.

A competitive REE model is employed as in Hirshleifer, Subrahmanyam, and Titman (1994). A mass of M long-term informed traders and a mass of $N = 1 - M$ short-term traders submit limit orders to the limit order book. The aggregate order size of the liquidity traders is random and is given by u_1 in $t = 1$ and Δu_2 in $t = 2$. A group of risk neutral market makers observes only the publicly available information and the noisy aggregate demand schedule, that is, the limit order book. Like in Hirshleifer, Subrahmanyam, and Titman (1994) the market makers act competitively and they are risk neutral. Hence, their information sets determine the prices.

Analyzing the equilibrium backwards, the mass of short-term traders, N, and of long-term traders M, is kept fixed at the second stage and is endogenized at the first stage. Backward induction is also applied within the trading subgame for deriving the optimal stock holdings of informed risk averse traders. At $t = 2$, the stock holding demand is standard for the long-term informed traders,

$$x_2^l = \frac{\delta^{\text{long}} + \delta^{\text{short}} + \eta - P_2}{\rho \sigma_\epsilon^2}$$

and for the short-term informed traders,

$$x_2^s = \frac{E[\delta^{\text{long}}|\mathcal{F}_2^s] + \delta^{\text{short}} + \eta - P_2}{\rho[\sigma_\epsilon^2 + \text{Var}[\delta^{\text{long}}|\mathcal{F}_2^s]]} = 0.$$

$x_2^s = 0$, since the market makers have the same information set as the short-term-informed traders and, therefore, the numerator in the above equation is zero. In economic terms, it would not make a lot of sense for risk averse short-term investors to hold risky stocks if the risk neutral market makers have the same information. Since x_2^s is zero, x_1^s is the same as in a myopic setting:

$$x_1^s = \frac{E[P_2|\mathcal{F}_1^s] - P_1}{\rho \, \text{Var}[P_2 \mid \mathcal{F}_1^s]}.$$

Short-term informed traders try to exploit the expected price change $(P_2 - P_1)$ and they close their position at $t = 2$. Long-term traders' stock holding at $t = 1$ is

$$x_1^l = \frac{E[P_2|\mathcal{F}_1^l] - P_1}{\rho \mathcal{S}_1} + \varrho E[x_2^l|\mathcal{F}_1^l],$$

where $\mathcal{S}_1$ and ϱ are nonstochastic quantities.

Holden and Subrahmanyam (1996) derive the REE only for a special case and continue their analysis with numerical simulations. In equilibrium, long-term traders reduce their period 1 demand if the variance of η is very high. η's realization is announced at $t = 2$. Early-informed traders do not want to expose themselves to the announcement risk generated by η (which is reflected in P_2). They engage in heavier trading after a large part of the uncertainty about the asset's value is resolved.

Holden and Subrahmanyam (1996) endogenize M and, thus, $N = 1 - M$. The equilibrium mass M can be derived by comparing the ex-ante utilities of short-term informed traders with the utility of long-term informed traders. They show that for certain cases the ex-ante utility from collecting short-term information is higher for $M \in [0, 1]$ than the utility from gathering the long-term signal. Thus, all traders search for the short-term signal in equilibrium. This is the case if the traders are sufficiently risk averse and σ_ϵ^2 is substantially high. Intuitively, short-term informed investors can only make use of their information from the price change $(P_2 - P_1)$ provided there are noise traders in $t = 1$ distorting P_1. Since η makes P_2 risky, high variance in η reduces their aggressiveness. Long-term informed traders can exploit their information from both price changes, $(P_2 - P_1)$ and $(P_3 - P_2)$. As described above, high variance of η makes long-term informed agents delay their purchase. Therefore, they are more active at $t = 2$ and they exploit $(P_3 - P_2)$ to a greater degree. If the variance of ϵ is very high, that is, speculating at $t = 2$ is very risky, long-term informed traders are very cautious at $t = 2$. Thus, they cannot make as much money out of their information as short-term informed traders can.

Holden and Subrahmanyam (1996) further show that as the degree of liquidity trading increases, both types of information are more valuable. Short-term investors profit more from higher variance in noise trading, at least for the case where it is the same in both periods.

The authors also address the question of whether long-term information can be made more valuable by making it short-term. In other words, is it profitable for long-term informed investors to disclose their information already in $t = 2$? The impact of early credible disclosures is discussed in the last section of their paper.

6.2.3. Unwinding due to Principal–Agent Problems

A wealth constrained trader who has discovered a profitable trading strategy might have to borrow money in order to trade on his superior information. However, the lending party might fear that the trader could default on loan repayment. The trader might be overconfident and his trading strategy might not be as profitable as he claims. In order to reassure the lender, the trader has to signal in the early stages that his trading strategy is paying off. If this is (accidentally) not the case, the lender will withdraw his money and the trader will be forced to liquidate his position early. Consequently, the trader will care a lot about short-term price movements.

Portfolio delegation leads to a similar principal–agent problem. It leads to a principal–agent relationship between the individual investor and the fund manager. Many individual investors delegate their portfolio management to fund managers. The share of investments undertaken by institutional investors is steadily increasing. Pension funds, mutual funds, as well as hedge funds are becoming predominant players in both the stock market and foreign exchange market. These professional traders conduct the bulk of informed trading.

It is very hard for an individual investor to find out whether a certain fund manager is really able to make extra profits. Bhattacharya and Pfleiderer (1985) show that optimal incentive contracts for the remuneration of fund managers might alleviate this problem by screening good from bad managers. Nevertheless, a linear remuneration contract is often the optimal one and full screening is not possible. Portfolio delegation might also induce managers to "churn bubbles" as shown in Allen and Gorton (1993).

The threat of early withdrawal of their funds is a much more powerful device for individual investors than is designing the optimal ex-ante remuneration contract. The fund manager might then be forced to liquidate part of his acquired position. The power of early withdrawal of funds changes the fund managers' incentives dramatically. Shleifer and Vishny (1990, 1997) show that it limits traders' ability to exploit arbitrage opportunities and thus has a profound impact on the assets' price process. Paradoxically, a good manager is most likely to be forced to liquidate his position when it is most profitable to extend the arbitrage opportunity.

Limits of Arbitrage

In Shleifer and Vishny (1997) only liquidity traders and fund managers are active in the stock market. Individual investors do not trade directly. They entrust their money F_1 to a fund manager who trades on their behalf. The fund manager's ability to pick the right stocks is not known to the investors. Good fund managers have found a riskless arbitrage opportunity. They know the fundamental value v of the stock with certainty. Bad fund managers have no additional information and just want to gamble with others people's money. Investors cannot screen the good managers from the bad ones, by assumption. There are two trading rounds, $t = 1$ and $t = 2$. In period $t = 3$ the true value of the stock v is common knowledge and the price adjusts accordingly to $P_3 = v$. The price in $t = 2$, P_2, in this limit order model is determined by the aggregate demand from fund managers and liquidity traders. The fund manager faces a liquidation risk in $t = 2$. Individual investors can withdraw their funds conditional on P_2.

Shleifer and Vishny (1997) focus on the case where (1) investors have entrusted their money to a "good" fund manager, and (2) the asset price goes even further down in $t = 2$ even though the asset was already under-valued in $t = 1$, that is, $P_1 < v$. This is due to sell orders submitted by the uninformed liquidity traders in $t = 2$. In the eyes of the individual investors, the additional price drop can be the result of three factors: (1) a random error term, or (2) sell orders by liquidity traders, or (3) sell orders by other informed traders in the case that the true value of the stock is lower. If the latter case were true, then the fund manager would have made the wrong decision and most probably he has no extraordinary skills to find arbitrage opportunities. Given that the individual investors can only observe the price process, it is rational for them to conclude that they probably gave their money to a bad fund manager. Consequently, they will withdraw some of their money. Shleifer and Vishny (1997) assume in their reduced form model that the fund size in $t = 2$ is $F_2 = F_1 - aD_1(1 - P_2/P_1)$, where D_1 is the amount of money the fund manager invested in the stock. The higher the coefficient a is, the more sensitive are individual investors to past performance. If the price does not change, the money in the fund remains constant. If the price increases, even more investors provide money to the fund, that is, $F_2 > F_1$. But in the case where the arbitrage opportunity becomes even more profitable, that is, when $P_2 < P_1$, investors withdraw money for fear of having entrusted their money to a bad fund manager. If the fund manager fully exploited the arbitrage opportunity, that is, he invested the whole fund into the stock, $D_1 = F_1$, he is forced to unwind part of his position although he is sure that the price will come back in $t = 3$. He incurs a loss by unwinding his position at an even lower price. Knowing that the investors will withdraw some money if the price goes down in $t = 2$, the fund manager will invest only part D_1 of the fund F_1 in the undervalued asset in $t = 1$. In general, the fund manager does not fully exploit the arbitrage opportunity. He will only invest the whole fund F_1

if the mispricing is very large thus making it very unlikely that the price will go down further.

This shows that even pure long-run arbitrage opportunities are risky since investors might withdraw their money early. Fund managers face the risk of interim liquidation. Pure arbitrage opportunities are very rare in reality and traders mostly discover expected arbitrage opportunities. Therefore, risky arbitrage is not only risky for fund managers because they cannot exactly replicate the payoff stream but also because they face an "early liquidation risk."

The consequence is that fund managers search for less risky arbitrage opportunities. In order to minimize the "early liquidation risk," they can either concentrate their research efforts on short-run information which will be made public very soon, or on information which is the focus of sufficiently many other arbitrageurs. This makes it more likely that information is reflected in the price soon. Professional arbitrage is concentrated in a few markets like in the bond market and foreign exchange market but is hardly ever present in the stock market. This is the same "arbitrage chain" argument which is formalized by Dow and Gorton (1994). Given that fund managers focus only on short-run arbitrage opportunities, long-run assets, whose positive dividend pay-offs will be in the far future, are more mispriced in equilibrium. No fund manager will exploit long-run arbitrage opportunities out of fear that he has to liquidate the position early when individual investors with-draw their funds. Put differently, long-run arbitrage opportunities must provide much higher returns than short-run arbitrage opportunities in order to compensate for the additional liquidation risk. This might also explain why stock market returns – contrary to what the capital asset pricing model (CAPM) suggests – do not only depend on systematic risk but also on idiosyncratic risk. The risk of wrong intermediate price movements makes arbitrage trading less attractive and thus must lead to higher returns.

Induced Collection of Short-Run Information

Gümbel (1999) explicitly models the principal–agent relationship and its implication in the stock market. He shows that the individual investors actually prefer that fund managers primarily search for *short-term information* and exploit short-term arbitrage opportunities. This allows the investors to quickly infer the manager's ability and to lay off an unable manager.

In Gümbel (1999) the risk neutral investor delegates his investment decision to a risk neutral fund manager whose ability to choose the right trading strategy is unknown. There are two underlying risky assets in this economy which pay a dividend of either 0 or 1 in each period $t \in 0, 1, 2, \ldots, \infty$. Let us assume for illustrative purposes that the individual dividend payments are securitized and are traded. In addition, there are traded bonds whose fixed return is r. The fund manager can gather either *short-term* information *or long-term information* without cost. He always receives one noisy signal {up, down} for each of the two stocks. Short-term information provides two noisy signals about the dividend payments of both assets in the next period $t + 1$, whereas long-term information provides two noisy signals about the dividend payments of both assets in $t + 2$.

There is a pool of potential fund managers, who invest on behalf of the investor. A fraction γ has high ability and the rest is of low ability. In contrast to Shleifer and Vishny (1997) neither the principal nor the fund managers know their type and both learn the manager's type at the same speed. Fund managers receive one signal for each of the two stocks. Each signal's realization is either "up" or "down." Bad fund manager's signals are always correct for one stock and incorrect for the other one. Either the signal for stock A is correct and the one for stock B is incorrect or vice versa with equal probability. Good fund managers' signals have the same structure with probability $(1 - v)$. However, with probability $v(\mu)$, their short-term (long-term) signals $S_t^{\text{short},j}(S_t^{\text{long},j})$ are correct for both assets $j \in 1, 2$. The trading game for each asset is a binary version of Kyle (1985). Liquidity traders in both markets as well as informed fund managers submit market orders to the market makers. The market makers only observe the aggregate order flows X_t^j of the asset j and set informationally efficient prices P_t^j. The liquidity trader submits a random order of fixed size $-x$ or $+x$ with equal probability. Whether the fund manager submits a buy or sell order depends on his signal. As long as the probability that he is of high type is sufficiently high, he will submit a buy (sell) order if he gets a positive (negative) signal. In order to disguise his order behind the liquidity traders' orders, his order size is also either $-x$ or x. The market maker could immediately identify any other order size as an order originating from the fund manager. The aggregate order flow is thus $-2x$, 0, $+2x$. If the aggregate order flow is $-2x$ or $2x$, the market maker can perfectly infer the fund manager's information. The market maker cannot figure out whether the manager submitted a buy or sell order only if the aggregate order flow is zero. Only in this case does the fund manager make a nonzero trading profit. This feature of the model simplifies the analysis.

The fund manager's trading activity depends on whether the fund manager has collected long-term information or short-term information. In the case that the manager is induced to collect *long-run information* about the dividend payments in $t+2$, he submits an order in t. This order will be executed at the price P_t, which the market maker sets based on the observed aggregate order flow in t. The market maker receives a private signal signal $S_{t+1}^{mm,j} \in \{up, down\}$ after he has executed the order at the price P_t. This signal predicts the correct d_{t+2} with probability $q \in [\frac{1}{2}, 1]$. The fund manager has the opportunity to unwind his acquired position prior to trading in $t+1$. Unwinding perfectly reveals his signal to the market maker. Consequently, the "unwinding price" is determined by the fund manager's information together with the market maker's signal $S_{t+1}^{mm,j}$. The manager is indifferent between unwinding and holding the asset until it pays the dividend in $t+2$. This is because the competitive risk neutral market maker sets the (semi-strong) informationally efficient price and the manager has the same information as the market maker about d_{t+1}. That is, they expect d_{t+1} to be zero. De facto, a fund manager with long-run information trades an asset in t whose "unwinding value" prior to trading in $t+1$ is

$$\frac{1}{1+r} E[d_{t+2}^j | S_{t+1}^{mm,j}, q, S_t^{long,j}].$$

The informational advantage for the manager with respect to the market maker in t results from his knowledge of $S_t^{long,j}$. Note since d_{t+2} is only paid out in $t+2$, the unwinding value has to be discounted by one period. $S_{t+1}^{mm,j}$ generates an additional noise term for the fund manager's "unwinding price" and thus does not affect the manager's expected profit.

Managers who gather *short-term information* trade an asset in t whose value in $t+1$ is d_{t+1}^j. The fund manager's best estimate in t is $E[d_{t+1}^j | S_t^{short,j}]$. The manager's informational advantage is, however, smaller since the market maker also holds some information about d_{t+1} prior to trading in period t. This is because (1) the market maker received a private signal $S_t^{mm,j}$ about d_{t+1}^j, and (2) he might have learned something from other fund managers who unwind the long-term position that they acquired by observing the signal about d_{t+2} in t.[12]

In summary, long-run information is advantageous for the manager since the market maker does not know it yet, i.e. he has not observed

---

[12] This will not occur in equilibrium since the fund manager will gather short-term information in equilibrium.

the signal $S_{t+1}^{mm,j}$ yet. On the other hand, short-run information of good fund managers is assumed to be more precise, that is, $v > \mu$, and one trades an asset whose dividend of 0 or 1 is paid out in $t + 1$ rather than $t + 2$. This reduces the loss from discounting. Proposition 1 of the paper shows that a high type manager trades more profitably with long-run information if $\mu > v(1 + r)4q(1 - q)$.

The decision whether to gather short-run or long-run information not only affects the direct trading profits, but also affects how quickly one learns the manager's ability. Short-run information not only has the advantage that it is more precise since $v > \mu$ but it also provides the principal a better update about the manager's ability already in $t + 1$. This again influences the employment decision of the principal, that is, when to fire the manager and hire a new agent from the pool of potential managers. If the manager traded in the right direction for both assets, he is of high quality with probability one, since a bad manager always trades in the wrong direction for at least one asset. If he has traded in the wrong direction for one asset, it is more likely that he is a bad manager.[13] If one of the manager's two first trades is wrong, it is better for the principal to replace him with a new manager from the pool.

If the manager collects long-run information, the principal's ability to evaluate the agent in $t + 1$ by observing his unwinding decision depends on the quality q of the market maker's signal, $S_{t+1}^{mm,j}$. Let us consider the two polar cases $q = \frac{1}{2}$ and $q = 1$. If $q = \frac{1}{2}$ the market maker's signal is worthless. Since $S_{t+1}^{mm,j}$ has no informational content, the market maker only learns the fund manager's signal if he unwinds it prior to trading in $t + 1$. He cannot evaluate whether the manager received a correct long-term signal or not. If $q = 1$ the market maker receives a perfect signal about the dividend payment in $t + 2$. Hence, he can infer whether the manager received a correct long-term signal or not. If he has received such a signal, then he is for sure of high ability; if not, it might still be the case that he received bad information because he was unlucky. Note that since $v > \mu$, it is more likely that a good manager who gathers long-run information is unluckier than one who gathers short-run information. Nevertheless, trading in the wrong direction makes it more likely that he is a bad manager and thus the principal fires him and hires a new manager from the pool. Note that a higher q makes long-run information more attractive for two reasons: (1) it allows a quicker evaluation of the manager's ability, and (2) it makes the short-run information

---

[13] Note that if the manager himself knows that he is of low ability, his trades would always contradict one of his signals.

less valuable since the market maker already knows part of the private information that the fund manager will collect.

The paper assumes that the decision to collect long-run versus short-run information is contractible and thus is decided by the principal. The main result of this paper is that for certain parameter values, learning about the manager's ability induces the principal to search for short-term information even though long-term information would be more valuable. Short-run information allows the principal to dismiss bad managers early. Focusing exclusively on short-run information leads to long-run mispricing.

6.3. Firms' Short-Termism

Mispricing of assets is not very harmful if it does not affect the real decision making within firms. This section illustrates that short-sightedness of investors leads to short-termism in firms' investment decisions.

Shleifer and Vishny (1990) argue convincingly that managers care about the stock price of their company. Corporate managers' remunerations are very closely linked to the stock price via stock options. They risk being fired because of a possible take-over if the company's equity is underpriced. Corporate managers have a vital interest that their investment decisions are reflected correctly in the stock price. Investors' focus on short horizons leads to systematically less accurate pricing of long-term assets, for example, stocks of firms whose investment projects only lead to positive return in the far future. Corporate managers who are averse to mispricing, therefore, focus on short-term projects.

In Brandenburger and Polak (1996) managers ignore their superior information and follow the opinion of the market. The market can observe the corporate manager's action and try to infer the manager's superior information, which is then reflected in the stock price. Since the manager cares about the short-run stock price, he has an incentive to manipulate his action and thus the market's inference. The result is that the corporate manager does not follow his superior information in equilibrium.

In the first part of Brandenburger and Polak (1996), a single risk neutral manager has to choose between action L(left) and R(right). The payoff of his action depends on the state of the world. In state λ, action L pays off \$1 and action R pays nothing. In state ρ, the payoff structure is exactly the opposite. Action L's payoff is 0 and action R pays off 1. The true state is ρ with prior probability $\pi > \frac{1}{2}$. The prior distribution might reflect public (short-run) information which is known to the whole market. The manager receives an additional signal $S^i \in \{l, r\}$ which tells him the true state with precision $q > \pi$, that is, $q = \Pr(l|\lambda) = \Pr(r|\rho)$. Since the signal is more precise than the prior, a manager who maximizes the long-run value of his company should follow his signal. However, it takes a while until the true payoffs are realized and reflected in the stock price. In the meantime, the market tries to infer the manager's signal and updates the short-run market price. If the manager could truthfully announce his signal to the market, he would always follow his signal and the market price would adjust accordingly. The trading game is such that the price reflects the posterior probability of the market. Note that the market price would be higher if the manager received signal r instead of signal l. This is due to the biased prior $\pi > \frac{1}{2}$.

In Brandenburger and Polak (1996) the manager cannot truthfully announce his signal. The market participants try to infer the signal from the manager's observed action R or L. However, there exists no pure strategy equilibrium in which the manager would follow his signal. If such an equilibrium existed, then the market participants would believe that the manager's strategy is to always follow his signal. Therefore, they would think that they can perfectly infer the manager's signal from his action. Consequently, they would update the stock price accordingly. The stock price after observing action R would be higher than that after observing L. This occurs because of the bias in the prior $\pi > \frac{1}{2}$. Since the manager cares about the current stock price, he has an incentive to deviate from the strategy that always chooses action R. Always choosing R is indeed the best BNE in pure strategies. The manager ignores his signal completely and – since in equilibrium the market participants know this – the stock price reflects the fact that the manager's action is always R. Even though the stock price is informationally efficient, the manager's decisions are clearly (allocatively) inefficient.

There are, however, mixed strategy equilibria in which the manager at least partly uses his information. The manager ignores part of his information since he sometimes chooses R even though he has received signal l. In the mixed strategy equilibria, the market participants know which strategy the manager applies but they cannot fully infer his signal. Mixed strategies can, therefore, be thought of as "garblings" of signals.[14] Traders can partly infer the manager's signal. The mixing probabilities have to be such that the market participants' posteriors

---

[14] Note the similarity to Crawford and Sobel (1982). In Crawford and Sobel (1982) the sender of the message cares about the receivers' opinion since it affects his action. In

that the manager has chosen the right action are the same. In other words, the market conjecture is such that the short-run stock price does not depend on the action of the manager. Consequently, the manager is indifferent between both actions in equilibrium and has no incentive to deviate from his mixed strategy. The bias in the unbalanced prior $\pi > \frac{1}{2}$, which drives the nonexistence result of informative pure strategy equilibria, has to be counterbalanced by the mixed strategy. Observing an action L has to be a stronger indication of signal l than observing R is for signal r. The stronger the bias, the more mixing is necessary and thus the higher the loss of information. The key is actually not the skewness or bias of the prior but the fact that the two decisions yield unequal posteriors about the expected profit of the firm.

In the second part of the paper, a dynamic model is introduced. Many firms receive a signal about the state λ or ρ and have to sequentially choose action L or R. Informational cascades like in the herding model à la Bikhchandani, Hirshleifer, and Welch (1992) arise. One might suspect that by applying mixed strategies the information aggregation problem due to herding might be alleviated. On the contrary, Brandenburger and Polak (1996) show that with share price maximization, equilibrium choices are strictly less efficient than under herding behavior. The successors can infer less information from their predecessor's decision but it is still optimal for them to herd on the inferred information and to disregard their own private signal.

There are numerous other papers dealing with short-termism of firms induced by the stock market. Grant, King, and Polak (1996) provide a good survey of this literature.

6.4. Bank Runs and Financial Crisis

Bank runs and bank panics are special forms of herding behavior. A bank run occurs when the deposit holders of a bank suddenly withdraw their money. If a run on a single bank spreads over to other banks, it can cause a panic in the whole banking system. Strong spillover effects can lead to contagion where many banks get into solvency problems.

This section focuses solely on the herding aspect of bank runs and thus ignores a large part of the banking literature. Interested readers are directed to Freixas and Rochet (1997) for a comprehensive coverage of

---

Brandenburger and Polak (1996) the sender cares about the action and thus the market participants' opinion because it affects the short-run stock price.

the banking literature. Although withdrawals by deposit holders occur sequentially in reality, the literature typically models bank runs as a simultaneous move game. An exception is Chen (1999) who explicitly models a bank run in a sequential setting.

Banks as Liquidity Insurance Providers

One role of banks is to transform illiquid technologies into liquid pay-offs, and also to provide liquidity insurance. Diamond and Dybvig's (1983) seminal paper illustrates this role of banks and builds on initial insights presented in Bryant (1980). In their model, banks offer demand deposits to match the agents' liquidity needs with projects' maturities. However, these demand deposits open up the possibility of bank runs.

In Diamond and Dybvig (1983) there are two technologies in which money can be invested for future consumption: an illiquid technology and a storage technology. The illiquid technology is a long-run investment project that requires one unit of investment. It can be liquidated early in $t = 1$ at a salvage value of $L \leq 1$.[15] If one carries on with the project until $t = 2$, the project pays off a fixed gross return of $R > 1$. In addition to the productive long-run investment project, agents also have access to a costless storage technology. Agents can devote a fraction of their endowment to the illiquid investment project and store the rest in the costless storage technology. The savings opportunities are summarized in Table 6.1.

There is a continuum of ex-ante identical agents who have an endowment of one unit each. Each agent faces a preference shock prior to $t = 1$. Depending on this shock, each agent consumes either in $t = 1$ or in $t = 2$. They are either "early diers," who consume in $t = 1$ or

Table 6.1.

Investment projects	$t = 0$	$t = 1$	$t = 2$
Risky investment project			
(a) continuation	−1	0	$R > 1$
(b) early liquidation	−1	$L \leq 1$	0
Storage technology			
(a) from $t = 0$ to $t = 1$	−1	+1	
(b) from $t = 1$ to $t = 2$		−1	+1

---

[15] Diamond and Dybvig (1983) restrict their analysis to $L = 1$. To illustrate the utility improving role of asset markets, we consider the more general case of $L \leq 1$.

"late diers," who consume in $t = 2$. In other words, early diers derive utility $U^1(c_1)$ only from consumption in $t = 1$, whereas late diers derive utility $U^2(c_2)$ only from consumption in $t = 2$. Since the agents do not know ex-ante whether they will die early or not, they would like to insure themselves against their uncertain liquidity needs.

Without markets or financial intermediaries each agent would invest x in the long-run investment project and store the rest $(1 - x)$. Early diers who liquidate their project consume $c_1 = xL + (1 - x) \in [L, 1]$, while late diers consume $c_2 = xR + (1 - x) \in [1, R]$. The ex-ante utility of each agent is given by $qU(c_1) + (1 - q)U(c_2)$, where q denotes the probability of dying early. This utility can be improved if trading of assets is allowed in $t = 1$.

Financial markets allow agents to sell their stake in the long-run investment project in $t = 1$. In this case, the higher consumption levels $c_1 = 1$ and $c_2 = R$ can be achieved even if $L < 1$ as long as a fraction $(1-q)$ is invested in the illiquid asset on aggregate. Instead of liquidating the long-run asset in $t = 1$, early diers can sell their asset to the late diers in exchange for c_1-consumption at a price of $P = 1$. Note that the price of the asset in $t = 1$ has to be 1 in order to ensure that agents are indifferent between storage and investing in the investment project in $t = 0$.

However, the consumption pattern of $c_1 = 1$ for early diers and $c_2 = R$ for late diers is typically not ex-ante optimal since it does not provide an optimal insurance against the ex-ante risk that one can be either an early or late dier. Ex-ante optimal consumption levels must satisfy

$$\frac{\partial U}{\partial c_1}(\cdot) = R\frac{\partial U}{\partial c_2}(\cdot).$$

The allocation $(c_1 = 1, c_2 = R)$ is ex-ante optimal only for special utility functions. Within the class of HARA utility functions, this allocation is only ex-ante optimal for the log-utility function. For utility functions with a relative risk aversion coefficient, γ, larger than unity,

$$\frac{\partial U}{\partial c_1}(1) > R\frac{\partial U}{\partial c_2}(R).$$

Thus, a contract which offers $c_1 = 1$, and $c_2 = R$ is not ex-ante optimal. In other words, given $\gamma > 1$, a feasible contract $c_1^* > 1$ and $c_2^* < R$ which satisfies

$$\frac{\partial U}{\partial c_1}(c_1^*) = R\frac{\partial U}{\partial c_2}(c_2^*)$$

is ex-ante preferred to $c_1 = 1$ and $c_2 = R$.

A bank can commit itself to perform this transfer of resources from c_2 to c_1. Competitive banks offer deposit contracts (c_1^*, c_2^*) which maximize the agents' ex-ante utility. Free entry in the banking sector and the absence of aggregate risk ensures this. In equilibrium, the bank makes zero profit, invests x^* into the investment project, and stores the rest $(1-x^*)$. The stored reserves are enough to satisfy the early diers demand in $t = 1$, that is, $qc_1^* = (1 - x^*)$, while the rest is paid out to the late diers in $t = 2$. Thus, $(1 - q)c_2^* = Rx^*$.

In Diamond and Dybvig (1983) the bank can observe neither the consumer type nor his private storage activity from $t = 1$ to $t = 2$. Therefore, the bank has to provide the right incentives such that late diers do not withdraw their money early and store it for later consumption in $t = 2$. As long as only early diers withdraw their demand deposit c_1 from the bank in $t = 1$, the bank is prepared for this money outflow and does not need to liquidate the long-run asset. In this case, no late dier has an incentive to withdraw his money early and hence deposit contracts are optimal.

Bank Runs as a Sunspot Phenomenon

However, if other late diers start withdrawing money early, then the bank does not have enough reserves and is forced to liquidate its long-run projects. For each additional late dier who withdraws c_1^* units from the bank, the bank has to liquidate more than one unit. The bank promised a payment of $c_1^* > 1$, which was optimal given the deposit holder's relative risk aversion coefficient $\gamma > 1$. If the salvage value L is strictly smaller than 1, the bank has to liquidate even a larger fraction of the long-run investment project. This reduces the possible payments in $t = 2$ and thus the incentive for late diers not to withdraw their money early. Diamond and Dybvig (1983) assume that the bank must honor a *sequential service constraint*. Depositors reach the teller one after the other and the bank honors its contracts until it runs out of money. The sequential service constraint gives depositors the incentive to withdraw their money as early as possible if they think that late diers will also withdraw their demand deposits early in $t = 1$ and make the bank insolvent. This payoff externality triggers the herding behavior. The authors assume the sequential service constraint even though they formally employ a simultaneous move game. In short, there also exists a bank run equilibrium in which all agents immediately withdraw their deposits in $t = 1$ and the bank is forced to liquidate its assets. In the bank run case deposit contracts are not necessarily optimal. Whether the Pareto inferior bank run equilibrium arises or the full insurance equilibrium arises might depend on sunspots. Sunspots, as explained in Section 2.3, are commonly observed extrinsic random variables which serve as a coordination device.

Suspension of convertibility eliminates the bank run equilibrium as long as the fraction of early diers q is deterministic. If the bank commits itself to serve only the first q customers who show up to withdraw their demand deposits, no assets need be liquidated and the bank has enough money to pay c_2^*. Consequently, no late dier has an incentive to withdraw any money in $t = 1$ in the first place. In short, the anticipation of suspension of convertibility prevents bank runs.

If the fraction of early diers q is random, the suspension of convertibility does not prevent bank runs since the bank does not know when to stop paying out money in $t = 1$.[16] On the other hand, a governmental *deposit insurance* financed by an inflation tax can eliminate the bank run equilibrium even for a random q. If the deposit guarantee of c_1^* is nominal, an inflation tax that depends on early withdrawals can reduce the real value of the demand deposit. This provides the late diers with the necessary incentive not to withdraw their money early.

Jacklin (1987) shows that agents can achieve the same optimal consumption level (c_1^*, c_2^*) with dividend paying equity contracts instead of bank deposits. Furthermore, dividend paying equity contracts eliminate the Pareto inferior bank run equilibrium. However, the optimal consumption level cannot be achieved with equity contracts in a more general setting with smooth preferences where both types of agents consume in both periods.

Possibility of Information-Induced Bank Runs in a Unique Equilibrium

Jacklin and Bhattacharya (1988) compare demand deposits with equity contracts. In their model bank runs are not due to sunspots, but changes in the fundamental variables. The payoff of the long-run investment project $\tilde{R}$ is random in Jacklin and Bhattacharya (1988) and some traders receive information about $\tilde{R}$ prior to their withdrawal. In contrast to

---

[16] The randomness of q also affects the bank's investment decision x. In Diamond and Dybvig (1983) this has no impact since $L = 1$ and thus investing in $t = 0$ and liquidating in $t = 1$ provides the same return as storage.

Table 6.2.

Investment projects	$t = 0$	$t = 1$	$t = 2$
Illiquid risky project	-1	$L = 0$ $R = \begin{cases} R_H & \text{Pr } 1 - \theta \\ R_L & \text{Pr } \theta \end{cases}$	
Storage technology			
(a) from $t = 0$ to $t = 1$	-1	$+1$	
(b) from $t = 1$ to $t = 2$		-1	$+1$

Diamond and Dybvig (1983), there is only one unique equilibrium. In this equilibrium bank runs occur in some states of the world.[17]

Another distinction between Diamond and Dybvig (1983) and Jacklin and Bhattacharya (1988) is that the latter authors assume smooth preferences $U^i(c_1, c_2) = u(c_1^i) + \beta^i u(c_2^i)$. Hence, agents want to consume a positive amount in both periods. Impatient agents put more weight on consumption in $t = 1$ and patient agents put more weight on consumption in $t = 2$, that is, $1 \geq \beta^2 > \beta^1 > 0$. Smooth preferences rule out the possibility that the optimal consumption profile can be implemented with dividend paying equity on a bank instead of demandable deposits.

The payoff structure in Jacklin and Bhattacharya (1988) is summarized in Table 6.2. The payoff structure differs from the one in Diamond and Dybvig (1983) in two ways. First, the salvage value of the illiquid investment project, L, is zero in $t = 1$. Second, the final payoff of the illiquid project R in $t = 2$ is random. The probability of a high return R_H is $(1 - \theta)$ and the probability of a low return R_L is θ. In the latter case, the bank can pay at most a fraction R_L/R_H of the maximum payment in $t = 2$. Agents learn their time preference β in $t = 1$. That is, they discover how strongly they prefer to consume the bulk of their endowment in $t = 1$ instead of in $t = 2$. A fixed fraction α of the more patient "late consumers" also receive a signal about the payoff of the illiquid project. This signal allows the informed late consumers to update their prior θ to $\hat{\theta}$.

Nonpatient consumers with low β^1 always withdraw a large fraction of their deposits from the bank in $t = 1$. Uninformed patient consumers keep their deposits with the bank, while informed patient consumers withdraw their money early if the posterior of the bad event R_L, $\hat{\theta}$, is above the threshold level $\bar{\theta}$. Jacklin and Bhattacharya (1988) show that the bank run threshold level $\bar{\theta}$ decreases as the variance of R increases.

---

[17] In this respect, their model is similar to Postlewaite and Vives (1987) who develop an alternative setup with a unique equilibrium over a range of parameter values.

Chari and Jagannathan (1988) analyze information induced bank runs where uninformed late consumers infer information from the aggregate withdrawal rate. In their setup, all agents are risk neutral with a utility function $U^i(c_1, c_2) = c_1 + \beta^i c_2$. Type 1 agents are early consumers and their β^1 is close to zero. Type 2 agents with high β^2 are late consumers. Risk neutrality eliminates the bank's role as a liquidity insurer. The fraction $q \in \{0, q_1, q_2\}$ of impatient early consumers is random in Chari and Jagannathan (1988). As in Jacklin and Bhattacharya (1988), a fraction α of late consumers receive a signal about the random return of the illiquid investment project $R \in \{R_L, R_H\}$. However, this fraction is also random with $\alpha \in \{0, \bar{\alpha}\}$. In short, in Chari and Jagannathan (1988) the fraction of impatient consumers q, the return R, and the fraction α of informed late consumers is random. In contrast to Diamond and Dybvig (1983), the authors do not assume the sequential service constraint. In their model all deposit holders arrive simultaneously and there is a *pro rata* allocation of the funds. If short-term funds are not sufficient, the bank can prematurely liquidate the long-run project. As long as the total aggregate withdrawals do not exceed some threshold $\bar{K}$ the salvage value of the long-run investment project is $L = 1$. Otherwise, premature liquidation is costly, that is, $L < 1$.

A large withdrawal of deposits can be (1) due to a large fraction of impatient consumers, that is a high realization of q, or (2) due to the fact that informed patient consumers received a bad signal about R. Since uninformed patient consumers cannot distinguish between both forms of shocks, they base their decision solely on aggregate withdrawals. Uninformed patient consumers might misinterpret large withdrawals due to a high q as being caused by a bad signal received by informed late consumers. This induces them to withdraw their funds and forces banks to liquidate their investment projects. Wrong inference by the uninformed deposit holders can lead to bank runs even when $R = R_H$. The liquidation costs erode the bank's assets and the possible payouts in $t = 2$. In Chari and Jagannathan (1988), the early withdrawal by deposit holders causes an information externality and a payoff externality. The early withdrawal sends a signal to the uninformed deposit holders that the return of the long-run asset is probably low (information externality) and also forces the bank to conduct costly liquidation (payoff externality).[18]

---

[18] In Gorton (1985) a bank can stop a bank run if $R = R_H$. By paying a verification cost, it is able to credibly communicate the true return R_H and suspend convertibility.

Potential bank runs can also serve as a discipline device for bank managers to make the right investment decisions. Calomiris and Kahn (1991) focus on this aspect in a model with endogenous information acquisition by the deposit holders. Their analysis explains why demand deposit contracts are the dominant form of savings.

Financial Crisis

A single bank run can easily spill over to other banks. A bank panic involves runs on many banks and might lead to a collapse of the whole banking system. Bhattacharya and Gale (1987) provide a model illustrating bank panics in a setting that focuses on the role of the interbank loan market. Chen's (1999) paper illustrates contagious runs on multiple banks in a herding model where deposit holders can decide sequentially. The analysis highlights the crucial role of information externalities and payoff externalities. The latter is due to the sequential servicing constraint.

In a broader context, all these problems arise from short-run financing of long-run high-yield investment opportunities. A fund manager who invests on behalf of individual investors also faces the same problem. As discussed in Section 6.2.3, the fear of early withdrawal of funds makes him reluctant to exploit profitable long-run arbitrage opportunities.

The discrepancy of maturities between investment projects and their short-term financing might explain the scope of the financial crisis in Southeast Asia at the end of the 1990s. Bad news about the lack of an efficient corporate governance structure might have justified a certain correction. However, it triggered a significant outflow of funds from these countries due to herding behavior, as in a bank run. This resulted in a plummeting of share prices and large-scale currency devaluations, thereby forcing these countries to also liquidate useful long-run investment projects.

Radelet and Sachs (1998) contrast this reasoning with other possible causes of the recent Asian crises. Each cause leads to different predictions of the price path and requires different remedies. No measures should be taken if the crash is just a price correction, for example, the bursting of a bubble. On the other hand, if the crisis is due to herding behavior as in bank runs, capital controls are a useful device to avoid the Pareto inferior bank-run equilibrium. Policy makers who are able to differentiate between these different causes can develop the right remedies to reduce the impact of future crises and minimize the social hardship faced by large fractions of the population.

REFERENCES

Admati, Anat R. (1985): "A Noisy Rational Expectations Equilibrium for Multi-Asset Securities Markets," *Econometrica*, 53, 629–657.

—— (1989): "Information in Financial Markets: The Rational Expectations Approach," in *Financial Markets and Incomplete Information*, ed. by Sudipto Bhattacharya and George M. Constantinides, pp. 139–152. Rowman and Littlefield Publishers, Inc., Totowa, NJ.

Admati, Anat R., and Paul Pfleiderer (1986): "A Monopolisitic Market for Information," *Journal of Economic Theory*, 39, 400–438.

—— (1988): "A Theory of Intraday Patterns: Volume and Price Variability," *Review of Financial Studies*, 1(1), 3–40.

—— (1990): "Direct and Indirect Sale of Information," *Econometrica*, 58, 901–928.

Akerlof, G. A. (1970): "The Market for 'Lemons': Quality Uncertainty and the Market Mechanism," *Quarterly Journal of Economics*, 84, 488–500.

Allen, Beth (1981): "A Class of Monotone Economies in which Rational Expectations Equilibria Exist but Prices do not Reveal all Information," *Economics Letters*, 7, 227–232.

—— (1982): "Strict Rational Expectations Equilibria with Diffuseness," *Journal of Economic Theory*, 27, 20–46.

—— (1985): "The Existence of Fully Rational Expectations Approximate Equilibria with Noisy Price Observations," *Journal of Economic Theory*, 37, 213–253.

Allen, Franklin, and Douglas Gale (1994): *Financial Innovation and Risk Sharing*. MIT Press, Cambridge, MA.

—— (2000): "Bubbles and Crises," *Economic Journal*, 110, 236–255.

Allen, Franklin, and Gary Gorton (1993): "Churning Bubbles," *Review of Economic Studies*, 60, 813–836.

Allen, Franklin, Stephen Morris, and Andrew Postlewaite (1993): "Finite Bubbles with Short Sale Constraints and Asymmetric Information," *Journal of Economic Theory*, 61, 206–229.

Anderson, Robert M., and Hugo Sonnenschein (1982): "On the Existence of Rational Expectations Equilibrium," *Journal of Economic Theory*, 26, 261–278.

Anderson, T. W. (1984): *An Introduction to Multivariate Statistical Analysis*. John Wiley & Sons, New York, Chapter 2.

Arrow, Kenneth (1953): "Le Rôle des Valeurs Boursières pour la Répartition la Meilleure des Risques," *Econometrie*, 31, 91–96; Colloques Internationaux du Centre National de la Recherche Scientifique 40 (Paris 1952), pp. 41–47; discussion, pp. 47–48, C.N.R.S. (Paris 1953), pp. 41–47; English translation in *Review of Economic Studies* (1964), 31, 91–96.

Aumann, Robert J. (1976): "Agreeing to Disagree," *Annals of Statistics*, 4, 1236–1239.

—— (1987): "Correlated Equilibrium as an Expression of Bayesian Rationality," *Econometrica*, 55, 1–18.

Aumann, Robert J., and Adam Brandenburger (1995): "Epistemic Conditions for Nash Equilibrium," *Econometrica*, 63(5), 523–541.

Ausubel, Lawrence M. (1990): "Partially-Revealing Rational Expectations Equilibria in a Competitive Economy," *Journal of Economic Theory*, 50, 93–126.

Ausubel, Lawrence M., and Peter Cramton (1995): "Demand Reduction and Inefficiency in Multi-Unit Auctions." Mimeo, University of Maryland.

Avery, Christopher, and Judith Chevalier (1999): "Herding Over the Career," *Economics Letters*, 63, 327–333.

Avery, Christopher, and Peter Zemsky (1998): "Multidimensional Uncertainty and Herd Behavior in Financial Markets," *American Economic Review*, 88(4), 724–748.

Azariadis, Costas (1981): "Self-fulfilling Prophecies," *Journal of Economic Theory*, 25, 380–396.

Back, Kerry (1992): "Insider Trading in Continuous Time," *Review of Financial Studies*, 5, 387–409.

Back, Kerry, and Jaime P. Zender (1993): "Auctions of Divisible Goods: On the Rationale for the Treasury Experiment," *Review of Financial Studies*, 6(4), 733–764.

Back, Kerry, H. Henry Cao, and Gregory A. Willard (1997): "Imperfect Competition among Informed Traders," *Journal of Finance* (forthcoming).

Bagehot, Walter (pseud.) (1971): "The Only Game in Town," *Financial Analysts Journal*, pp. 12–14, 22.

Bagnoli, Mark, S. Viswanathan, and Craig Holden (1994): "On the Existence of Linear Equilibria in Models of Market Making." Discussion Paper 9421, Duke University.

Banerjee, Abhijit V. (1992): "A Simple Model of Herd Behavior," *Quarterly Journal of Economics*, 107, 797–817.

Bergemann Dirk, and Juuso Välimäki (1996): "Market Experimentation and Pricing." Cowles Foundation Discussion Paper, Yale University.

Bewley, Truman (1980): "The Optimum Quantity of Money," in *Models of Monetary Economics*, ed. by J. Kareken and Neil Wallace. Federal Reserve Bank, Minneapolis.

Bhattacharya, Sudipto, and Douglas Gale (1987): "Preference Shocks, Liquidity and Central Bank Policy," in *New Approaches to Monetary Economics*, ed. by William A. Barnett and Kenneth J. Singleton. Cambridge University Press, Cambridge, UK.

Bhattacharya, Sudipto, and Paul Pfleiderer (1985): "Delegated Portfolio Management," *Journal of Economic Theory*, 36(1), 1–25.

Bhattacharya, Sugato, and Barton L. Lipman (1995): "Ex ante versus Interim Rationality and the Existence of Bubbles," *Economic Theory*, 6(3), 469–494.

Bhattacharya, Uptal, and M. Spiegel (1991): "Insider, Outsider, and Market Breakdown," *Review of Financial Studies*, 4, 255–282.

Biais, Bruno, and Jean-Charles Rochet (1997): "Risk Sharing, Adverse Selection and Market Structure," in *Financial Mathematics*, ed. by Bruno Biais, Tomas Björk, Jakša Cvitanić, N. El Karoui, and M. C. Quenez, pp. 1–51. Springer-Verlag, Berlin.

Biais, Bruno, David Martimort, and Jean-Charles Rochet (1997): "Competing Mechanisms in a Common Value Environment," (forthcoming) Econometrica.

Bikhchandani, Sushil, David Hirshleifer, and Ivo Welch (1992): "A Theory of Fads, Fashion, Custom, and Cultural Change as Informational Cascades," *Journal of Political Economy*, 100, 992–1026.

Blanchard, Olivier J., and Mark W. Watson (1982): "Bubbles, Rational Expectations, and Financial Markets," in *Crisis in the Economic and Financial Structure*, ed. by P. Wachtel. Lexington, Lexington, MA, 295–315.

Blume, Lawrence, and David Easley (1990): "Implementation of Walrasian Expectations Equilibria," *Journal of Economic Theory*, 51, 207–227.

Blume, Lawrence, David Easley, and Maureen O'Hara (1994): "Market Statistics and Technical Analysis: The Role of Volume," *Journal of Finance*, 49(1), 153–181.

Bolton, Patrick, and Christopher Harris (1999): "Strategic Experimentation," *Econometrica*, 67(2), 349–374.

Brandenburger, Adam (1992): "Knowledge and Equilibrium in Games," *Journal of Economic Perspectives*, 6, 83–101.

—— and Ben Polak (1996): "When Managers Cover their Posteriors: Making the Decisions the Market Wants to See," *Rand Journal of Economics*, 27, 523–541.

Bray, Margaret M. (1982): "Learning, Estimation, and the Stability of Rational Expectations," *Journal of Economic Theory*, 26, 318–339.

—— (1985): "Rational Expectations, Information and Asset Markets: An Introduction," *Oxford Economic Papers*, 37, 161–195.

Bray, Margaret M., and David Kreps (1987): "Rational Learning and Rational Expectations," in *Arrow and the Ascent of Modern Economic Theory*, ed. by Georg R. Feiwel, pp. 597–625. New York University Press, New York.

Brennan, Michael J. (1990): "Latent Assets," *Journal of Finance*, 45, 709–730.

Brock, W. A. (1979): "An Integration of Stochastic Growth Theory and the Theory of Finance," in *General Equilibrium, Growth and Trade*, ed. by Jerry Green and José Scheinkman. Academic Press, New York.

—— (1982): "Asset Prices in a Production Economy," in *The Economics of Information and Uncertainty*, ed. by J. McCall. University of Chicago Press, Chicago.

Brown, David P., and R. H. Jennings (1989): "On Technical Analysis," *Review of Financial Studies*, 2, 527–552.

Brunnermeier, Markus K. (1998): "Buy on Rumors – Sell on News: A Manipulative Trading Strategy." Mimeo, London School of Economics.

Bryant, John (1980): "A Model of Reserves, Bank Runs, and Deposit Insurance," *Journal of Banking and Finance*, 4, 335–344.

Bulow, Jeremy, and Paul Klemperer (1994): "Rational Frenzies and Crashes," *Journal of Political Economy*, 102(1), 1–23.

Bulow, Jeremy, and Paul Klemperer (1999): "The Generalized War of Attrition," *American Economic Review*, 89(1), 175–189.

Bulow, Jeremy, John Geankoplos, and Paul Klemperer (1985): "Multimarket Oligopoly: Strategic Substitutes and Complements," *Journal of Political Economy*, 93(3), 488–511.

Calomiris, Charles, and Charles Kahn (1991): "The Role of Demandable Debt in Structuring Optimal Banking Arrangements," *American Economic Review*, 81(3), 497–513.

Cass, David, and Karl Shell (1983): "Do Sunspots Matter," *Journal of Political Economy*, 91(2), 193–227.

Cass, David, and Joseph Stiglitz (1970): "The Structure of Investor Preferences and Asset Returns, and Separability in Portfolio Allocation: A Contribution to the Pure Theory of Mutual Funds," *Journal of Economic Theory*, 2, 122–160.

Chamley, Christophe, and Douglas Gale (1994): "Information Revelation and Strategic Delay in a Model of Investment," *Econometrica*, 62, 1065–1085.

Chari, V., and Ravi Jagannathan (1988): "Banking Panics, Information, and Rational Expectations Equilibrium," *Journal of Finance*, 43(3), 749–761.

Chen, Yehning (1999): "Banking Panics: The Role of the First-Come, First-Served Rule and Information Externalities," *Journal of Political Economy*, 107(5), 946–968.

Cho, In Koo, and David M. Kreps (1987): "Signaling Games and Stable Equilibria," *Quarterly Journal of Economics*, 102, 179–221.

Cochrane, John (2000): *Asset Pricing*, forthcoming book.

Copeland, Thomas E., and Dan Galai (1983): "Information Effects on the Bid–Ask Spread," *Journal of Finance*, 38(5), 1457–1469.

Crawford, Vincent P., and Joel Sobel (1982): "Strategic Information Transmission," *Econometrica*, 50(6), 1431–1451.

De Long, J. B., A. Shleifer, L. H. Summers, and R. J. Waldmann (1990): "Positive Feedback Investment Strategies and Destabilizing Rational Speculation," *Journal of Finance*, 45, 379–395.

Debreu, Gerard (1959): *Theory of Value*. Wiley, New York, Cowles Foundation Monograph, vol. 17.

Dekel, Eddie, and Faruk Gul (1997): "Rationality and Knowledge in Game Theory," in *Advances in Economics and Econometrics: Theory and Applications, Seventh World Congress*, ed. by David M. Kreps and Kenneth F. Wallis, vol. 1, pp. 87–172. Cambridge University Press, Cambridge, UK.

DeMarzo, Peter, and Costis Skiadas (1998): "Aggregation, Determinacy, and Informational Efficiency for a Class of Economies with Asymmetric Information," *Journal of Economic Theory*, 80, 123–152.

—— (1999): "On the Uniqueness of Fully Informative Rational Expectations Equilibria," *Economic Theory*, 13, 123–152.

Dennert, Jürgen (1993): "Price Competition between Market Makers," *Review of Economic Studies*, 60, 735–751.

Diamond, Douglas, and Philip Dybvig (1983): "Bank Runs, Deposit Insurance, and Liquidity," *Journal of Political Economy*, 91(3), 401–419.

References 225

Diamond, Douglas W., and Robert E. Verrecchia (1981): "Information Aggregation in a Noisy Rational Expectations Economy," *Journal of Financial Economics*, 9, 221–235.

Diamond, Peter (1965): "National Debt in a Neoclassical Growth Model," *American Economic Review*, 55, 1126–1150.

Diba, Behzad T., and I. Grossman, Herschel (1988): "The Theory of Rational Bubbles in Stock Prices," *Economic Journal*, 98, 746–754.

Dow, James, and Gary Gorton (1994): "Arbitrage Chains," *Journal of Finance*, 49(3), 819–849.

Dubey, Pradeep, John Geanakoplos, and Martin Shubik (1987): "The Revelation of Information in Strategic Market Games: A Critique of Rational Expectations Equilibrium," *Journal of Mathematical Economics*, 16, 105–137.

Duffie, Darrell (1996): *Dynamic Asset Pricing Theory*, 2nd edition. Princeton University Press, Princeton, NJ.

Duffie, Darrell, and R. Kan (1991): "Universal State Prices and Asymmetric Information." Mimeo, Stanford University.

Duffie, Darrell, and Rohit Rahi (1995): "Financial Market Innovation and Security Design: An Introduction," *Journal of Economic Theory*, 65, 1–42.

Dutta, Jayasri, and Stephen Morris (1997): "The Revelation of Information and Self-Fulfilling Beliefs," *Journal of Economic Theory*, 73, 231–244.

Easley, David, and Maureen O'Hara (1987): "Price, Trade Size, and Information in Securities Markets," *Journal of Financial Economics*, 19, 69–90.

—— (1992): "Time and the Process of Security Price Adjustment," *Journal of Finance*, 47, 577–605.

Fama, Eugene F. (1970): "Efficient Capital Markets: A Review of Theory and Empirical Work," *Journal of Finance*, 25, 383–417.

—— (1976): *Foundations of Finance*. Basic Books, New York.

Feldman, M., and C. Gilles (1985): "An Expository Note on Individual Risk without Aggregate Uncertainty," *Journal of Economic Theory*, 35, 26–32.

Fleming, W. H., and R. W. Rishel (1975): *Deterministic and Stochastic Optimal Control*. Springer-Verlag, New York.

Foster, Douglas F., and S. Viswanathan (1996): "Strategic Trading When Agents Forecast the Forecasts of Others," *Journal of Finance*, 51(4), 1437–1478.

Freixas, Xavier, and Jean-Charles Rochet (1997): *Microeconomics of Banking*. MIT Press, Cambridge, MA.

Froot, Kenneth A., David S. Scharfstein, and Jeremy C. Stein (1992): "Herd on the Street: Informational Inefficiencies in a Market with Short-Term Speculation," *Journal of Finance*, 47, 1461–1484.

Fudenberg, Drew, and Jean Tirole (1986): "A Signal-Jamming Theory of Predation," *Rand Journal of Economics*, 17(3), 366–376.

—— (1991): *Game Theory*. MIT Press, Cambridge, MA.

Gale, David (1973): "Pure Exchange Equilibrium of Dynamic Economic Models," *Journal of Economic Theory*, 6, 12–36.

Gale, Douglas (1996): "What Have We Learned from Social Learning?" *European Economic Review*, 40, 617–628.

Garber, Peter M. (1990): "Famous First Bubbles," *Journal of Economic Perspectives*, 4, 35–54.

Geanakoplos, John (1994): "Common Knowledge," in *Handbook of Game Theory II*, ed. by Robert J. Aumann and Sergio Hart, pp. 1437–1496. Elsevier Science B.V., Amsterdam.

Gennotte, Gerard, and Hayne Leland (1990): "Market Liquidity, Hedging, and Crashes," *American Economic Review*, 80(5), 999–1021.

Gervais, Simon (1997): "Market Microstructure With Uncertain Information: A MultiPeriod Analysis." Working paper.

Glosten, Lawrence R. (1989): "Insider Trading, Liquidity, and the Role of the Monopolist Specialist," *Journal of Business*, 62, 211–235.

Glosten, Lawrence R. (1994): "Is the Electronic Open Limit Order Book Inevitable?" *Journal of Finance*, 69, 1127–1161.

Glosten, Lawrence R., and Paul R. Milgrom (1985): "Bid, Ask and Transaction Prices in a Specialist Market with Heterogeneously Informed Traders," *Journal of Financial Economics*, 14, 71–100.

Gorman, W. (1953): "Community Preference Fields," *Econometrica*, 21, 63–80.

Gorton, Gary (1985): "Bank Suspension of Convertibility," *Journal of Monetary Economics*, 15, 177–193.

Graham, John R. (1999): "Herding Among Investment Newsletters: Theory and Evidence," *Journal of Finance*, 54(1), 237–268.

Grant, S., S. P. King, and Ben Polak (1996): "Information Externalities, Share-Price Based Incentives and Managerial Behaviour," *Journal of Economic Surveys*, 10, 1–21.

Grossman, Sanford J. (1976): "On the Efficiency of Competitive Stock Markets Where Traders Have Diverse Information," *Journal of Finance*, 31, 573–585.

—— (1978): "Further Results on the Informational Efficiency of Competitive Stock Markets," *Journal of Economic Theory*, 18, 81–101.

—— (1981): "An Introduction to the Theory of Rational Expectations under Asymmetric Information," *Review of Economic Studies*, 48, 541–559.

—— (1988): "An Analysis of the Implications for Stock and Futures Price Volatility of Program Trading and Dynamic Hedging Strategies," *Journal of Business*, 61, 275–298.

—— (1995): "Dynamic Asset Allocation and the Informational Efficiency of Markets," *Journal of Finance*, 50(3), 773–787.

Grossman, Sanford J., and Joseph E. Stiglitz (1980): "On the Impossiblity of Informationally Efficient Markets," *American Economic Review*, 70, 393–408.

Grossman, Sanford J., and Zhongquan Zhou (1996): "Equilibrium analysis of Portfolio Insurance," *Journal of Finance*, 51(4), 1379–1403.

Grundy, Bruce D., and Maureen McNichols (1989): "Trade and Revelation of Information through Prices and Direct Disclosure," *Review of Financial Studies*, 2, 495–526.

Gul, Faruk, and Russell Lundholm (1995): "Endogenous Timing and the Clustering of Agents' Decisions," *Journal of Political Economy*, 103, 1039–1066.

Gümbel, Alexander (1999): "Trading on Short-Term Information." Oxford Financial Research Center, Working Paper 1999-FE-10.

Harris, Christopher, M. Stinchcombe, and W. Zame (1997): "Resolving the Closure Problem in Normal Form Games." Mimeo.

Harrison, J. Michael, and David Kreps (1978): "Speculative Investor Behavior in a Stock Market with Heterogeneous Expectations," *Quarterly Journal of Economics*, 89, 323–336.

—— (1979): "Martingales and Arbitrage in Multiperiod Securities Markets," *Journal of Economic Theory*, 2(3), 381–408.

Hayek, Friedrich (1945): "The Use of Knowledge in Society," *American Economic Review*, 35, 519–530.

He, Hua, and Jiang Wang (1995): "Differential Information and Dynamic Behavior of Stock Trading Volume," *Review of Financial Studies*, 8(4), 919–972.

Hellwig, Martin F. (1980): "On the Aggregation of Information in Competitive Markets," *Journal of Economic Theory*, 22, 477–498.

—— (1982): "Rational Expectations Equilibrium with Conditioning on Past Prices: A Mean-Variance Example," *Journal of Economic Theory*, 26, 279–312.

Hirshleifer, David, Avanidhar Subrahmanyam, and Sheridan Titman (1994): "Security Analysis and Trading Patterns When Some Investors Receive Information Before Others," *Journal of Finance*, 49, 1665–1698.

Hirshleifer, Jack (1971): "The Private and Social Value of Information and the Reward to Inventive Activity," *American Economic Review*, 61, 561–574.

Ho, T., and Hans R. Stoll (1981): "Optimal Dealer Pricing Under Transactions and Return Uncertainty," *Journal of Financial Economics*, 9, 47–73.

Holden, Craig W., and Avanidhar Subrahmanyam (1992): "Long-Lived Private Information and Imperfect Competition," *Journal of Finance*, 47, 247–270.

—— (1994): "Risk Aversion, Imperfect Competition and Long-Lived Information," *Economics Letters*, 44, 181–190.

—— (1996): "Risk Aversion, Liquidity, and Endogenous Short Horizons," *Review of Financial Studies*, 9, 691–722.

Holmström, Bengt (1999): "Managerial Incentive Problems: A Dynamic Perspective," *Review of Economic Studies*, 66(1), 169–182.

Holmström, Bengt, and J. Ricart I Costa (1986): "Managerial Incentives and Capital Management," *Quarterly Journal of Economics*, 101, 835–860.

Holmström, Bengt, and Roger B. Myerson (1983): "Efficient and Durable Decision Rules with Incomplete Information," *Econometrica*, 51(6), 1799–1819.

Huang, Chi-fu, and Robert H. Litzenberger (1988): *Foundations for Financial Economics*. Prentice Hall, Upper Saddle River, NJ, Reprint.

Ingersoll, Jonathan E. (1987): *Theory of Financial Decision Making*. Rowman and Littlefield, Savage, MD.

Jacklin, Charles J. (1987): "Demand Deposits, Trading Restrictions and Risk Sharing," in *Contractual Arrangements for Intertemporal Trade*, ed. by Edward C. Prescott and Neil Wallace. University of Minnesota Press, Minneapolis.

Jacklin, Charles J., and Sudipto Bhattacharya (1988): "Distinguishing Panics and Information-based Bank Runs: Welfare and Policy Implications," *Journal of Political Economy*, 96(3), 568–592.

Jacklin, Charles J., Allan Kleidon, and Paul Pfleiderer (1992): "Underestimation of Portfolio Insurance and the Crash of October 1987," *Review of Financial Studies*, 5(1), 35–63.

Jackson, Matthew O. (1991): "Equilibrium, Price Formation and the Value of Private Information," *Review of Financial Studies*, 4, 1–16.

Jordan, J. S. (1983): "On the Efficient Markets Hypothesis," *Econometrica*, 51, 1325–1343.

Jordan, J. S., and Roy Radner (1982): "Rational Expectations in Microeconomic Models: An Overview," *Journal of Economic Theory*, 26, 201–223.

Keller, Godfrey, and Sven Rady (1999): "Optimal Experimentation in a Changing Environment," *Review of Economic Studies*, 66, 475–507.

Keynes, John Maynard (1936): *The General Theory of Employment, Interest and Money*. Macmillan, London.

Kindleberger, Charles P. (1978): *Manias, Panics and Crashes: A History of Financial Crises*. Macmillan, London; 3rd edition, 1996.

Klemperer, Paul (1999): "Auction Theory: A Guide To the Literature," *Journal of Economic Surveys*, 13(3), 227–286.

—— (2000): *The Economic Theory of Auctions*. Edward Elgar, Cheltenham, UK.

Klemperer, Paul, and Margaret Meyer (1989): "Supply Function Equilibria in Oligopoly under Uncertainty," *Econometrica*, 57(6), 1243–1277.

Kreps, David (1977): "A Note on Fulfilled Expectations Equilibria," *Journal of Economic Theory*, 14, 32–43.

Kyle, Albert S. (1985): "Continuous Auctions and Insider Trading," *Econometrica*, 53, 1315–1335.

—— (1989): "Informed Speculation with Imperfect Competition," *Review of Economic Studies*, 56, 317–356.

Laffont, Jean-Jacques (1985): "On the Welfare Analysis of Rational Expectations Equilibria with Asymmetric Information," *Econometrica*, 53(1), 1–29.

Laffont, Jean-Jacques, and Eric S. Maskin (1990): "The Efficient Market Hypothesis and Insider Trading on the Stock Market," *Journal of Political Economy*, 98, 70–93.

Leach, J. Chris, and Ananth Madhavan (1993): "Price Experimentation and Security Market Structure," *Review of Financial Studies*, 6, 375–404.

Lee, In Ho (1993): "On the Convergence of Informational Cascades," *Journal of Economic Theory*, 61, 395–411.

—— (1998): "Market Crashes and Informational Avalanches," *Review of Economic Studies*, 65, 741–759.

LeRoy, S. F., and R. D. Porter (1981): "The Present Value Relation: Tests Based on Implied Variance Bounds," *Econometrica*, 64, 555–574.

Lipster, R. S., and A. N. Shiryayev (1977): *Statistics of Random Processes I, II*. Springer-Verlag, Berlin.

Lyons, Richard K. (2000): *The Microstructure Approach to Exchange Rates*. MIT Press, Cambridge, MA (forthcoming).

Madhavan, Ananth (1992): "Trading Mechanisms in Securities Markets," *Journal of Finance*, 47, 607–641.

—— (2000): "Market Microstructure: A Survey," *Journal of Financial Markets* (forthcoming).

Madrigal, Vicente, and José Scheinkman (1997): "Price Crashes, Information Aggregation, and Market-Making," *Journal of Economic Theory*, 75(1), 16–63.

Magill, Michael, and Martine Quinzii (1996): *Theory of Incomplete Markets*, vol. 1. MIT Press, Cambridge, MA.

Marcet, Albert, and Thomas J. Sargent (1989*a*): "Convergence of Least Squares Learning in Environments with Hidden State Variables and Private Information," *Journal of Political Economy*, 83, 1113–1144.

—— (1989*b*): "Convergence of Least Squares Learning Mechanism in Self Referential Linear Stochastic Models," *Journal of Economic Theory*, 48, 337–368.

Marin, José M., and Rohit Rahi (1996): "Information Revelation and Market Incompleteness." Working paper, University of London.

Maskin, Eric S., and John G. Riley (1989): "Optimal Multi-unit Auctions," in *The Economics of Missing Markets, Information, and Games*, ed. by Frank H. Hahn, pp. 312–335. Oxford University Press, Oxford.

Matthews, Steven (1995): "A Technical Primer on auction Theory I: Independent Private Values." Mimeo, Northwestern University.

McAfee, R. Preston, and John McMillan (1987): "Auctions and Bidding," *Journal of Economic Literature*, 25, 699–738.

McAllister, Patrick H. (1990): "Rational Behavior and Rational Expectations," *Journal of Economic Theory*, 52, 332–363.

Milgrom, Paul R. (1981): "Good News and Bad News: Representation Theorems and Applications," *Bell Journal of Economics*, 12(2), 380–391.

—— (1989): "Auctions and Bidding: A Primer," *Journal of Economic Perspectives*, 3(3), 3–22.

Milgrom, Paul R., and Nancy Stokey (1982): "Information, Trade and Common Knowledge," *Journal of Economic Theory*, 26, 17–27.

Milgrom, Paul R., and Robert J. Weber (1982): "A Theory of Auctions and Competitive Bidding," *Econometrica*, 50(5), 1089–1122.

Morris, Stephen (1994): "Trade with Heterogeneous Prior Beliefs and Asymmetric Information," *Econometrica*, 62, 1327–1347.

Morris, Stephen, Andrew Postlewaite, and Hyun Song Shin (1995): "Depth of Knowledge and the Effect of Higher Order Uncertainty," *Economic Theory*, 6, 453–467.

Muth, J. R. (1960): "Optimal Properties of Exponentially Weighted Forecasts," *Journal of the American Statistical Association*, 55, 229–305.

—— (1961): "Rational Expectations and the Theory of Price Movements," *Econometrica*, 24, 315–335.

Myerson, Roger B. (1981): "Optimal Auction Design," *Mathematics of Operations Research*, 6, 58–73.

O'Hara, Maureen (1995): *Market Microstructure Theory*, Blackwell Publishers, Cambridge, MA.

Osborne, Martin J., and Ariel Rubinstein (1994): *A Course in Game Theory*. MIT Press, Cambridge, MA.

Ottaviani, Marco, and Peter Sørensen (1999*a*): "Herd Behavior and Investment: Comment," *American Economic Review* (forthcoming).

—— (1999*b*): "Reputational Cheap Talk." Mimeo, University College London.

Pagano, Marco (1989*a*): "Endogenous Market Thinness and Stock Price Volatility," *Review of Economic Studies*, 56, 269–288.

—— (1989b): "Trading Volume and Asset Liquidity," *Quarterly Journal of Economics*, 104, 255–274.

Pagano, Marco, and Ailsa Röell (1992): "Auction and Dealership Markets – What is the Difference?" *European Economic Review*, 36(2–3), 613–623.

Pfleiderer, Paul (1984): "The Volume of Trade and the Variability of Prices: A Framework for Analysis in Noisy Rational Expectations Equilibria." Working paper, Stanford University.

Pollak, R. A. (1971): "Additive Utility Functions and Linear Engel Curves," *Review of Economic Studies*, 38, 401–414.

Postlewaite, Andrew, and Xavier Vives (1987): "Bank Runs as an Equilibrium Phenomenon," *Journal of Political Economy*, 95(3), 485–491.

Prendergast, Canice, and Lars Stole (1996): "Impetuous youngsters and Jaded Old-Timers: Acquiring a Reputation for Learning," *Journal of Political Economy*, 104(6), 1105–1134.

Radelet, Steven, and Jeffrey Sachs (1998): "The East Asian Financial Crisis: Diagnosis, Remedies, Prospects." Mimeo, Harvard Institute for International Development.

Radner, Roy (1979): "Rational Expectations Equilibrium, Generic Existence and the Information Revealed by Prices," *Econometrica*, 47, 655–678.

Rao, K. P. S. B., and M. B. Rao (1983): *Theory of Charges*. Academic Press, New York.

Riley, John G., and William F. Samuelson (1981): "Optimal Auctions," *American Economic Review*, 71, 381–392.

Rochet, Jean-Charles, and Jean Luc Vila (1994): "Insider Trading without Normality," *Review of Economic Studies*, 61, 131–152.

Röell, Ailsa (1998): "Liquidity in Limit Order Book Markets and Single Price Auctions with Imperfect Competition." Mimeo, Princeton University.

Romer, David (1993): "Rational Asset-Price Movements Without News," *American Economic Review*, 83, 1112–1130.

Rothschild, M. (1974): "A Two-Armed Bandit Theory of Market Pricing," *Journal of Economic Theory*, 9, 185–202.

Rothschild, M., and Joseph E. Stiglitz (1976): "Equilibrium in Competitive Insurance Markets: An Essay on the Economics of Imperfect Information," *Quarterly Journal of Economics*, 90, 629–649.

Rubinstein, Mark (1974): "An Aggregation Theorem for Securities Markets," *Journal of Financial Economics*, 1, 225–244.

Samuelson, Paul A. (1958): "An Exact Consumption-Loan Model of Interest with or without the Social Contrivance of Money," *Journal of Political Economy*, 66, 467–482.

Santos, Manuel S., and Michael Woodford (1997): "Rational Asset Pricing Bubbles," *Econometrica*, 65(1), 19–57.

Sargent, Thomas J. (1979): *Macroeconomic Theory*. Academic Press, New York.

—— (1991): "Equilibrium with Signal Extraction from Endogenous Variables," *Journal of Economic Dynamics and Control*, 15, 245–273.

Scharfstein, David S., and Jeremy C. Stein (1990): "Herd Behavior and Investment," *American Economic Review*, 80, 465–479.

Scheinkman, José (1988): "Dynamic General Equilibrium Models – Two Examples," in *Mathematical Economics*, ed. by A. Ambrosetti, F. Gori, and R. Lucchetti. Springer-Verlag, New York.

Shiller, Robert J. (1989): *Market Volatility*. MIT Press, Cambridge, MA.

Shleifer, Andrei, and Robert W. Vishny (1990): "Equilibrium Short Horizons of Investors and Firms," *American Economic Review Proceedings*, 80, 148–153.

—— (1997): "The Limits of Arbitrage," *Journal of Finance*, 52(1), 35–55.

Singleton, Kenneth J. (1987): "Asset Prices in a Time-Series Model with Disparately Informed, Competitive Traders," in *New Approach to Monetary Economics*, ed. by William A. Barnett and Kenneth J. Singleton. Cambridge University Press, Cambridge, UK.

Smith, Lones, and Peter Sørensen (1997): "Informational Herding and Optimal Experimentation." Mimeo, Massachusetts Institute of Technology.

—— (2000): "Pathological Outcomes of Observational Learning," *Econometrica*, 68(2), 371–398.

Spiegel, Matthew (1998): "Stock Price Volatility in a Multiple Security Overlapping Generations Model," *Review of Financial Studies*, 11(2), 419–447.

Spulber, Daniel F. (1999): *Market Microstructure*. Cambridge University Press, Cambridge, UK.

Subrahmanyam, Avanidhar (1991): "A Theory of Trading in Stock Index Futures," *Review of Financial Studies*, 4, 17–51.

Tirole, Jean (1982): "On the Possibility of Speculation under Rational Expectations," *Econometrica*, 50, 1163–1182.

—— (1985): "Asset Bubbles and Overlapping Generations," *Econometrica*, 53(6), 1499–1528.

Tobin, J. (1958): "Liquidity Preference as Behavior Towards Risk," *Review of Economic Studies*, 26, 65–86.

Townsend, Robert M. (1983): "Forecasting the Forecasts of Others," *Journal of Political Economy*, 91(4), 546–588.

Treynor, Jack L., and Robert Ferguson (1985): "In Defense of Technical Analysis," *Journal of Finance*, 40, 757–775.

Trueman, Brett (1994): "Analyst Forecasts and Herding Behavior," *Review of Financial Studies*, 7, 97–124.

Vayanos, Dimitri (1996): "Strategic Trading and Welfare in a Dynamic Market." Research Paper 1416, Stanford University.

Verrecchia, Robert E. (1982): "Information Acquisition in a Noisy Rational Expectations Economy," *Econometrica*, 50, 1415–1430.

Vickrey, William (1961): "Counterspeculation, Auctions, and Competitive Sealed Tenders," *Journal of Finance*, 16(1), 8–37.

Viswanathan, S., and James J. D. Wang (1997): "Market Architecture: Limit-Order Books versus Dealership Markets." Mimeo, Duke University.

—— (1999): "Optimal Bidding in Multi-unit Discriminatory Auctions." Mimeo, Duke University.

Vives, Xavier (1993): "How Fast Do Rational Agents Learn?" *Review of Economic Studies*, 60(2), 329–347.

Vives, Xavier (1995*a*): "Short-Term Investment and the Informational Efficiency of the Market," *Review of Financial Studies*, 8, 125–160.

—— (1995*b*): "The Speed of Information Revelation in a Financial Market Mechanism," *Journal of Economic Theory*, 67, 178–204.

—— (1997): "Learning from Others: A Welfare Analysis," *Games and Economic Behavior*, 20, 177–200.

Wang, Jiang (1993): "A Model of Intertemporal Asset Prices Under Asymmetric Information," *Review of Economic Studies*, 60, 249–282.

—— (1994): "A Model of Competitive Stock Trading Volume," *Journal of Political Economy*, 102(1), 127–168.

Welch, Ivo (1992): "Sequential Sales, Learning and Cascades," *Journal of Finance*, 47(2), 695–732.

Wilson, Robert (1979): "Auctions of Shares," *Quarterly Journal of Economics*, 93(4), 675–689.

Zhang, Jianbo (1997): "Strategic Delay and the Onset of Investment Cascades," *Rand Journal of Economics*, 28, 188–205.

Zwiebel, Jeffrey (1995): "Corporate Conservatism and Relative Compensation," *Journal of Political Economy*, 103, 1–25.

INDEX

traders 28, 69, 73, 74, 86, 89, 93, 94,
96, 148, 178, 179, 203, 205,
208; *see also* noise traders
non-discretionary 137–9
discretionary 137–9
see also market depth, bid ask spread
Litzenberger, R. H. 38 n.
Long Term Capital Management
(LTCM) 171
Lundholm, R. 154, 156, 157
Lyons, R. K. 97

Madhavan, A. 81, 97, 153
Madrigal, V. 181
Magill, M. 38 n.
managers of firms 211–3
see also fund managers
Marcet, A. 116
marginal rate of substitution 49, 99
Marin, J. M. 26
market:
breakdowns 36–7
clearing 75, 131
completeness *see* completeness of
markets
depth 77, 94, 139–40
for lemon 36
makers 90, 179–82, 184, 196–7,
200–1, 208–11
competitive fringe, risk neutral 70–1,
111–2, 199, 203
monopolistic 87–8
microstructure models 60–97
classification dimensions 60–2
sequential move models 79–97
simultaneous demand schedule
models 65–79
order 60; *see also* limit order; stop
(loss) order
order driven 61
quote driven 61
timers 170–1
Markov:
perfect linear recursive equilibrium
145
perfect equilibria refinement 143, 144
process 91, 101
see also Gaussian Markov process
Martimort, D. 82–4
martingale 39, 43, 48–9, 51–3, 90–2,
140, 180, 200
Maskin, E. S. 79, 96

matching models 62
Matthews, S. 187 n.
McAfee, R. P. 185 n.
McAllister, P. H. 29
McMillan, J. 185 n.
McNichols, M. 103–6, 109, 112, 124,
129, 130, 131–2
mean–variance utility function 78, 79, 86
Meyer, M. 74
Milgrom, P. R. 11, 35, 83 n., 87–93, 96,
105, 177, 178, 181, 182, 184,
185 n.
Mississippi Bubble 47
MLRP *see* monotone likelihood ratio
property
monotone likelihood ratio property
(MLRP) 10, 11, 182
Morris, S. 7, 10, 21, 37, 50, 56, 57–8,
131
multi-unit auctions *see* share auctions
mutual knowledge 5–6, 7, 10, 21, 32,
55, 57, 58, 136
see also knowledge; common
knowledge
Muth, J. R. 1
Myerson, R. B. 23, 35, 185
myopia 111, 192
see also short horizons; short- termism
of firms; myopic REE

NASDAQ 61, 81
Nash equilibrium 73, 194 n.
symmetric 75–6
see also Bayesian–Nash equilibrium
net present value 53, 59, 118
New York Stock Exchange 80, 81
no-arbitrage condition 38, 51
see also arbitrage
noise traders 28
see also liquidity traders; noisy REE
noisy REE 28–9, 68–70
see also rational expectations
equilibrium
no-trade (no-speculation) theorems
30–7, 105, 106, 129, 136,
176 n., 182
agree to disagree 32–4
asymmetric information 36–7
Aumann's result 32–4
common knowledge 31–2
for Bayesian–Nash equilibrium 36